CHASING A
CONSPIRACY
CHARLES ANDERSON

To: Bill

From: Charles Anderson-
Williams

Charles
9-15-15

PAGE PUBLISHING, INC.
New York, NY

First originally published by Page Publishing, Inc. 2015

ISBN 978-1-68213-005-6 (pbk)
ISBN 978-1-68213-006-3 (digital)

Printed in the United States of America

This book is dedicated to my mother, Rosa Lee Anderson-Dunlap, who was born on January 15, 1914. She and Martin Luther King were born on the same day. Her strength, love, discipline, and hard work made everything possible for me. When I finished this book, she was living with me and fairly healthy. It is also dedicated to my grandfather who died two years prior to my birth. He was born on 1865, shortly after the Civil War in America. He was a courageous man and stood tall against racism. Credit is granted to my grandmother who was born around 1885. Her name is Pheny Davis-Anderson, who died around 1950.

She portrayed a tremendous amount of love toward me. It was mutual. The last person was my paternal aunt whose name is Bossie Williams-Baker. She was born on 1913 and died in 2010. She did all that she could in getting me to know my father's relatives. After her death, I attended the Dunbar-Williams family reunion in 2011". It was held in Miami, Florida. I met a substantial amount of my paternal relatives. My grandfather, Grossman's niece, resides in New Jersey. She is my cousin and her name is Grace Dunbar-Lincoln. In 2014, she was one hundred and seven years old. Everybody call her Aunt Grace. She is agile and healthy. She can even dance. Most of her children live in New Jersey. I met all of them at the family reunion.

CHASING A CONSPIRACY

This is an autobiography that relates to me and my family. The majority of it relates to my maternal family members. It is because I was raised by my mother and grandmother. My father did not have any impact on my life. Some of the information in this book was researched on the Internet. A lot of it was given to me by my relatives. My mother gave me a substantial amount of information. On the paternal side, Bossie Williams-Baker gave some information. She was my father's sister. The information in this book is based upon my research. It includes factual information given to me by family members. In my opinion, it is an interesting book to read. Many people in this book had a nickname, and a few of them did not like their birth name. They informally changed their first name. A couple of names were spelled the way it sounded to your ear. For instance, my maternal grandmother changed her first name to Fennie or Phenora. Several more versions were documented. In her death certificate, Fannie was documented. Her marriage license documented her name as Pheny. All of those names related to her were based on my research. One of her daughters changed her first name too. Anna was her first name. She did not like it. She informally changed it to Fannie. Several names were found about my grandfather. Documents were found under Jeff and Jefferson. He was documented as Jefferson

Anderson on his marriage license. The Census Bureau documented his name as Jeff. Their names were not legally changed.

In my opinion, this is an exciting and interesting book. I am listing the names and nicknames of my relatives, as follows:

(1) Rosa Lee Anderson-Dunlap, mother. Nigger was her nickname.

(2) Try-Fennie Davis (Fennie, Pheny, Phenora, and Fannie). Her nickname was Mi.

(3) Jeff Anderson (Jefferson). His nickname was Pi.

(4) Rutha Anderson-Phillips-Hall (Ruthie). Her nickname was Love.

(5) Charlie Anderson (Charley). His nickname was Bay.

(6) Edmond Anderson. His nickname was Spudge.

(7) Anna Anderson (Fannie). Her nickname was Little Sister.

(8) Fannie Ivy Williams-Anderson, aunt-in-law, nicknamed Fannie Ivy.

(9) Fannie Bell Anderson-Crittenton, first cousin, nicknamed Bay.

(10) James Willie Anderson (Willie James), first cousin, nicknamed Honey.

(11) Alonzo Williams (Lonzo), father, nicknamed Par-Gross.

(12) Grossman Williams, grandfather, nicknamed Gross.

My mother was the youngest among her siblings. Her name is Rosa Lee Anderson. She was born in Leary, Calhoun, County, Georgia, on January 15, 1914. The U.S. Census Bureau, Georgia, in 1920, showed that she was five years old. According to that report, she could have been born on 1914 or 1915. She was the fifth child among eight children and had two brothers and two sisters. They called her Nigger, and sometimes, they would say Nig. She is from a very close tight-knit family that earned their living by farming. My mother is a few inches taller than five feet but have the heart of a person seven feet tall. She was approximately thirty-five years old when she realized that she was short. My friend and neighbor by the name of Johnny Gates made Rose realize that she was short. Johnny lived directly across the street from us. All of the neighborhood kids loved to visit us, tease, and have fun with my mother. I call her Rose because she is like a sister to me.

My father was around six or seven years younger than my mother. He was about thirty-five years old when he died. My mother is still alive and well. My father's name is Lonzo or Alonzo Williams. I am not sure which one it is. Some people call him Lonzo and the others call him Alonzo. He was more than six feet tall and a very handsome, good-looking man. He looked like an Indian. He had nice skin with real black curly hair. Sometimes, he would wear two ponytails that hung to his back. His skin was the color of tan. He was born in Wellborn, Florida. Just like my mother, he and his family made a living by working on farms. I am not sure whether he could read or write.

My name is Charles Lee Anderson. Just like my mom, I was born in Leary, Georgia. I was born on September 26, 1941. My mother informed me that I was born on the 27th, instead of the 26th of September. However, my vital statistics shows the 26th of September. Rose insisted that the midwife must have made a mistake about my birthday. Her name was Dale Williams.

My mother's sister decided to name me after their older brother, whose name was Charley Anderson, and after one of their nephews, whose name was Charlie Anderson. My aunt's name was Ana Anderson, and she named me Charlie Lee Anderson, which was similar to my maternal uncle and first cousin.

Unlike my parents, I was not reared by a father. I always wished I had been raised by both parents and had brothers and sisters. I do not have any brothers or sisters. I understand that Ana did not like her name and chose to go by Fannie instead of Ana Anderson. I knew her by Fannie and not Ana. During those days, it was not uncommon for blacks to change their birth name without going through the court system. Birth certificates did not exist. Prior to the inception of birth certificates, people went by information recorded in bibles or gathered by representatives from the United States Census Bureau.

Similarly to Ana, I did not like my birth name. My friends and relatives called me Charlee, for short. I have never liked being called Charlee. I used my birth name throughout elementary and high school. I graduated from high school in 1961, and I started using Charles Lee Anderson. The opportunity arose for me to legally change my name to Charles after ordering a birth certificate from Atlanta, Georgia.

When I received the birth certificate, it was upsetting, and it pissed me off. They did not include the name of my father. My last name should have been Williams instead of Anderson. The birth certificate listed me as No Name Boy Anderson, and that is when I changed it to Charles Lee Anderson, with appropriate notarized documentation.

I only know a few of my maternal or paternal relatives. For some years I have been asking my mother questions concerning my maternal relatives. My paternal aunt Bossie Williams-Baker provided me with valuable information about my paternal relatives. She was born in Wellborn, Florida, on March 5, 1913. Bossie died in 2010. She was ninety-six years old. She was cremated in Miami, Florida. At one hundred years old in 2014, my mom Rose is witty and very talkative. She is a fun loving, very friendly lady. I was born on 1941, two years after the death of my mother's father. I asked my mother to further describe him.

PI

Rose meticulously described her father to me. She stated, "Your granddaddy's name was Jeffrey Anderson, and he was from some part of Alabama." His nickname is Pi. She said, "I am not sure which town he was from but, I believe he said it was Dothan, Alabama." According to the best recollection by Rose, her father was seventy-four or seventy-five years old when he died in 1939. He told his family that he was born shortly after the Civil War ended. The war ended around 1865. Although, Jeffrey was not born during the slave era, he told his family that he had a half-white sister born during slavery. She had small feet and wore a size five shoe. She was beautiful and very fair in complexion. Rose did not remember her aunt's name, and she never saw or met her. She believed that her name was Lela Anderson.

She described her father as a strict disciplinarian and a very hard working farmer. He did not like to share crop. He rented his land. He did not like the idea of splitting his profits with the owner of the land. Another reason for renting the land was because he did not trust white people. Rose stated, "He was illiterate and could not read nor write. Even without education, he was a very gifted and talented man. He hated education and made it hard for me and my sister, Fannie, to go to school."

My mother has a very keen memory about her family members and other things that happened during her lifetime. She is a remarkable person. Her memory continues to be keen even at age ninety-four in 2008. I question her usually when she is in a good and talkative mood. It does not take much to fire her up. That is a blessing for me, and the interview continues another day.

She told me that "the folks from Leary called him Uncle Jeff. His family members gave him the nickname Pi." To me, my grandpa was unique and special. He appeared to be an interesting man. It is too bad that he passed two years prior to my birth. I was born on 1941, and he died in 1939. It is heartbreaking that I never had a chance to know him. I believe in spirituality, and I believe that we will meet one day.

According to my mother's version, he was born around 1865. Pi stood about six feet six inches tall and had very dark skin. My mother said, "He was jet black. His eyes were red all the time. They looked like they were bloodshot. He was very muscular. He had two knuckle bones located near his wrist on each arm. His friends and family members said that he was double-jointed. Double-jointed means having two knucklebones near the wrist. That means having the strength of two people. Obviously, Pi had the strength of two people. He was very mean and had a violent temperament. "He was very violent. I really thought that he would die in a violent death. He kept me scared and nervous but died in a natural death." He was a family man with excellent morals and values. When he spoke to his family, his words were his law. We had to abide by them. If you did not, it was best to hit the highway. He always said, "God damn it if one of ya'll ever raise your hand to hit me, I will blow your brains out or cut your head off with my knife." He meant every word he said because the police would say, "By George by golly you did the right thing." Dig a hole and bury him or her. That is all that would be done. Pi had a pocket knife that was as sharp as a razor. It was sharp enough to get a shave. If my daddy was mad at you, he could put his hand in his pocket and pull it out with the blade open. He was fast as lightning. Seven days a week, he wore a pair of overalls. He was an expert shot with his pistol rifle or shotgun. And he had an arsenal of weapons to use, living far out in the country.

Several weeks later, the interview continues with my mother. She stated, "Charlee, your granddaddy could do just about anything." That meant he was a jack-of-all-trades. That's exactly what it meant for an uneducated man, especially for a black man. Most of the things he knew were taught by his parents. Searching for my unknown relatives is a reason for this story. I refer to it as pieces missing to our family tree. It is similar to parts missing from a puzzle. He told his family that he was a fast learner, and that his parents taught him a lot. He learned just about everything about wildlife. Pi knew the names of all plants and animals. He was an excellent hunter and fisherman. He was an excellent farmer too. He knew how to make medicine and tea from the wild herbs. In the modem era, he would be called a botanist.

My granddad was very strong. He was an excellent athlete. He would hunt rabbits by chasing them on feet. For a short distance, he could outrun a mule or a horse. My mom believed that he could have been a great fighter or track runner. He was a great swimmer. He could tread the water and could light his pipe while floating on his back. He was the best at everything he did. Nobody could win an argument with him. He was the boss, and you could not tell him anything according to Rose. Most of them were afraid to challenge him. He was very domineering. Rose replied, "My dad was like a dictator, and he demanded respect. He built his own house from the oak trees in Leary, Georgia, on the rented land. He made furniture and wood shingles from the oak wood. The house had a fireplace that was made by him. He dug and built his own well and stables for his mules and horses. Grandpa made his own gigs and trapped monster alligators and crocodiles. He trapped otters and beavers and plenty of other wildlife. The hide and meat were sold as a business. People would hire him to dig wells for them. He had a large smokehouse to smoke his meat. He even had beehives for honey. She stated, "He had a moonshine still and made the best moonshine in Leary. His was made from copper pipe, and he had that good moonshine. He had many white customers. They made their syrup and butter. He was a very good farmer and grew just about everything. They had enough food stored to last long periods of time. He would hitch his wagon to his mule or horse and deliver food to widows living long distances away. He gave it to them. He could have been a wealthy man had he listened to my mother," Rose replied. "Obviously, he did not listen to her."

His parents were born during slavery or kidnapped from Africa. They passed along a great deal of knowledge, wisdom, and experience to him when he was young. Rose believed that her paternal grandfather's name was Edmond Anderson. He would be my great-grandfather who lived in Dothan, Alabama, after slavery on a large plantation. He was just as gifted as his son, Jeffrey. He grew just about everything on his property including having a rice farm. She firmly believed that her grandfather was Edmond because of having an older brother named Edmond Anderson. She believed her brother was named after his grandfather. Edmond II was my mother's eldest brother. He was born around 1898 in Leary, Georgia. My grandmother was Tripheenie Davis. She got married to my granddad at the age of twelve. She had her first child a year later around 1898. She was born in Dawson, Georgia. Therefore, she had to be born around 1885. My grand-dad was twenty years older than my grandmother. He was thirty-two when they got married.

My grandparents had eight children. Three of the eight children died due to miscarriage or shortly after birth. The eldest child was Edmond Anderson who died in Orlando, Florida, in 1989. He was ninety-one years old when he died. Edmond II was my uncle. I knew him very well and loved him dearly. My mother told me, "When you see your uncle, that is a perfect picture of your granddad." She said the only difference is your granddad was tall and your uncle is short. Your uncle was five feet and a few inches taller. His nickname was Spudge. Uncle Spudge was tough just like his father. He could not read or write.

Uncle Spudge was married to Fannie Ivy Williams in Leary, Georgia. She had a very strong big double-jointed mother. I understand that men could not beat her. Rose said that Fannie Ivy's mother could pick a man up in the air with one hand and beat the shit out of him with the other hand. Her name was Fronnie Williams. Miss Fronnie was married to Frank Williams. Fannie Ivy died in 2003 in Orlando, Florida. She was around 108 years old and born around 1895. Rose went to school with aunt Fannie Ivy's sister in Leary. They called her Willie Lee. Fannie Ivy could not read nor write.

Uncle Spudge and Aunt Fannie Ivy had three children. They had two boys and a girl. Rose would babysit the boys when they were not home. She was their aunt. They loved her dearly as if their mother. The eldest son was Charlie Anderson, who was a taxicab driver in Orlando. He died in the 1990s. He was a tough man and could fight like a heartbeat. His punch was harder than one by George Foreman or Mike Tyson. Many white people wanted to be his agent, but he chose not to box. He could have been a champion. I only know two of his children, and they are Nettie and Will. I admired and liked Charlie as if my brother. I do not know if he could read or write. Rose said that as a young lad, he was mean. He was quiet. He kept a sharp switch blade knife in his overalls. Willie James, his brother, never could beat him. She told me that one day they got into a fight while babysitting them. Willie James continued to harass his brother. Charlie said, "leave me alone!" He would not stop. Charlie hit his brother in the chest with one punch and knocked him out. Rose said she thought he was dead. He was bleeding from the mouth, nose, and ears. Charlie knocked the shit out of him. She got a bucket of cold water from the well and poured it on her nephew. He gained his consciousness. She spanked Charlie for hitting his brother so hard. He did not like that and didn't forget it.

Charlie really liked his brother and named him Honey. When Willie James was picking on him, he would say, "Honey, leave me alone!" Honey would not leave him alone and got knocked out. I know that Willie James could read and write but not sure about Charlie. Charlie told me that shortly after moving from Leary to Orlando, he got into a fight at a black bar on Church Street. Charlie said, "This guy kept picking on me because I was a stranger at the bar. I hit him with one punch in the chest. The man's body rocked back and forth. He fell on the floor and knocked unconsious. The folks in Orlando got to know him after that fight. He never had any more problems from the bullies." He drove a taxi until his death. He had two more children who are my second cousins. They are Zelma and Ozzie. I do not know them.

Rose explained that her nephews were young kids. Sometimes, she would stay with them. That would allow her brother and wife to go out on the weekend. She said that little hammer knocker, Charlie, never forgot about that spanking. She said he was mean just like her father. "Charlie would look at me and roll his eyes at me while on their farm. His brother was not like that. One day, when I was getting water from the well, Charlie threw a dry corncob, and it hit me in the face. The bucket of ice cold water from the well and me hit the grown. That little hammer knocker ran toward the house which was quite a distance from the well. He could run fast and so could me, but I could run faster than him. I should have been faster and quicker because I am older. I got up and chased him to the house. As he reached the porch of the wood house, I caught up with him. My brother and sister-in-law were working on the farm and could not see us. I grabbed him and gave him an ass whipping of the century. He cried. He ran away from the house crying and heading toward the farm. While running and crying, he said, "I am going to tell my mama and daddy about you, and we will be back. I double-dog dare you to be there." I told him to bring them back, and I will be here.

I looked in the direction of the farm. I could see all of them walking hurriedly to the house. Spudge, Fannie Ivy, and their boys entered the house together. I went inside. All of them rushed into the house. They approached me. Spudge inquired about the spanking of his son, Charlie. While Spudge and Fannie Ivy were trying to tell me that I should not have spanked him, he put his hand in his overall pocket and came out with his knife. Charlie held the switch blade knife in his hand along his side while they argued with me. I explained to them the reason for chastising him. I said, "If I had to do it all over again, the punishment would be equally as good or worse." They started walking closer to me. Then I grabbed the steel rod from the fireplace. I got it to defend myself. The steel rod is used to stir or pick up hot ashes to make it warmer in the winter season. This was not during the winter season. The fireplace was not used because of the weather. I told them that they would get hurt badly when I drew the rod backward. I yelled, "You betta not come up on me!" And they backed away. They knew not to attack me because boys could not beat me or my sister, Fannie. Working on the farm made us strong. We worked as hard as men. All of the boys would say, "Do not bother Uncle Jeff's girls unless you want to get a butt whipping." I put the steel rod down and walked home. It was during the night.

Rose said her dad rented land from George Colley and lived in it. Spudge and his family lived in Albert Dozier's farm. The two farms were about six miles away from each other, and I walked in the pitch-black darkness. It was a full moon, and the light from it enabled me to see the road. The clay road in the woods led me to my parent's home on George Colley's property. In those days, there was no electricity. People burned kerosene lamps. No homes were within eyesight until I reached home.

The Colleys were considered as "big shot" white people because of their wealth. Pi, my dad, always said, "Guns and money create power."

It was rare to see an automobile. People usually walked or rode in a wagon or buggy pulled by a mule or horse. Only a few black folks owned a horse. Pi and another black man owned a horse. His name was Rich Rutledge. He bought his horse from a circus owner who came to town. Rose said she was scared of Mr. Rutledge's horse because of his fancy walk. Sometimes, the horse would stand on two legs prior to pulling the buggy.

When Rose entered the wood house, everybody was up. They had not gone to bed. She told her mom and dad the reason she walked home at night. His nickname was Pi and pronounced it with a long I. Her mother's nickname was Mi. and pronounced with a long I. Pi said he would straighten out the mess. He must have because we never talked about it anymore and remained friends or relatives. Several weeks later, I had to babysit the boys again without any problems.

Spudge and Pi resolved the altercation we had at his house. They really never got along with each other. People would say they resembled each other too much to get along. That was one reason he moved out of the house at a young age. Rose informed me that she can only remember living with her sister, Fannie, and their parents.

Uncle Spudge had three children. The last one is a female named Fannie Bell Anderson Crittenton. She resides in Orlando, Florida.

Fannie Bell and I grew up together in Georgia. Her nickname was Bay. She is like a sister to me, and I am crazy about her. I love her like a sister. The reason is because I do not have sisters or brothers. That is one of my dreams that will never come true. I know three of her children but none of her grandchildren. All of them are my cousins. Rodney and Jamie are two of her children. I do not know their last name. I do not know if Rodney is using Crittenton as his last name nor do I know what last name is used by Jamie. I believe that Jamie and Terry have the same father. Terry Murphy is her eldest son. Jamie may very well use Murphy for her last name. I do not know whether or not she is married.

I met Rodney when he was a young kid a couple of times. He went into the navy or air force. I understand he lives in Atlanta, Georgia, and is married to a white lawyer. In 2008, his mother gave me that information concerning her son, Rodney. I was thrilled to know that because I am a lawyer too. I made approximately ten phone calls to Rodney in 2008. Messages were left on the voice mail. He never returned the phone calls. His sister and brother live in Orlando.

Prior to writing this story, I had the occasion to communicate with two of my cousins by phone. Their father is Willie James, previously mentioned. I spoke with them at his funeral in Orlando. Coincidently, one of them was working on a family tree. She is Sherry Anderson-Taylor and resides in the Orlando area. She did not know the names of her paternal great-grandparents. I gave her their names to put on her family tree. That would be Uncle Spudge and Fannie Ivy, her grandparents. I informed her that I was writing an autobiography, which would include our descendants.

I spoke with her sister several weeks later by phone, and her name is Juanita Anderson-Murphy. I told her the same thing. Both of them live in Orlando. I met them at their father's funeral including their other sisters and brothers. One of their brothers is a carbon copy of their dad. When I saw him, I told him that he was my second cousin. "I said you look just like Willie James, and you are a carbon copy of him. His name is Frank Anderson.

Willie Edward Anderson, Minnie Anderson, Gloria Anderson-Jackson, Mary Anderson-Callahan, and Leola Anderson-Davenport are the rest of his children. I do not know them that well, but I would love to because we are closely related to each other.

I spoke to their dad by phone a week prior to his death, and he did not tell me that he was ill. We discussed making plans for a family reunion. That is something the Anderson family need to do. It broke my heart to learn about his death. I do not believe in shedding tears, but I went in the corner of my bedroom and let a few out.

I realize that life is not easy, and we must work hard to be successful. Sometimes, we have to sacrifice and take time out for a family reunion. That will help prevent the kin from getting into intimate relationships with each other. An example of that is a conversation between me and Fannie Bell at her brother's funeral. She said, "Charlee, you know we had two cousins in the military, and they were dating each other. They did not know they were kin to each other. They came to Orlando while on military leave. We told them they were cousins, and they broke off."

We are all equally guilty of this problem, but someone should take the initiative and do something about it. When I finish this project, I intend to try and organize one.

MI

As mentioned previously, the vowel (i) in my grandmother's nick-name is pronounced with the long sound. The same sound is applicable to my grandfather. I did not use her nickname, but I did call her mommy. She took care of me. Rose, who is my mother, had to work. She worked on different farms. We were crazy about each other. Today, I continue to call her Rose. Referring to Rose, as mommy, just do not sound right. I would tell my friends that she was my sister.

My grandmother was born and reared in Dawson, Georgia. Rose told me it was in Terrell County. Her name was Tripheenie Davis. Many people called her Fennie Anderson. She was born around 1885 and had her first child around 1898. Her nickname was Mi. She was thirteen when she had her first child. Her last child was born on 1914, who is my mother. She had eight children between 1898 and 1914. Only five of them lived. Their names are listed as follows:

(1) Edmund or Edmond Anderson, nicknamed Spudge, was born on 1898 in Leary, Georgia, and died in Orlando, Florida in 1989. He was married to Fannie Ivy Williams, his first and only wife. A few years after his death, she was 108 years old when she died.

(2) Charley Anderson, nicknamed Bay, was born 1901 in Leary and died in Pompano Beach, Florida on November

08, 1958. The death certificate listed him as born on April 30, 1908.

(3) Rutha or Ruthie Anderson, nicknamed Love, was born in Leary in 1905 and died around July 1987 in Glenwood, Georgia. Death records show that she was born on July 1, 1907. Her first husband was Jake or Jacob Phillips. Her second husband was Charlie Hall. They lived in Leary, Georgia.

(4) Anna Anderson, nicknamed Lil Sis was born on 1908 in Leary, Georgia. Her first husband was Thomas Colley. He was half white and black. He was related to the prominent wealthy white Colley family in Leary. They were given a ranch in Leary. They moved to Albany, Georgia, and bought a house on Van Buren Street. Years later, they got a divorce. The Albany property was awarded to her. She relocated to Pompano Beach, Florida. Her second husband was Willie Gilbert. He was a retiree who worked for Chrysler Corporation as a janitor. Both of them are buried in Pompano Beach.

(5) Rosa or Rosie Lee Anderson, nicknamed Nigger was born on January 15, 1914 in Leary. Her birthday is the same as Martin Luther King's birthday. Her first husband was Johnny Wright, a much older man. He was very light-skinned. He loved to dance. When not working on the farm, he worked as an electrician. Willie Lee Dunlap became her second husband.

The U.S. Census Bureau, taken in 1910, shows:

(1) Jeff Anderson was forty-five years old, which means he was born on 1865. It indicated that his mother was born in Alabama while his father was born in Kentucky.

(2) Fennie Anderson, his wife, was thirty years old, which showed she was born on 1880.

(3) Anna (Fannie) Anderson, child, was two years old; therefore, she was born on 1908.

(4) Rutha Anderson, child, was five years old and was born on 1905.

Rose and her brother Edmond (Spudge) are the only two siblings who had children. I have seen all of my uncles and an aunt except Rutha. Around 1939, she became mentally ill and was institutionalized. Aunt Rutha was married twice before losing her mind. Her first husband was Jake Phillips. Jake was an expert shot as were my granddad, Pi. They would practice shooting at targets. However, my granddad was slightly a better shooter than Jake. Both were experts. Jake had a mouth full of gold and would smile and talk at the same time. It was hard to detect if he were mad at you. Rutha broke up with Jake and married Charlie Hall. She and her second husband lived in the city limits of Leary. She became mentally incapacitated.

Subsequently, law enforcement officials with the Sheriff Department were advised that Rutha was mentally unstable. They arrived in the country portion of Leary and spoke with her parents. They probably had a court order to place her in a mental institution. They placed her in the police car along with her husband and parents. She was driven to the nearest psychiatric facility. She ended up in the state facility in Milledgeville, Georgia. That was the last time her relatives would ever see or have any contact with her. Rose wrote several letters to her when I was in sixth grade. I read the reply letters, and she was still alive.

Rose described her as tall and attractive. She was a very good farmworker. It was hard to do more work than her. Years later, she got a social security card and worked at the peanut mill in Leary. She worked better and picked up peanuts faster than the other workers. The peanut mill was owned by Willie Jordan. He was one of the wealthy white families in town. My mother had a card and worked at the mill too. That is where they got their social security cards.

Rose stated that they called her sister's husband, Buddy Jake. He was her first husband. She alleged that he was an expert shot along with being a dangerous man. He did not like it when she married Charlie Hall. Rose heard him make a statement about it. She contends that Buddy Jake said, "Love, will never do Charlie Hall any good." She was afraid that he was talking about her sister. However, it did not happen that way. His statement was somewhat true because she never did her second husband any good. Today, she would be more than a hundred years old. I believe she is dead. We need to get a court order to get some answers about her demise.

Jake Phillips and my granddad were friends, and they did many things together. He had a hot and mean temperament. He was violent and did not believe that he would lose a gun fight. However, my granddad was a better fighter and slightly meaner than Jake. Jake was an expert shooter but not as good as my grandpa because he was the best at everything he did.

Major Davis and Rutha Davis were my grandmother's parents. They were my great-grandparents. They were dead when my mother was born on 1914. Uncle Spudge ran away from home when he was very young and lived with his grandmother. He lived with Rutha until old enough to get married to Fannie Ivy. My great-grandmother was from Dawson, Georgia. My grandmother, Tripheenie's sister and brothers are Fannie Davis, John Henry Davis, Sylvester Davis, Amos Davis, Andy Davis, and Major Davis II. All of them lived in Dawson until the death of their father.

Years later, my great-grandmother, Rutha, met a man by the name of Jim Jones. He lived in Dawson, Georgia. They got married and lived in Dawson, on Lemon Street. She and her children lived with her husband. Jim Jones and Rutha Davis-Jones had two girls. Their names are Lela Jones and Willie Mae Jones. Lela became a teacher in Georgia.

My mother did not know any of them. After Rutha Davis-Jones' death, her husband had to take care of the family. Rose told me things that her mother told her about Jim Jones. She stated that Jim Jones was a farmer, and they had to work hard on the farm. He believed in getting an education. When his two biological children became old enough to go to school, Jim refused to let his stepchildren go to school. He made sure that Lela and Willie Mae got good education. He made his stepchildren work hard on his farm. When he took my grandmother out of school, she was in the eleventh grade. She had a good education at that time. She had better education than my mother. My grandmother studied out of the Webster's Blue Back Spelling Book. She was an excellent speller.

My grandmother told my mother that she was going to leave and marry the first man to have an interest in her. That was due to their stepfather's unfair treatment toward her sister and brothers. She was twelve years old when she met Jeffrey Anderson. There were no laws pertaining to young children getting married. They were married in Dawson, Georgia. They moved and lived in Leary until my grandfather's death.

The following information is about my grandmother's sister and brothers. Aunt Fannie Davis met a man and got married. They lived in Arlington, Georgia. I knew Aunt Fannie. Amos Crawford was her husband. She went in the name of Fannie Davis-Crawford. I lived with her in Georgia when I was about two years old. My mother alleges that she had to do that to wean me off her breast. She said I would not suck milk from a bottle. My mother lived in Florida and worked on the farm while I lived with her in Arlington.

My great-aunt kept me when I was in the first grade. She would fix food in a bucket, and I would walk to the school held in a church. I did not like the idea of going to school. My cousin went to the school too. I called him Billy Joe. I do not know whether that is his correct name. After going to school for two days, I told Billy Joe, that I was not going to go to school. I encouraged him to play hooky with me. We would play and hide on the farm until school turned out. When school had turned out, we would walk with the other students as if we had gone to school. Both of us failed the first grade because we played the whole year.

My grandmother came to her sister's house and got me. She took me back to Florida with her. She figured that I would go to school in Florida. The same thing happened in Pompano. I played hooky in the first grade and stayed back in the first grade again. I played hooky in the Oak Field, which was the equivalent of 9th Avenue. However, the next year, I decided to go to school. I did not play hooky anymore.

Aunt Fannie's children are named Willie D. Crawford, Hattie Crawford, and Pearl Crawford. I believe Hattie was Billy Joe's mother. I ascertained that Billy Joe is a truck driver and live in New York. I had his phone number but lost it. He gave it to my mother when she came to Hattie's funeral in Orlando. Hattie was residing in Orlando when she died. I met her several times. However, I was unable to go to her funeral. She was buried in Georgia.

Hattie had two daughters living in Miami. Rose gave me their phone numbers too. One of them is a teacher. Somewhere between 1978 and 1981, I paid them a visit while married to my first wife. I lost their phone numbers and on many occasions attempted to locate their home to no avail. They are my maternal cousins, and I would love to see them.

Hattie had a son who was killed in Orlando. His name was Charlie Rainey. Someone shot or stabbed him while sitting in his car. He died. I was in my twenties when it happened. His father was Willie Rainey. Willie Rainey was one of the best black baseball pitchers in the nation. He could throw a baseball very hard and fast. The white ball players alleged that they could not see it. The white people in Arlington and Dawson would pay him to pitch for them.

Willie D. Crawford was not married and did not have any children. While living in Arlington, with his mother, people referred to him as Dee. He had puffy eyes and was not handsome. However, he was a talented, gifted organ player. He was a self-taught organ player and could play anything on it. Single and married women loved him. He was a real player with the women. I remember him because of playing the organ all the time. He tried to teach me how to play it the year I missed school.

When I was a young kid and living in Pompano, Dee, was set afire and killed. It was during the winter, and he was with friends around a fire. In the winter, people would burn fires outdoors to stay warm. I understand that they were drinking moonshine. Dee was wearing a long overcoat at the gathering and had his back to the fire. Someone poured some gasoline on his coat, and he burned to death. No one was ever charged with the crime because the people refused to talk. That crime took place in Arlington.

My great-aunt Fannie had a daughter, and everyone called her by the name of Sista Rose. My mother never got the chance to meet her. She did not know her correct name. Sista did have a daughter who was in a wheelchair. Her daughter's name is pronounced the way it is spelled Schood. My mother believes she moved to the northern states.

Pearl Crawford was another daughter. She lived in Albany, Georgia, until her death. Her nickname was Tom. Pearl had a son named Dewey. Dewey lived in Orlando when I met him. He appeared to be blind. I met him at Uncle Spudge's funeral. Now, he is dead. Everyone called her daughter by the name of Jo. That is all we know, except that she lived in Miami. She was married to someone from one of the islands. She had some children who lived in Miami with her. She had a daughter who moved to the northern states, and her name is Alice Mae.

The 1930 U.S. Census Bureau had a report of their ages in 1930. The names are as follows:

Primas Crawford, age 65, born on 1865, husband
Fannie Davis-Crawford, age 41, born on 1889, wife
Pearline Crawford, age 23, born on 1907, daughter
Willie Dee Crawford, age 21, born on 1909, son
Hattie B. Crawford, age 19, born on 1911, daughter
Louise Crawford, age 10, born on 1920, daughter
Elizabeth Crawford, age 8, born on 1922, daughter
Willie C. Crawford, age 7, born on 1923, son
Alice Mae Crawford, age 3, born on 1927, daughter
Charlie Crawford, age 2, born on 1928, son

Charlie Crawford lived in Orlando, Florida. He died in 1998. Hattie had several daughters or grandchildren living in Miami, Florida. One of them was employed by Miami-Dade County Public School.

Great-aunt Fannie Crawford lived in Arlington, Georgia. I lived with them when I was very young. My mother left me with them when I was about two years. Then she went to Pompano Beach, Florida. She was a migrant farmworker. My grandmother took me to Pompano when I was about four years old. When I was six or seven years old, I lived with Aunt Fannie to attend first grade. The school was at a small church. I would walk to school with my lunch bucket. A boy about my age lived there too. We would walk to school together. We went to school a few days in the term. We played "hooky" in the corn fields. I named him Billy Joe. He probably was her grandson. I do not know his real name. I understand that he is a tractor-trailer driver in New York.

Great-aunt Fannie's oldest daughter was named Bernice, and she lived in Arlington. She worked in Florida. She would board the train in Smithville, Georgia, and go to Florida. She probably was a Crawford too.

Uncle Amos Davis was my grandmother's oldest brother. He and his brother, Andy Davis, were in the mason lodge. They had thirty-three degrees in the lodge. That was something special for a black those days. It was considered as a big accomplishment. It was recognized all over the nation. Both of my uncles got into trouble while living with their stepfather, Jim Jones. They were very mad at someone and waited until Sunday to get even with that person. On Sunday, they went to church with their guns. They shot someone in the church and killed the wrong person. They fled to a friend's home who were masons and explained their problem to them. They were hidden to prevent the police from apprehending them. Their masonic friends made arrangements with a funeral home director to ship them to the northern states. They were placed in a casket with an assumed name as if they were dead and transported on a train. The masonic friends, in one of the northern states, helped them to get jobs and a place to live. We do not know if they changed their names. More than likely, they did. My grandmother lost contact with them.

However, she would go to Dawson and visit her stepfather, Jim Jones. He would tell her that her brothers were mailing letters to him. He refused to ever show her any of the mail. He would tell her, "I will let you read them on your next visit." The last time she attempted to visit him, he was unavailable. He was dead, and the wood house had been burned down. My grandma always said that he did not treat them fairly.

Uncle John Henry Davis moved to Atlanta, Georgia. He got a live-in job with a white family. He lived in the servant's home on their property. He had keys to their home so he could enter when they were away. Rose said that he told the white folks that he would be out of town over the weekend. He allegedly changed his mind and remained on their property. He did not put them on notice. Rose contended that he entered their home on a Sunday night and was shot to death. The owner of the home told the police that he was mistaken as a burglar and shot him to death. There have been many unanswered questions about his death. This happened before my birth.

Uncle Major Davis, Jr., was the oldest. He moved to Jacksonville, Florida. He worked as a chef cook at a hotel. On the weekend, while riding on a boat, he got drowned. The passengers told authorities that he was drinking alcohol and fell overboard and drowned. My grandma believed that he was murdered. All of my grandmother's brothers are probably dead, and no other information is available about them. I do know that I am related to some Davis family. The same is applicable to the Crawford and Jones families.

MI AND PI

The above nicknames are the ones given and used by my mother's parents. They got married at an early age, especially my grandmother. They were married in Dawson and settled down in Leary, Georgia. My grandfather grew up in Dothan, Alabama, on his parents' land. It is what my mother told me. I believe that he was born in Alabama. I am not sure if the city was Dothan. Dothan is not very far away from Leary, Georgia. He told his family that he was born shortly after the Civil War. He left his parents at an early age and traveled to parts of Florida. He did farm labor and odd jobs for white people. When he got married, he had saved enough money to rent his own land. He did not believe in the concept of sharecropping. He rented land far in the rural section of Leary, from the Colley family. Since he was a very skillful young man, he built a large wooden house made from oak trees. The house had a large double fireplace. It was built with clay dirt and red clay bricks. Automobiles and electricity had not been invented yet.

The house had a front and rear door. The rear door had a hole at the bottom of it so their cat could go in and out. They refer to it as the cat's hole in the door. "The home had open spaces without glass for the windows. Wooden shutters were built from oak wood that hung above the open spaces. The shutters would be closed at night and opened during the day.

I did some research on the Internet under Ancestry.com, and it showed when he got married. It coincided with what my mother told me. The marriage record showed the following information:

Jefferson Anderson - husband
Pheny Davis - wife
Married on February 12, 1897
Dawson, Terrell County, Georgia

My mother is the last one of the old-timers, and she is the one who gave me this information. It took me many years to get this information. She told me that her father made shingles from oak wood for the roof of their home. Just about everything was made from cypress, oak, and hickory trees. He even made furniture for the house.

My granddad had a reputation as the best well digger and fire-place builder in that locale. He would hitch his mule to the buggy or wagon and go to the local hardware store in Leary. At the store, he would purchase his tools, such as shovels, hoes, and others. If the handle would break on one of the tools, he was skillful enough to make his own. His axe, shovel, and hoe handles looked identical to ones sold at the stores. They were made from oak wood. The small roads were made of reddish looking clay and were very hard.

There were swamps in the area where they lived and plenty of wildlife, both plants and animals. There were many ponds and lakes. Fish and animals were plentiful. There were many springs in the wooded areas. All types of herbs were in the woods, and Rose told me that her dad knew all of them. He used his tools on his farm and dug his own well with them. After digging real deep through the clay, he was able to get to the spring waterline. The water was as cold as ice and tasted very good. During the process of digging his well, grand-dad would have a rope line tied to him. If something went wrong, he could be pulled out to prevent a tragedy. He was successful and did not have any problems. Once the well was dug successfully, shelter was built around it. On the inside of the shed was a metal pulley. It was anchored to the top of it. A metal chain ran through the pulley with a bucket attached to it. I believe the chain was very long to reach the depth of the well. As a young boy, my grandma would take me back and forth to Georgia with her. She would visit her brother who was Uncle Spudge. He lived in the rural area of Leary. I remember getting water from a well built by my granddaddy. Also, I have many other memories and experiences, which I will share later.

Rose told me that everybody had certain daily chores or tasks to do, including her parents. It was difficult to go to school and get an education because of the work. Pi did not believe in getting an education and made it difficult to get one. However, my grandma had a decent education and wanted her kids to get one. Rose and her sister Fannie managed to slip away from home and obtain some elementary education. It was taught at a Baptist church, and they had to purchase their books and pay tuition. When they were promoted to seventh grade they had to quit school.

The land rented by my granddad adjoined and was contiguous to hundreds of wooded acres of land. He was allowed to use as much as needed to farm on. They did not have a clock to know the time of day; however, they listened for the chickens to crow. The chickens would crow during the day and night. They crowed at one, five, and twelve o'clock. He had chickens, turkeys, peacocks, quails, and other foul birds.

They were fenced in on the property. Grandpa and his sons built barns to store corn, watermelon, and other fruits and vegetables for long periods. They stored hay in the barns. Their peanuts were stacked around tall poles to get dry. Stables were built for their animals.

When the chickens crowed at five in the morning, my grandparents would get out of bed. The children had to be up prior to daylight. Pi would start the fire for the stove. The stove was called a wood stove because it used wood to derive its energy. Mi would make coffee and cook food for the family. During the winter, Pi would make sure the fireplace was burning most of the time. He would sit back in his rocking chair near the fireplace and smoke his pipe while drinking coffee.

Rose told me that she was very young when she learned how to work. When she was approximately six years old, she had to work. That was in the early 1920s. Only she and her sister Fannie were living with their parents. Their brothers ran away at an early age. Rutha was married and lived in the town of Leary. Fannie had to help her mother cook and clean the house and work on the farm. My mother was responsible for feeding the animals and giving them water to drink. She had to work on the farm too.

Every year, the four of them would clear new farming land. Each year, they would use the process of rotation by farming on different land. The girls had to use the plow behind their mule along with their father. Pi told my mother and aunt that he did not care how much food they would eat because of working so hard. There was something to do all the time.

When not working on the farm, they had to cut down cypress, hickory, and oak trees. The oak and hickory wood was used to heat and cook food. Rose and her sister had to cut and split the wood. It had to be cut to the correct size and stored at their home. They used manual saws with a handle on each end to cut the trees down. Everything was done manually, and it was hard work.

Pi carried his rifles and shotguns to hunt while they cut and gathered wood. He carried traps in his wagon. The traps would be placed in special locations to catch wild animals, such as raccoons. Rose told me that raccoon meat is delicious. Sweet potatoes would be cooked around the meat. Pi was a very good hunter. He hunted deer and birds.

They smoked beef and pork in their smokehouse. Pi had beehives and stored plenty of honey. He sold honey to his customers. He was the only person in Leary, having beehives. He robbed the hives for honey without hardly any stings. He knew how to attract the bees when they flew over his property. Rose said he would have some sort of tin cans in each hand and beat them together to attract the bees. The bees would hear the noise, and the colony of them would enter the cages and live on their property. They were attracted by the noise made with the tin cans. He even made horns to call deer, wild boar, turkeys, and quail birds.

Fannie had to milk the cows. She made butter manually in the churn. They kept plenty of butter and buttermilk the whole year. She helped her mother prepare and cook food. They would make jelly and preservatives from different types of fruits. Rose said her mother was an excellent cook. She made flaky biscuits that were very light. She cooked her own flour bread in a skillet because her mother's bread was not heavy enough to get full. Fannie, her sister, always said that Rose was greedy and ate too much. However, their father told them that they could cook and eat any amount of food. They kept plenty of food the whole year.

Pi grew very large watermelons. It took almost a year to grow them. Some of them were too heavy for one person to lift. They were super melons. Rose told me they were very sweet. You could almost see the sugar inside them. The ones we eat today are no comparison. They used horse and cow manure. Today, they are harvested in approximately three months with fertilizer. It is rare to eat a sweet one. It is doubtful to see any super ones that would take more than one person to lift. The melons were stored between hay in the barn for nearly a year.

Rose told me that when she had spare time, she would clear an area of land for her small farm. She grew sweet potatoes and watermelons. By having her own farm, she thought that would prevent Fannie from calling her greedy. However, that did not stop her sister. She continued to call her greedy.

According to my mother, when they became ill, my grandfather would gather herbs from the woods and make a remedy for their ailment. Other black families would come for medical treatment too. In the town of Leary, there was a white doctor. He gave everybody the same medicine. They would be given some black pills to take for their problem. So all of the rural blacks stopped going to town for treatment from the white doctor. They went to my granddad for treatment. All of the folks referred to the white doctor as the white doctor with the black pills.

Pi was really a botanist in reality. He knew which wild herb to use for a medical complaint. He knew how to make medicine to treat bad colds and flu. He would mix eggs and sugar with some of his moonshine He referred to it as his homemade eggnog. He knew how to mix and beat it up. Rose stated that a bad flu epidemic came when she was in her teens. The only survivors were the ones who drank her dad's eggnog. The white doctor and the others came to the farm and got some of it. He gave it to people and did not charge any money for it.

He had several remedies for the flu and bad colds. A vine grew in the pecan trees. Pi said it was ladyfinger. Rose said that the vine had joints on it similar to the joints on a finger. They would boil the ladyfinger until it turned to oil. It resembled mineral or castor oil. They would drink it to help build their immune system to fight off the flu and bad colds.

Pork salad was an herb that grew on rich soil. It grew near cow and horse pastures. It resembled collard greens. It was edible once a year and used to cleanse your blood. It grew berries that would turn dark blue. When it produced berries, it became poisonous and not edible. The berries were used on babies and small children to treat thrash. They would use the dark blue juice from the berries. To treat the thrash, the juice would go on the child's mouth and tongue.

They made a toothbrush from the branches of a tree which was called the knotty tree. It grew about five feet in height. Nodules that were on the tree limbs are the reason for calling it the knotty tree. The branches would be cut about the length of a toothbrush. They would chew the round nodules at the end of the stick until it became soft. Then it would be dried out by the sun. That would be their toothbrush. Rose stated that it worked better than the modem-day toothbrush. An herb was made from the roots of a tree referred as rattlesnake tree roots. The rattlesnake tree root herbs and other medicinal herbs were used to cure syphilis. They referred to it as the bad disease. Another tree was called the sweet gum tree. It had nodules on its branches. The nodules had a sweet flavoring agent. They would chew them the way one would chew gum.

They made their tea from "lifalastic and sassafras" bushes. Both of them had a delicious flavor. Corn husks were used to help make mops. Brooms were made from a plant that grew in the woods. Along with various tool handles, my granddad made rub boards. Rub boards were used to help clean and wash clothes. My grandmother would boil their clothing in a metal washpot outdoors. She made her soap with lye and animal oils in the washpot. They named it lye soap. It was similar to octagon soap. There were many other herbs according to Rose. Those are the only ones she can remember. She told me that her father treated many people for diseases and illnesses. He was better than the white doctor in the town of Leary.

Pi died in 1939. He was living in the country in Leary, Georgia. My grandpa was seventy-four years old when he died. He is buried at Mt. Zion Missionary Baptist Church in Leary. He was not a member of the church. He was a member of St. Mary Baptist Church. They did not have a cemetery on their church grounds. Mt. Zion had one. He attended church services at Mt. Zion, a few times a year with his family. They were members of Mt. Zion. My grandmother, Pheny, is buried there too.

According to my mother, Try-Fennie Davis, was my grandmom's name. Her marriage license on February 12, 1897 documented her name as Pheny Davis. That was in Georgia. Rose alleged that she informally changed her name to Fennie. That was done when she was young. The 1920 U.S. Census Bureau documented it as Fennie. Whereas, the 1910 report listed it as Phenora. In 1949, her death certificate documented her as Fannie Anderson. She died on March 10, 1949, and was 64 years old. Her body was transported to Leary, Georgia. She was buried in the cemetery at Mt. Zion Missionary Baptist Church.

She was a faithful member of that church. Her husband Jeff is buried there too. He was not a member of Mt. Zion.

I was eight years old when she died. We had a wonderful relationship. To me, she was my mother. It really shocked me when she died. I remember when she became sick. The doctor treated her and discharged her. His name was Dr. George. I think she had a stroke. She was not bedridden, but she would be in it most of the time. The room was next to the front porch. Sometimes, I went in the room to spend time with her. She would hold my hand while we chatted. I remember telling her, "Ma, please don't die. She responded and said, "Son, you don't have to worry; everything will be all right." There were two windows between the bedroom and front porch. Sometimes, I would sit on the porch and raise the window up. Then I would talk with her. I remember rubbing her head a few times. I took some soup for her a few times.

After a few weeks, she died in the bed. It took me aback and into shock. I stopped going into that bedroom. I would go into the woods to be alone. I would cry and shed tears. I just wanted to be by myself. I had lost my best friend.

At her funeral, I remember seeing my grandmother the very last time. Her body was in a casket. It was open to view her body. I remember walking to the casket shedding tears. Someone placed their arms around me. Then I placed one of my hands on her face and rubbed it. Her skin was very hard. Mentally, I feel it today. After the church services, she was buried in the cemetery. The cemetery belonged to the church. It was next to it. She was buried next to her husband. Their son, Charley, is also buried there.

My grandmother loved to eat vegetables, chicken feet, pig tails, ears, and pig feet. She was an excellent cook. She could bake some real good large homemade biscuits. I really liked her chicken with dumplings.

When we returned to Pompano, I refused to go back to school. My mom, Rose, had to get up early in the morning to work on the farm. Uncle Charley went to his construction job. I would leave the house with my lunch bucket. There were three Avenues in New-Town. They were 9th, 10th, and 11th Avenue. Two of them were a mixture of dirt and rocks. The other one was a short dirt road which was 9th Avenue. The road was a short road with five or six homes. I remember a few of the families. One man we called him Geechy Black. His daughter was a year behind me in high school. She is a retired teacher and currently resides in my neighborhood. Another man was a short man, and we called him a little Shorty. We called an elderly lady Aunt Gertrude. The road was short and did not go through to Hammondville Road. When the road ended, we had to walk through a path in the woods. It led us to Hammondville Road. Every one called that area The Oat Field.

Instead of going to school, I went to The Oat Field. I would play until I became tired. Then I would sit in the shade under a tree. When I thought it was near time for lunch. I would eat my food from my lunch bucket. I would join the children walking from school. Then I would go home as if I had been to school. At the end of the term, I was demoted to first grade.

My grandmother was a very quiet woman. She was not talk-ative. Sometimes, my mother would ask her, "When are you going to talk?" Grandma would reply, "There is nothing to talk about." She was about five feet tall and medium built. She wore a strawhat most of the time. One was purchased for me. We would walk together to the store or visit friends. She would hold one of my hands. Sometimes, we would go the store or visit a few friends. One of her friends was Mrs. Jake. Her husband's nickname was Mr. Fat. He had a farm and some hogs. Mr. Fat sold "Cuba Numbers" too. Sometimes, she would buy a few numbers. Two of their sons or grandsons lived with them.

They had to get slop for the hogs. One of them is Charles Ellington who is a friend. We call him The Boogie-Man. His brother is older than him. Everybody call him Hicky. He is a few years older than Charles. The majority of families would save leftover food in cans. It was left behind their homes. That would be the slop for the hogs.

My grandma had a friend in New-Town whose name was Miss Washington. She lived next door to Miss Daisy Brown. Her grandson whose name is Renard Brown lived with her. Renard is a cousin and classmate. David Wiggins lived with Miss Washington. He was her grandson. She was a mean lady. She chastised David all the time. The children in New-Town, were afraid of her.

The Gates families lived across the street from us. My friend was Johnny Gates. Sometimes, I would go to their house. Johnny and I would play and have fun. A few times when I went home, my grandmother would not be home. She had walked to the store. When I returned home, I would inquire about her to my mother. I would leave the house running and yelling her name. "Grandma is scared to walk alone." I would get with her at the store. We would walk to the house. She would be holding one of my hands.

In Leary, she had a friend whose name was Carrie Carter. Her husband was a preacher. One of the church members was his mistress. Her name was Jane Figgin. Both of the women were friends. Often, she ate some of Carrie's food. Someone put some poison in her food. She died. Most of the folks believed that Carrie killed Jane. Willie Figgin was Jane's husband. Clarence Figgin was their son. He was very slew-footed. Doll Baby was his wife's nickname.

My grandfather cheated on my grandmother a few times. They were separated during the 1920s. She moved to Daytona Beach, Florida. She was a maid at a motel or hotel. Wilbert-By-The-Sea was its name. She eventually moved to Arlington and lived with her sister, Fannie. After a few weeks, she returned to Leary. She and her husband went back together.

During the 1930s, he contracted a sexually transmitted disease. The folks called it a Bad Disease. It had to be syphilis. Grandma stated that the woman was ugly, skinny, and had real dark skin. Her name was Alice Boyd. She was married. Her husband was Albert Boyd. Alice had a brother named Lewis Boyd. My grandmother remained with Jeff. But she never had any more sex with him.

Sometimes, I would walk to the business section in the black community. My grandmother would hold my hand. We wore straw-hats on our head. When we got near people, I would snatch my hand away from my grandmother. I would say to her "Grandma, I am a big boy. I can take care of myself. Some of the folks would laugh. Some of them would be her friends. You do not have to hold my hand around people." She would get pissed off with me. My grand-mother would not let nobody spank me. That included my mother, Rose. One day, my mother spanked me, and that was her last time. Grandma picked up a broomstick and hit her on the back with the stick. She almost fell on the floor. My grandma told her, "You know that I told you that I'm the only person allowed to chastise this boy." When my grandma spanked me, she would pat me with her hand a few times. Then she would say, "Stop being a bad boy. Be a good boy."

My grandmother lived with her stepfather in Dawson, Georgia. Her brothers and sister lived with him. Jim Jones was his name. He raised them after their mother's death. Jim had some other children by another woman. They lived in the house with them. He had a daughter who became a teacher. Lela Jones was her name. He sent his children to school. I do not know the names of the other children. His stepchildren were not allowed to attend school. They had to work on his farm.

My grandmother managed to get an education. She attended high school. It was at a church. They had to pay a tuition fee. She told me that one of her books was referred to as *The Webster Blue Back Speller*. It taught them how to use a syllable when spelling words. She was an excellent speller of words. She had more education than her children. It is possible that she finished high school. The names of her relatives are as follows:

(1) Major Davis, father
(2) Rutha Davis, mother
(3) Fannie Davis, daughter
(4) Fennie Davis, daughter
(5) Amos Davis, son
(6) Andy Davis, son
(7) John Henry Davis, son
(8) Major Davis Jr., son

(9)   Jim Jones, step-father
(10) Lela Jones, step-sister
(11) Willie Mae Jones, stepsister
(12) Additional Jones children, unknown

All of them realized that they were treated unfairly by their step-father. He made them do most of the farmwork. His children did not have to work on it. As they grew older, they moved away from him.

Two of the boys were named after the black comedians on the radio. They are Amos Davis and Andy Davis. The legendary famous radio show was called The Amos and Andy Show. Amos Davis was the oldest sibling. He and his brother were members of the all Black Masonic Lodge. Someone did something to one of them. They waited for the people to attend church on Sunday. While the people were in the church, they shot into it. One or two people were injured or killed. They fled to some of their masonic members. The masonic members hid them. Contact was made with a black mortician, who was a mason. "Amos and Andy were put in caskets, as if they were dead. The caskets were placed on a train and shipped to an unknown state. Members of the Mason Lodge in Dawson, Georgia, had informed the other lodge, about them. For a while, both of them lived with masonic friends in a Northern State or perhaps Canada. They sent letters to their stepfather, Jim Jones. He refused to give them to their sisters.

The crime took place between 1896 and 1898 at the church. Rose informed me that her mother told her that because of her step-father's treatment, she had planned to get married and move. Jeff became her first boyfriend. She was twelve years old. They got married, and she moved in with him. She had her first child when she was thirteen years old.

From time to time, she would visit her stepfather, Jim Jones. She was aware about the particulars with her brothers. He would tell her that her brothers had written a letter. Then he would say, "I will let you read them on your next visit." That went on for a few visits. In my opinion, that was a terrible way to treat a stepdaughter. He could have given her one of the letters. Perhaps, he was mad because she had eloped and gotten married. On her last visit, he had died and was buried. The wood house had caught fire and burned up. She lost contact with her brothers. She believed that they were living in New York or Canada.

John Henry Davis, another brother, had a live-in job in Atlanta, Georgia. He worked for a couple who was married. He had a key to the house. He informed the white family that he was going out of town. This was on the weekend. For some reason, he returned to the house on a Sunday. When he entered the house, he was shot and killed. Rose alleged that her mother told her that "they believed the husband thought, John Henry, was having an affair with the wife." He told the police that he thought John Henry was a burglar. They believed him. He was not charged with a crime.

Major Davis Jr. was employed as a cook in Jacksonville, Florida. He worked on a ship. One day, after a few drinks while on the deck, he fell off the ship. He was drowned in the water. My grandmother believed that he was pushed off the ship. That left her with bad feelings about Jasonville. She swore that she would never enter that town again. And she did not during her lifetime. Fannie Davis, her sister, got married to Primas Crawford. They lived in Arlington, Georgia. The two of them had a large number of children.

UNCLE JEFF

Jefferson Anderson is my maternal grandfather. That name was documented and recorded on a marriage license. He got married to my grandmother in Georgia. It was in 1897. The 1910 and 1920 Census Bureau recorded his name as Jeff Anderson. One of them documented his place of birth in Alabama and the other one listed Georgia. He told everyone that he was born in Alabama. According to the records, he was born on 1865. He stated many times that he was born after the Civil War.

Pi was his nickname. The majority of the white folks called him Uncle Jeff. A few blacks called him that too. He died in Leary, Georgia, in 1939 or 1940. I was born on 1941. However, my mother talked about him numerous times. I would take notes on paper. He had a half black and white sister. She was born during slavery. Her name was Lela Anderson.

According to my mother whose name is Rose, the slave master would beat his mother and force her to have sex with him. She was forced to have sex many times. She became pregnant and had his daughter. The child was very light skinned.

I was told by Rose that his parents became successful farmers after slavery was abolished. They owned their home and the land. It was a significant amount of land. The land had water on it. They grew rice on the farm along with many more plants and vegetables.

Also, cows, hogs, chickens, and mules were owned by them. Based upon that information, they must have been free slaves. He told his wife and children that some of the white people were jealous about their success.

When he was a teenager, he decided to go for a stroll on their wagon. He hitched up the mule to the wagon. He was in his late teens or twenties or more. That would have been between 1880 through 1885. He parked the mule and wagon next to a tree in the woods. Three to four young white men approached him. Afterward, they got into an argument. The white folks said, "We are gonna kill a nigger today." The white thugs attacked him. That was a big mistake. He was fearful for his life and shot and killed a couple of them. The other ones were cut to death with his pocket knife. He went home and told his parents about it. He headed to the woods to get out of Alabama. He was a genius concerning wildlife. He had learned a lot about plants and animals. His father had taught him how to survive in the woods. He was an excellent hunter and an expert shot. My grandfather was an excellent swimmer too.

He was scared and knew that the Klan and the white folks would lynch and kill him. He hoped that they would not ascertain who killed those thugs. They would burn his parent's home up and kill all of them. It was no such thing as self-defense for a black man. He got the hell out of Alabama and never looked back. He hit the woods and the swamp lands.

He walked through the woods and entered the swamps. He ate what he had to eat to survive. He knew which plants were edible. He knew the poisonous ones too. Sometimes, he had to swim across deep water. He came out of the swamps and ended up in Georgia. He was able to get to work on the farms in the small towns. He told the folks that his parents had died during slavery. Most of the folks thought he was just one of the hobos. He didn't have any trouble getting jobs. He could make logs by cutting trees. He knew how to build fireplaces. He dug a few wells to get drinking water. Sometimes, he would fish and hunt wildlife. It was sold to some of the folks. He did not have any education but was very talented.

Some of the farms were in Dawson, Arlington, Leary, and Williamsburg, Georgia. He was young, energetic, and adventurous. He had gotten away with murder in Alabama. After saving a few dollars, he would quit his job. He told his bosses that he wanted to go to Florida. He knew how to hitch a ride on the freight trains. He rode on one to Tallahassee, got a few jobs, and ended up in a small town near the Okefenokee Swamp. He got a job in one of the small towns. His boss liked the way he worked. According to Rose, her father was allowed to live in one of the buildings.

The boss, who was white, had a young son who liked to talk with Jeff. One Sunday, his father went to buy something from a hardware store. The little boy went to the building where Jeff lived. He said, "You know my dad really like you, and I do too. Then he said, "I want to show you something." He took him to another building that was near a lake. They went into the building. All of the buildings were made out of wood. The young boy pointed at a man-made door in the center of the floor. It had a padlock on it. Then the boy said, "Uncle Jeff, this is where my father brought the bad niggers." When he got pissed off with them, this is where he brought them. My dad would get his rifle and make them walk into the basement. Then he would make them lift the door and walk down the steps below the building. He said that his father would go down there with his gun too. Then he said, "The bad nigger would not be seen again. He would be missing, and that would be it.

Jeff had a hot temper and knew it. He made plans to move while his boss and family were sleeping. He had packed some food and his belongings. During the night, he left into the woods. Rose told me that her father said he knew that he was not going to open the door and go down into the basement. He said, "The white man would have had to kill him. One of them would have died in a terrible fight."

Jeff traveled and worked in the northern portion of Florida. He did the same thing in southern Georgia. He was afraid to return to Alabama. He lost contact with his parents and sister. They were never seen again. He hoped that the Klu Klux Klan did not find out who killed the white men. He knew what they would do. If they knew that he had killed them. The Klan would have killed all of his kin. Then they would have burned up their home. Based upon that premise, he refused to return to Alabama.

He became tired of working and living in Florida. It was during the 1890s when he was more than thirty years old. He chose to migrate to Georgia. He walked and swam through the Okefenokee Swamp. When he came out of the swamp, he was a few miles away from Waycross, Georgia. The folks in those small towns were in disbelief. It was hard to believe that a person could survive in the swamp from Florida to Georgia. They told Jeff that he was a lucky man. "You are the first one that they knew was able to come out of it." Jeff was revered by the local folks. He worked on the nearby farms. On his spare time, he earned money from some of the skills he had. Enough money was saved to buy a mule and a wagon. All of the odds were stacked against him during the Jim Crow and segregation eras. He managed to be a jack-of-all-trades. He mastered them too. Most of his skills came from his parents. He always managed to get some friends who were Indians. He picked up a lot of skills from them too. A few of them lived in Alabama, Florida, and Georgia.

My granddad had made plans to return to Leary. He had to travel to the southwestern portion of Georgia. He traveled from town to town until he was nearly out of money. Then he would earn enough money to leave the area. Sometimes, he told the folks that he was from Florida. Then he would tell them that he wanted to travel to different parts of Georgia. Most of the folks said that he was very adventurous.

He knew some of the folks in Leary and in some of the surrounding towns. He got a job on George Colley's farm. They became friends. Then he rented some land from George. He grew cotton and peanuts to earn money. He lived in a small shack that was on the land. It was modified into a house by my grandfather.

On a weekend, he decided to ride on his buggy and mule to Dawson. It was in 1896, during the Christmas and New Year holidays. While visiting a few friends, he met my grandmother, Fennie Davis. She was twelve years old and became his girlfriend. He traveled from Leary to be with her. She did not like the treatment from her stepfather, Jim Jones. She had planned to get a boyfriend and get married.

In February 1897, she got married. She left her stepfather a note and returned to Leary with her husband. She became pregnant and had her first child when she was thirteen. A few months after the wedding, Jeff told her about the incident in Alabama. She made an attempt to encourage him to visit his parents. He would say, "Oh no, my lord, the dry paper will not rot." He meant what was written about him would continue to exist. I am quite sure that he was talking about a warrant.

Jeff got into a confrontation with a white man. It was about seven years after his marriage. The white man was poor. His name was John Mack. His son was Innis Mack. John was a sharecropper with the Jordan family. He and his wife lived in Jordan's property. One of the Jordans owned a peanut mill in Leary.

Some of Jeff's cows and hogs escaped from his property. They went to the property where John Mack lived. His wife had some clothes hanging on the clothing line. The animals entered the yard and chewed on the clothes. John chased the animals away from the property. John was able to ascertain the owner of the animals. He went to Jeff's house. He told Jeff to get his cows and hogs and put them in the fenced land. He said, "Uncle Jeff, they came to my house and went to the clothing line and chewed up our clothes. If they do it again, I will shoot and kill all of them." My grandfather told Mr. Mack, "That will be the day you will die. If you shoot one of my cows or hogs, I will kill you. The best thing to do is chase them off the property." Mr. Mack replied, "Uncle Jeff, I have been to prison. I went there because of shooting bad ass niggers like you. I shot a few of them." My grandfather told him, "That is the reason why I cannot return to Alabama because of killing crackers like you. You had better leave this property. If you do not, you are going to die today." John Mack went home. That was their last confrontation while living in Leary.

In Morgan, Georgia, the folks would get their corn grounded into meal. The name of the facility was Couldry Mill. There was a real tall hill in the road. My grandfather would hitch up his horse to the buggy. He named the horse Queen. He would gather his corn and make my mother ride with him. She was about five years old and afraid of heights. She said the tall hill was not very far from the Court House.

She was afraid to ride across the hill. She did not like to ride to the mill with her father. The reason was the tall hill in the road. He knew she was scared and would say, "Nig, don't be afraid."

My grandfather was a very courageous man. The Klu Klux Klan was terrible in those days. They did not bother him. He was given respect. Perhaps, it was due to his friendship with George Colley. He was very talkative and was an extrovert. On some Sundays, he would go to town. The business district was booming in those days. He would park his buggy and horse around the comer near the saloon. It was where the black folks would hang out. They would drink whiskey. Some of them would dance. All of the folks knew him. He was a popular man, especially with the women. One day, he had a little too much booze. The police confronted him and said, "Uncle Jeff, you've had too much to drink. Get on your buggy and go home." He said, "Yes, Mr. White Folks, I will do that." It was several police officers. I am sure that they were deputy sheriffs. The town was too small to have a police department. Instead of going home, my grandfather went and parked his buggy and horse at another spot. The law enforcement officials could not see him. About thirty minutes later, he was spotted by three of them. They walked and approached him. One of them said, "Uncle Jeff, we have given you a warning to go home. We are going to arrest you. When you become sober, you would be allowed to go home." Jeff was standing near his buggy and his horse, Queen. Leary did not have a jail. They used a small building similar to the size of an outdoor toilet. The name of it was a calaboose. The officers held both of his hands together in front of him. Then the handcuffs were put on. One of the officers unlocked the padlock. They said, "Uncle Jeff, we are going to keep you in the calaboose over the weekend. You will get sober in there. Then you will be able to get home." Jeff replied, "I am not going inside that little house, Mr. White Folks. It looks like a shit-house to me. They got into a fight. Jeff beat two of the officers with his hands cuffed in front of him. Two of them were knocked down. One of them was reaching for his gun to shoot Jeff. The other officers discouraged him from shooting Jeff. They said, "Uncle Jeff whipped us. It was fair and square. Even with the cuffs on him. He is too good of a man to kill." They managed to get him in the calaboose with the help of some of the folks. After getting sober, he was taken to the county jail in Dawson because of the fight. George Colley, his friend, got him out of jail. He got on his buggy and said, "Gitty-up!" to Queen. That meant for the horse to go. All of his horses were trained by him. Wooh meant for them to stop walking or running. Haw meant for them to turn to the left. Gee meant to turn to the right.

My mother told me that her father was a very hard working man. She and her sister, Fannie (Anna) were living with their parents. The other children had moved away from the house. Three females and one male lived in the house. When it came to work, he did not discriminate. Rose and her sister had to work as if they were men. They had to cut down trees and make logs for the house. The wood was used to cook with in the stove. Some of it were burned in the fireplace.

One day, he had to dig a well in the clay. He was an expert. It was tedious and dangerous work. He was a brave man. He could have been killed by an accident. The water was used to drink, and it was cold as ice. He had to dig to the waterline from the springs. Rose said that he would be very far in the hole. They could not see him. He would use ropes as a harness to get out of the well. It would be tied to a tree. Another one had a bucket connected to it. A small shed had been built. It was around the area where the well was dug. A pulley was attached inside of the shed. The rope hung across the pulley. It was the rope with bucket. It was a lifting mechanism built by him. When Jeff was fairly deep in the hole, he would fill the bucket with clay dirt. Rose and her sister had to pull the bucket to the surface. They would empty it and send it back to their father. That process would continue until he had struck the waterline. The rope which was tied to a tree would be used to climb out of the well. Some of the folks would hire him to dig a well for them.

My mother said that Jeff was a competitor and a positive thinker. He had to be number one and the best at any task or chore. When it came to farming, she said, "Pi had a real good green thumb." He was uneducated and hated school. She said that if he would have listened to them, he could have become wealthy. He could not read or write and refused to listen to them. He would put money in the bank. It was from the farm. She said that he was a very free-hearted man. He would give some money to strangers and friends. Then he would spend and give some to his women. Rose said, "He could have bought the land." He continued to rent it.

In those woods, he would hunt and set traps for animals. They lived off the land and the animals. He collected their hides. He knew how to dry and preserve them. Most of it was sold to Sears, Roebuck and Montgomery Ward. They had their magazines and bought items by mail. One of their representatives came and bought the hide. He collected sap from trees and sold it. He was an excellent cook. He baked a cake during the winter in the fireplace. He called it Pi's ash cake. The cake would be baked under the ashes in the fireplace. When it was cooked, it would be removed from under the ashes. A brush was used to remove the dust from it. Then the cake was wiped with a damp towel. His wife and children said, "The cake was real delicious."

He was not afraid of water. He was an excellent swimmer. He could do almost anything in the ponds. He loved to swim in the springs. He could tread the water and float on his back. Sometimes, he would smoke his pipe while floating. When freestyling, he was fast.

After building the house, a few barns were built. He had plenty of them to store many things. Some were used to store his moonshine. Everything was built from the trees in the woods. That included his furniture. He made his own shingles for the roof. Others were used to store corn, nuts, syrup, honey, and preservatives. One was used to store his hay. He built a smoke house for his meat. He knew how to smoke and preserve it. Watermelon and sweet potatoes were stored in a barn. They had plenty of food to eat. Rose said that Jeff grew real sweet large watermelons. They were as sweet as sugar. The melons were harvested once a year in July.

His fireplace was built with two chimneys. A lot of people would pay him to build one for them. My mother said that he was an excellent fisherman. He caught many species of fish. The white folks would buy all of the channel catfish. They were six feet or more long. He kept it a secret where they were caught. He caught otters and beavers and sold their hide. Jeff made his own "gig" to catch alligators and crocodiles. Some of them were monsters that grew up to twenty feet in length. He ate some of their meat. To him, it tasted like a combination of fish and chicken. Their hides were sold along with some of their meat. He killed and sold bear hide.

He built his honey beehives and knew how to attract the wild bees to them. Rose said that he would gather some metal cans. He would stand near his beehives. When he saw the wild bees flying, he would beat the cans together. He would make a humming noise along with the cans. My mother said that the bees would enter his hives. Sometimes, he would use smoke to run away most of the bees.

Then he would get some honey and wax from the hives. It was rare to get a sting.

Rose stated that her father was a compassionate man. He enjoyed helping people. He would buy seeds and grew a large variety of vegetables. Oftentimes, he said that he was growing some to help orphan children and widowed women. When it was harvested, he would load a wagon up and take it to them. Several times, he helped a few convicts who had escaped. They were working in the woods or along the side of the road. Some of them would escape. Rose told me that she had seen the convicts running toward them. They were working on the farm. They were black men. The uniforms had white with black stripes on them. Just looking at the uniforms made her scared. The men had managed to get the chains and balls from their legs. Jeff took them to one of his barns and hid them under the hay. He went back to the farm. He was using the plow when the convicts came on the farm. He plowed over all of their shoe prints. Shortly afterward, the police came with their bloodhound dogs. The police asked them if they saw the two convicts. Jeff replied that they were too busy working to see them. Then he pointed into an opposite direction from his house. He pointed in the opposite direction. He said, "They went to that area."

A lot of ponds are in that area. Then he said, "I will get in touch with you if I see them." They thanked him and took off with the dogs.

After a few days, he took them some clothes and food to eat. He burned the uniforms up. They hid about a month in the barn. He gave them some food and a few dollars. After things had gotten quiet, he hitched up the mule and wagon. It was during the night. The men were taken to one of the small towns where the trains were parked. They were not passenger trains. The trains were used to haul freight, and they were able to hitch a ride.

Another girlfriend was Daisy Smart. She was married to Clark Smart. They were separated when Jeff was dating Daisy. She had a sister whose nickname was Sister. They lived in Bozzie Keel's property. Daisy had a lot of children. Martin Smart was a big fat short man. He was Clark's father.

Rose alleged that her father caught a bad disease while cheating. He caught it from Alice Boyd whose husband was dead. His name was Albert Boyd. He had a brother whose name was Nedus Boyd. After that, my grandmother stopped having sex with him.

A man whose name was Rich Rutledge was another friend. He was married to Emma Rutledge. She appeared to be an Indian. He lived in the Colley's property. Rich bought a horse from a circus. He named the horse Son. When walking with the horse, Mr. Rutledge would say, "Ad — Son, Gitty it up!"

All of the folks said that the horse was a Show Horse. The horse walked like it was from a circus. Their daughter was called Shane.

Rose said that her father could really entertain people. He could sing, dance, and play some musical instruments. They were the harp, drums, guitar, and piano. He would sing music for the square dancers or any other type of dance. He could do any of the popular dances. The Charleston and the Frolic are a couple of them.

All of the folks in Leary called his farm Uncle Jeff's farm. He called his farm the one-back farm. He meant that his farm was very far in the woods. That is why he gave it that name. He was very courageous and was not afraid of anything. He was not afraid to threaten or challenge the white folks. He got into an argument with a young white man. The white guy said, "I will kick all of your teeth out of your mouth." Jeff was wearing his overalls. He kept a sharp pocket knife in one of the pockets. He grabbed the white guy and held him with one hand. He intentional fell backward with the white guy on top of him. While falling on the ground, he managed to get his knife. He held the white guy with one hand. Then he would cut him with the knife. It was in the other hand. The white guy was unable to get off Jeff. The young white man started screaming. He said, "Help! Help! I need someone to pull me off this nigger. Please, take me off him before he kills me." Jeff's family members took his knife. They took the young white man off him. He left the property bleeding from the cuts. Jeff told the white guy, "You are lucky. If my family had not been here, you would have been a dead cracker." They were not life-threatening. He never returned to that area in those woods.

One day, two white men walked on his property. They wanted to know his name. He told them that he was Uncle Jeff. They responded, "We are not going to call you Uncle Jeff." He politely asked them to leave the property. They were reluctant to leave. He went into the house and returned with a rifle. The men said, "We were joking. Do not shoot us, Mr. Jeff." They said, "We meant Uncle Jeff" and left in a hurry.

Rose said that he helped many people. When some of the black people got into trouble, they would come to his farm. A single woman whose name was Miss Carrie worked for Bozzie Keel Junior. He was a white man. She was his girlfriend. Her son was named Walter. They lived in the house with her boyfriend. He named the boy Walter. For some reason, some of the people would call him Sol.

Effie Keel was the boyfriend's mother. Effie worked at the cotton gin in Leary. The Keels may have owned it. One day, Ms. Carrie and her boyfriend got into a fight in the house. She pushed him and his head hit the fireplace. They cooled off from the fight. Then she went outside to get milk from the cows. After a few moments, Bozzie came outside. They got into another altercation and fight. Walter was working on the farm with the mule and plow. He heard his mother screaming for help. Walter grabbed the steel Beam used to weigh bales of cotton. They call it a P. Walter hit Bozzie on the head with the P. It killed him. All of the folks called his father Benny Melvin. I presume that his name was Benny Melvin Keel.

My mother told me that Benny Melvin Keel was killed by his father, Bozzie II, at the cotton gin. It could have been the opposite with Benny killing his father. It was one of the scenarios.

Walter was scared. He got on the mule and rode it to Jeff's farm. He told him what had happened. Jeff told Walter that he and his mother, to get the hell out of Georgia. He grabbed a bale or two of his cotton. They put them on the wagon. Queen, his horse, was hitched to it. Jeff told Walter, "You know his daughter is at the cotton gin. I am going to take you to your mother so you can leave. It will give you a chance to get out of Georgia." Jeff said, "If you do not leave, these whites will kill both of you. I want you and your mother to leave on a buggy and horse. Try to get to Williamsburg and get on a train." Then he said, "I know his daughter, Effie, will ask about him."

They arrived at the house and told Ms. Carrie to leave. She refused and told her son to leave. Jeff said to Ms. Carrie, "If you do not leave, the white folks are going to kill you. When they learn that Mr. Keel is dead, they will kill you." She told Jeff, "I did not kill him. They will not do anything to me. Walter got on the buggy and horse and left for Williamsburg. Jeff told him to hurry. Jeff took his time getting to the cotton gin.

When Jeff arrived at the cotton gin, Effie asked about her son. He said I am quite sure that he is fine. I did not stop to say hello, and I did not see him. He sold his cotton and went home. Many hours after Walter was gone, the white folks learned about the death. Miss Carrie told them about the fight. She told them that her son hit Bozzie on the head with the steel beam. She said that Walter was scared and ran into the woods. She told them that Bozzie was beating her. That was the reason her son had hit him on the head.

According to the U.S. 1910 Census Bureau, Bozzie was named after his father. His father was twenty three, and he was one year old. His mother, Effie, was twenty years old. He was probably killed during the 1920s.

A large group of white men and law enforcement officers looked for Walter. They had their guns and bloodhound dogs. He managed to get away. He went to Washington, D.C. on the trains. The next day, a group of white folks returned to the house. They grabbed Ms. Carrie and brutally attacked her. They took her in the woods a few feet away from a clay road. A mailbox was in the area alongside the road. Ms. Carrie was screaming and said, "I did not kill him. He was my boyfriend. My granddad told his family, "Ms. Carrie was a fool. I begged her to leave with her son." He said that he learned that one of the men had a steel rod. It was six or seven feet long. The men threw the woman on the ground. Some of them held her. He said, "They pushed that rod through her butt, and it protruded through her head." She was tied and hung from a tree. She was lynched and murdered in a scandalous manner. The white folks had plenty of alcohol to drink. They shot Ms. Carrie with their rifles. She was shot so many times until most of her meat fell on the ground. They left her body in the woods. A sign was posted "We dare any one to move her body. If it is moved we will kill you." That is what my grandfather's white friend told him. He was in the Colley family. Rose said he told her that the mail carrier made a complaint. The mail carrier met with officials from Leary. They were told that the odor was too bad to deliver mail. Those people were warned to move or allow someone to move the body. "If you do not move it, a complaint will be made to the federal government. After that, her body was removed and buried. Several years later, Walter returned with federal agents. He was allowed to get their belongings. Walter and the federal agents returned to the District of Columbia.

Jeff helped so many people when they were in trouble. One time, when the circus came to Leary, he helped a lady. She came with the circus and was a show lady. She was an attractive and shapely black woman. A married white man became her boyfriend. I do not have his name. She was discouraged from leaving with the circus. Her boyfriend got his mistress a place to live. The wife found out about the relationship and went to the Klan.

The show lady's boyfriend became aware of the Klan. When darkness came, he escorted his mistress to Uncle Jeff. He gave him some money and told him to hide her. I want you to take care of the show lady. He hid her in a barn. It was the barn that had corn in it. She was covered with the corn. An air pocket was left to get air to breathe.

The Klan got to her house too late. She was gone. Her boyfriend told them that she had moved. They did not believe him. For several weeks, the Klan stood on both sides of the clay road. They had their rifles and were looking for the lady. They would stop and check everybody traveling on the clay road. They were unable to find her.

Rose said that the woman hid in the barn nearly a month. Jeff thought the Klan had stopped searching for her. He was wrong. The woman had a fair complexion. At night, she was taken from the barn into the house. Her hair was cut very short to resemble a man. Jeff got some smut from the fireplace chimney. It was rubbed all over her skin. Then she was dressed into a pair of pants. The clothes were made for men. A hat was placed on her head. The wagon and horse were hitched up. He decided to use his young horse, Queen. He planned to take the lady to Williamsburg and to wait for a train. They rode on the clay road for a few miles. They could see the mob on each side of it. They had rifles in their hands. Queen was a young nervous horse. The mob knew about the horse's history of nervousness.

When Queen got near the mob, she became nervous and would not stop. The horse took off and ran fast on the road. The mob of white folks said, "That is Uncle Jeff with that nervous horse. It looks like his son is on the wagon with him." He managed to get the lady to the train station. They had to wait until it opened in the morning. He bought a ticket for her and away she went. My mother said when he returned home the next day, the horse stopped for the mob. "They said, "We did not shoot because we know about this horse. And we could see you and your son." He answered, "Yes, sir, it was me and my son." The white folks asked, "Where did you go, Uncle Jeff? He said, "Good old white folks, I took my son to Williamsburg to ride on the train. He is visiting some of his kinfolks. I waited for the hardware store to open to buy some equipment for my plow. Take a look at it on my wagon. He uncovered the equipment that he had previously bought. It was a brand-new steel beam. The mob of white folks acknowledged that it was new and believed him. Leary had a train station, but they were not foolish enough to go to it.

The mob asked him had he seen the show lady. He answered no. Jeff told them. "You know, good old white folks, I will bring that bitch to you." They said, "We believe you, Uncle Jeff. We know that you are a good man. But if we knew you were helping her, we will kill you right now." Rose said that was a very close call for her father. She said that he told them, "It was a blessing that Queen got nervous and ran. And thank *God* for not taking the new equipment off the wagon.

Rose told me that Jeff, her father, decided to take a bath. It was cold during the winter. He picked up the tub and put it in front of the fireplace. The tub was made with galvanized tin. He heated the water and poured it in the tub. The fireplace was already lit. He got into an argument with his wife, Mi. Then he threw the bar of home-made soap at her. The soap struck her on the ear. It was bleeding. Anna, who is also called Fannie, was about six years old then. She picked up the soap and walked toward her father. He thought she was bringing the soap to him. That was not true. She walked up to her father with the soap. Then she hit him with it. Jeff jumped out of the tub. He told her, "I am going to kill you with my pocket knife. Do not hit me unless you want to die." He grabbed his daughter and held her on the floor. When he reached for his overalls to get his knife, his oldest son came in the house. His name is Edmond with the nickname Spudge. Spudge had been hunting and chose to visit them. He had his rifle with him. Then he asked his father why he was holding Fannie on the floor. Pi told Spudge, "She hit me with the soap. I plan to cut her head off with my knife. I have always said that is what I will do if one of you should hit me." Spudge told his father, Pi, not to do that. He said, "You are my father, and she is my sister. If you kill her, I will have to kill you with my gun." The rifle was pointed at his father. Spudge chatted with his mother, Mi, briefly and left with Fannie. He and his wife kept her until matters cooled off. Afterward, Fannie returned home. She cared more about Spudge than any of the other siblings. He was her favorite brother. You can't blame her because he saved her life.

One of his friends was Clark Smart. His wife was Daisy Smart. Martin Smart was his father. Mr. Clark owned some land in Williamsburg, Georgia, between 1884 and 1887. He died in 1931 in Leary. Another friend was Rich Rutledge. Emma was his wife. She looked as if she was an Indian. Rich owned a horse that he bought from a circus. All of the folks said, "It was a show horse." He enjoyed walking with his horse. He would hold the rope in his hand. Rich named his horse Son.

George Colley was Jeff's best friend. He rented his land from George. George was a farmer and businessman. He owned a cotton gin too. His wife was Cora Colley. According to my research on Ancestry.com, Mr. George Colley was a mulatto. My grandfather and mother thought he was a white man. It revealed that some of the folks passed for white and others as black. Most of the white folks believed that they were white. The 1990 US Census Bureau listed the following information.

(1) George Colley, age 51 in 1910. Born: 1859
(2) Cora Colley, age 45 in 1910. Born: 1865
(3) John Colley, age 18 in 1910. Born: 1892
(4) Dewey Colley, age 10 in 1910. Born: 1900
(5) Marvin Colley, age 7 in 1910. Born: 1903

Dewey Colley moved to Albany, Georgia, many years after adulthood. The Census Bureau reported him as a white person. He died in Albany. Today, some of his relatives live in Albany.

John Colley rode a bicycle with a rifle attached to it. He was well educated. Most of the folks thought he had learned too fast in school. They thought that he had a few screws missing in his head. My grandfather had an altercation with him. It was on a Sunday.

Apparently, he was not aware that Jeff rented the land from his dad. He thought Jeff was a sharecropper with his father. John wanted to know the reason they were not working on Sunday. Jeff told him that he rented the land and did not work on Sundays. Then he was chased away from the farm.

Jeff had a reputation as one of the best moonshine makers. His stills were made with copper. Only a few of the makers used copper stills. He had a big business with black and white customers. He made moonshine until his last arrest by the U.S. Federal Revenue agents. His friend George Colley got him out of jail. I do not think he was ever prosecuted. He made it for many years prior to and during the liquor prohibition era. He ran out of the woods quite a few times when the agents were looking for the stills. They were unable to catch him. The Agents knew it was him. However they destroyed his stills. Then they would come to his house and threaten to arrest Jeff. The agents would search the house and property. The contraband was stashed away in a barn. It was hidden under the corn. He would move his stills to another location in the woods. The raids continued until his last raid and arrest. George Colley advised him to give the moonshine business up. He said, "Uncle Jeff, those revenue agents work for the federal government. The next time, you are going to prison." He listened to his friend and quit.

The majority of my relatives believed in spirituality. They alleged that they have seen ghosts. Sometimes, they would use the word "haint." It is synonymous to ghost. Jeff alleged that he could make them leave the property. He said my son, Spudge, was born to see them. But he was born to chase them. He taught his children the secret.

He told his children what to do in the event of a ghost. My mother told me that sometimes you can smell the ghost before seeing it. The majority of times, it will be a dead family member. If you can see it and know who it is, you are supposed to do the following:

(1) Tell the spirit his or her name
(2) Tell them that they are dead and how they died
(3) Tell them to leave your home or from where they are
(4) Tell them to go to their grave and rest in peace

(5) Sometimes, people get killed too fast to know they are dead, such as by accident or by murder

(6) Then pray to the *Lord* to keep the spirits away

Rose said that sometimes, the spirits are reluctant to leave around you. In that case, you are to do the following:

(1) Put a sharp knife with a pointed edge under your mattress or pillows

(2) Do that in every bedroom

(3) One can be placed in the window seals

(4) Purchase or get some pieces of new lumber

(5) Cut them into small pieces or buy them already cut

(6) Put the small pieces next to the knives

(7) The reason for the new wood is because the corpse is buried into new wood

(8) That will prevent them from coming to your home or chase them away

One of his friends owned and rented a few homes in Leary. A husband and wife rented one of their homes. They refused to pay the rent and would not move. Rose told me that the landlord came to their home and told them about the problem. The landlord told Jeff that he knew how to make them move. He paid Jeff to get him some graveyard dirt. The instructions were to get nine hands filled with dirt. It must come from a man's grave. It must be taken from the area of his chest. Jeff went to a grave and followed the orders.

Jeff told his family that he went home with the landlord. He was curious and wanted to observe him. The landlord told him, "When I finish with my formula, I bet you they will move." Rose said that the landlord did the following:

(1) Got some silver foil paper, usually wrapped around chewing gum, etc. Today, we use aluminum paper

(2) It was parched in the oven

(3) It was broken into small pieces

(4) And it was mixed with the graveyard dirt

(5) He mixed something white with the dirt and pieces of silver foil. He refused to reveal it to Jeff

(6)   When the people were at work, all of it was sprinkled around the house

Jeff told his family that the tenants came home from work. The husband and wife got into a violent argument. They fought like cats and dogs. The house was nearly destroyed by the tenants. They moved to another place.

One of George Colley's workers was murdered. The folks believed that George killed the man. He was not charged with the crime. A man named Doc-Jones was indicted and sent to prison. When Doc walked, his knees appeared to sink. The folks said that Doc-Jones was set up and framed for the crime. They believed that George Colley killed the man. George was Jeff's best friend. He did not smoke and cigarette butts were at the crime scene.

My grandfather attended St. Mary's Baptist Church. He was a member of it. The rest of the family attended Mt. Zion Missionary Baptist Church. Sometimes, he would visit it.

All of the folks in Leary said that he was better than the physician. The doctor gave all of the patients the same medicine. Rose said, "It was some black pills." After learning about that, all of the folks went to Jeff instead of the physician. Jeff knew what wild herbs to use for almost any sickness. He treated and cured many people with bad colds and the flu. If they had a bad cough, he would make a remedy for it. He made an eggnog to drink. The folks would get well. My mother continued to use it for colds. Instructions of how it is made are as follows:

(1)   A pint of moonshine or Gordon's gin
(2)   Beat up two or three eggs real good. Use a container large enough to hold the alcohol
(3)   Then pour the alcohol on the eggs slowly
(4)   Use a large spoon to stir slowly while pouring the alcohol
(5)   Use enough sugar or honey to suit your taste
(6)   If you prefer, pour a little vanilla flavor in it to fit your taste
(7)   If you prefer, pour a little of lime or lemon juice in it to fit your taste
(8)   The best time to drink it is at bedtime

(9) Try to drink a fourth of it and go to bed

(10) Make sure that your body is covered in the bed

(11) Put the rest of the drink in the refrigerator

I understand that my grandfather was able to cure a few sexually transmitted diseases. One of them was the claps. I am going to list a few of the wild herbs which he used:

(1) Ladyfinger vine grew on pecan trees. He boiled it into a thick oil to drink for colds. You should take several table-spoons of it

(2) A tea was made from a shrub named four leaf clove

(3) Rattle snake roots were used to cure diseases

(4) Pork salad leaves that resemble collard greens. Leaves are toxic when bearing berries

The leaves would be cooked similar to collard greens and eaten to cleanse your blood. Ham hocks, neck, bones, or bacon can be added

(5) Pork salad. When it have its berries, it is not edible. The berries are used to cure "thrash" on the tongue. Squeeze the juice and cover the tongue with it. Use it daily. It was used to cure ringworms. Cover the affected area with the juice from the berries

(6) Sasy-Fax tea is a delicious drink. There were two different types of it, and one of them is toxic. I do not know which one is not toxic

(7) Sweet gum tree was used to make a toothbrush. The branches grew some nodules on them. Break off a branch with a nodule at the end of it. Chew up the nodule and let it dry in the sun. Then spread the brittles to make the toothbrush

(8) Dry corn fodder was used to make mops. They would tie it at the end of a stick.

(9) Shrubs and small tree branches were tied together to make outdoor brooms. Rake them on the clay dirt

(10) Make soap with animal oils. It was mixed with lye and boiled in the firepot outdoors

(11) Lifalastic tea is a delicious drink. The shrubs grew about three feet tall. The leaves are black and white in color

(12) Pepper plant. The seeds and plants are used to make a tea and season food

There were many other plants used for medicinal purposes. In reality, Jeff was a botanist. He knew the names of all of the wild plants and how to use them. Some of them could not be used, and he knew them. His wildlife knowledge and skills seemed to be impeccable. He owned many traps that were made with iron metal to catch animals. He made a gig to catch alligators and crocodiles. A gig was made to catch rattlesnakes so that he could kill them. He made a rub board. It was used to scrub and clean their dirty clothes. Roofing shingles were made with the wood from oak trees.

Many more productive things were done by him. Queen knew how to get home without being steered. A few times, Jeff was too intoxicated to steer her home. He had been drinking in the town. It was quite a few miles away from his home in the country. Jeff would get in the buggy and pass out.

Queen would take off with the buggy. The horse would stop with the buggy in front of the house. Around 1938, he became drunk, got into the buggy, and passed out. While riding, he got a foot between the spokes on a wheel. It was severely injured, and he was taken to the hospital in Albany, Georgia. The doctors wanted to amputate his foot and a portion of his leg. He refused to let them amputate it. Pi told the doctors, "I was born with two legs and feet. I intend to die with both of my limbs." After recovering, he was discharged and sent home. When he died in 1939 or 1940, he had both of his limbs. He died from prostate cancer. In those days, I do not believe the medical profession knew about that disease.

Jeff was a shooting expert. He owned an arsenal of weapons. All of his children and wife were taught to use them. He bought all of them a gun and taught them how to use it. Oftentimes, he would target practice in the woods. Rose said that her father could write his name on a tree. He had a reputation as the best shooter in that county. Sometimes, he would make bets with some of the folks. He won majority of them. His shots would hit bull's-eye. His family was always fearful that he would die as a result of violence. However, he had a natural death. He contracted cancer in the private area of his body. More than likely, syphilis disease had something to do with it. Jeff and his wife Fennie and son Charley are buried at Mt. Zion Missionary Baptist Church in Leary, Georgia. His wife was a member of that church. Jeff attended it a few times per year although he was a member of St. Mary Baptist Church. His church did not have a cemetery. My grandfather died a few years before my birth. I would have been grateful to have met him. My mother alleged that our personalities are similar. When I was young, she did all she could to keep me out of trouble. A few years after his death, the rest of the family moved to Florida. All of his personal property were given to his children, Fannie and Spudge. Fannie was married and lived with her husband. Rose was the only sibling living with her parents. None of them took the initiative to ascertain whether any money was in his bank account.

My grandfather really wanted to return to Alabama. He wanted to know whether or not his kinfolks were lynched and killed. He prayed that they were not lynched by the Klan. He did not start the fight with those young white thugs. He was scared to return to Alabama to see them again. As a result of that incident, we were unable to trace my grandfather's family history. It does not take a "rocket scientist" to figure out who created the problem.

His wife and children would worry about him because of his temperament. He was a hotheaded violent man. They thought that he would be killed from a gun battle. But he died from a natural cause. He was transported in the casket on a two horse-drawn wagon. They traveled on the clay road to the church. The church was filled, and there were no sitting areas. All of the local folks, friends, and family members attended the services. He had his favorite pipe in his mouth. Most of his pipes were handmade. He wore a new pair of overalls and a nice long sleeved shirt.

LOVE

My mother replied and stated, "Love was the oldest daughter. One of her grandmothers was named Ruthie. It was either Ruthie Davis or Ruthie Anderson. Love was tall and very attractive. Her teeth were very white and gorgeous. Some men would give her money to see her smile. One day, she went to the nearest dentist to get a couple of gold teeth. The dentist refused. The dentist told her, "You have a perfect set of teeth in your mouth. They are even, and they are white as ivory. He told her that the gold would destroy her beautiful teeth."

Rose said that she vaguely remember when Love lived with them. She remembered when Love would work on her father's farm. We were a close-knit family who made a living by farming. That was the only thing we could do. Our parents grew up on a farm. They were too poor to own any land. Our father did not trust white people. He rented his land to live and farm on. He rented his land by the acre. He made enough money from farming to pay his rent by the year.

She said, "Love was a hard working young lady. She was the best worker on the farm. She was considered as one of the best workers in Leary." Wow, she could really get down when it comes to working. Our father did not discriminate when it comes to working. We had to hitch up the mule and walk behind the plow.

At that time, there were only two girls living with their mom and dad. It was me and my sister, Fannie. Her nickname was Lil Sis. Love was married and living in the town of Leary. The boys left at an early age. They ran away because of our father. They refused to let him beat them. He would whip them with the leather strap used to sharpen his razor. He did it in one of his barns while they were naked. The boys had gotten bigger and got tired of the beatings.

She was married to Jake Phillips. Jake was quite a few years older. He had a mean temperament. He was an expert gun shooter. He was a friend of our father. But he was not as mean as our father. He could not fight as good as Jeff. Dad was a better shooter too. The folks in Leary were afraid of Bro Jake. He was known as a killer if you crossed him the wrong way. My father probably was the only person who was not afraid of him. "My daddy was not afraid of the devil in hell."

Bro Jake, my dad, and other sharp shooters would target practice in the woods. That would be on the land he rented. That would be on Sundays, some hours after church. Sometimes, they would make bets. My dad would win the money the majority of times. Jake would win his share of bets too. They were the best shooters. They could write their names on the trees.

Bro Jake hung out with our daddy. He liked to drink moonshine with Dad. He could really talk when drinking. Our dad was considered one of the best moonshine brewers in the county. His stills were made with copper. He had many black and white customers.

Love did not have any children. Bro Jake would get abusive sometimes with Love. She was tall and beautiful. Her hair had a lot of body to it. It was thick and hung to her shoulders. Bro Jake would falsely accuse her of cheating. Rose remembered the last time he left their house in his buggy and horse. He went home and got into an argument with his wife. I think they got into a fight. Someone told our dad about it. Our dad got some of his guns and got on his one horse-drawn wagon. He went to their house. He confronted Bro Jake. He told Jake, "If you ever touch my daughter again, I will blow you to kingdom come!" Love got on the wagon. She took her belongings and moved with us. That occurred in the early 1920s. A few people owned cars in those days. The roads were made from clay dirt. The roads were primarily traveled by wagons and buggies.

Our daddy, Pi, was very popular and had quite a few friends. The next day, one of his friends came to our house on his mule and wagon. He was in a big hurry. His name was Mr. Zackary. A lot of people called our dad Uncle Jeff. We called him Pi. Mr. Zackary rushed to the door. He knocked and said, "Uncle Jeff, I have something to tell you." Pi went to the door and asked him what was wrong. He told Pi to be careful because he heard Jake talking with a relative. Bro Jake and a relative had planned to get their guns and come to your house. They plan to do it the next day. That would be on Sunday. They plan to sneak up on you armed with their guns. He intends to force his wife, Love, go back home with him. He said, "I want you to be careful because Bro Jake is a crazy fool." Pi responded and said, "Mr. Zackary, thank you! I know that you are a true friend." He told Mr. Zackary that he would be all right, and he can handle this problem.

Mr. Zackary and Pi walked to his wagon and mule. The man was nervous and shaken. Pi said, "If they bother you, come and get me, Mr. Zachary, and I will take care of them." He replied, "I get the point, Uncle Jeff. I appreciate that." He stated, "You know that he is a dangerous man. He had shot and killed his uncle." Pi replied, "I saw it when he shot Mr. Abe Bass. They were target shooting in the woods. They got into an argument about a bet. Bro Jake wanted his money. Abe claimed that he had won the bet. Bro Jake shot and killed him. This incident was reported to the police. Jake Phillips was arrested. He got out on bond. And Uncle Jeff said that he didn't make any time. The charges were dropped. I heard he went to see some root worker near Albany, Georgia. They told me she is a woman. Uncle Jeff said that he had heard about her. Mr. Zackary said, "I get the point." Uncle Jeff said, "I don't care how good she is. She will never be as good as Dr. Buzzard." Zack replied, "I see the point. You are right about doc."

Mr. Zackery stated, "You know I've heard a few stories about Doctor Buzzard. Uncle Jeff concurred. The police don't even mess with Doc. I heard the police arrested him and couldn't lock the handcuffs. When they put him in the police car, the engine would not start. They couldn't lock the jail cell. Man, they do not mess with him. Zack said, "I see the point Uncle Jeff. You know, Doc can turn into a bird at night and pay you a visit. Uncle Jeff, he is the best one to go to if you are in trouble."

Mr. Abe Bass was a sharecropper for the Colley family. The Colley family was wealthy and powerful. They owned a lot of lands and were big-time farmers. They owned some businesses. They even owned some plantations in Leary, referred as The Colley Place. I do not know where Abe lived in Leary. Rose stated, "I have forgotten whether or not he lived in The Colley's Place." She said she remembered that George Thomas Colley was really angry about the murder. Those rich white people were pissed off when he got out of jail and went free.

On Sunday, which was the next day, Pi and his family dressed for church. The church was Mt. Zion Missionary Baptist Church. Pi loaded a revolver and put it in his pant pocket. He hid one of his windchester rifles in the wagon. The wagon was a two horse wagon. He hitched up two of his horses to the wagon. Pi and his family prayed before leaving for church. They prayed for *God* to take care of them. He didn't want any trouble at the church. When the church services were terminated, they got on their wagon and went home.

Pi asked Love, "Do you want to go back home with Bro Jake?" He told his daughter, Love, "He is your husband." She replied, "I do not care. I plan to leave him forever. We can be friends. I do not want him anymore. I plan to get myself another man." Pi said, "That is all I need to know. I think all of us should change into our regular clothes and eat." And that they did. Pi told his youngest daughter, Rose, to eat last. Her nickname was Nigger. They called her Nig for shorthand. Pi said to Nig, "You watch out for us while we eat." He chose her because he knew she was very nosey.

Pi was the first one to finish eating. He got from the table and went to the bathroom. The bathroom was an outdoor toilet. The toilet was about twenty feet away from the house. The toilet was made from oak wood. Pi was the one who built it. He built their house too. Prior to using the toilet, "He yelled and told Nig, "You can eat when I come out!" Nig liked to play in the yard. Their house was the only one within eyesight. Around 6:00 PM, Pi observed Nig running toward the house. She was almost out of breath. He asked her what was wrong. It was daylight. The folks would call it dust darkness. Nig told her father that she saw Bro Jake and his cousin get off the wagon.

They tied the mule and wagon to a tree. She said that they did not see her. Nig said both of them have a rifle. "They are walking on the dirt road toward our house. Pi got his rifle and told them to be normal.

Pi got his pistol and extra rounds of cartridges. He was wearing his overall pants He put them in his pockets. Then he grabbed his rifle. Everybody was worried and scared except Pi. They told him it is two against one. Pi replied, "Never mind. I will go into the woods and circle around them." He said, "I have enough time to do it. Pi left the house and told them to arm themselves. It was plenty of them. Nig was really scared. She was trembling, afraid that something bad was going to happen.

Pi went through the rear door. They watched until he disappeared in the woods. Their mother whose nickname was Mi stated that all of us know how to shoot. "Arm yourselves with a gun." Mi and her three daughters picked up a rifle. The three daughters were Love, Nig, and Lil Sis. Pi walked in the bushes and leaves lightly. He walked until he could get a good view of the dirt road. Finally, he could see Bro Jake and his cousin. They were about one hundred feet away from him. He had not circled them. So he hid behind a huge oak tree. They could not see him. Pi watched them when they had stopped walking.

Bro Jake pulled a bottle of whiskey from his rear pocket. Bro Jake said, "This is some damn good white lightning. Take a sip, Cousin, it will build up your nerves." He said, "You know we may have to kill Uncle Jeff. And this is some of his moonshine. Bro Jake told his cousin, "I parked the horse and wagon far away for a reason. I want it to be almost dust darkness when we get to the house. Then we will sneak up on them with our guns. We will catch them by surprise. Both of them began to walk toward the house. They were close enough to see the house. They could see smoke coming from the chimney flues. And it smelled really good. The aroma in the air was so pleasant. Bro Jake said, "Someone is cooking a cake." The men walked slowly on the road. They walked beyond the point where Pi was hiding. Pi was cautious while walking. He did not make any noise. He eased on the dirt road. He was right behind Bro Jake and his cousin. He raised his rifle. Then he said, "Bro Jake, I want the two of you to stop. And do not turn and face me. Stop and don't move. Now drop your guns on the ground. Now take ten steps backward and face me. Then, Pi said, "Where are you headed with the guns in your hands? Bro Jake lied and said, "Uncle Jeff, we had planned to hunt for some rabbits and coons. Then we were going to go to your house. We were gonna visit you and my wife, Love." Bro Jake's cousin was scared. He said nervously, "Uncle Jeff, please don't shoot us. I want to live to see my grandchildren." Uncle Jeff told them that they were acting like cowards. "And ya'll were like two thieves in the night. That is what they do when they have guns. We call that stealing a person. You had planned to take advantage of me." He said man up to it. And to tell the truth.

Bro Jake did not show any fear in his heart. His cousin did. He was shitless scared. He was so scared and pissed all over his overalls. Pi did not show any fear in his heart either. He said, "I am not going to kill ya'll. You know it takes a fool to go on another man's property to harm him. But I'm a fool too. And the devil from hell sent me down here. Bro Jake, I am not gonna harm ya'll this time. You know that I'm your father-in-law." Pi said, "Bro Jake, remember that I saw you shoot and kill your uncle. I'm talking about Mr. Abe Bass." Pi made Bro Jake lay on the ground. He made his cousin remove all of the bullets from the rifles. Then he searched them for additional weapons. He made them walk to the house with him. While walking, Pi told them that this was a warning. The next time will not be like this. Pi was walking and talking. "You know I could have killed both of you a long time ago. That was when I was hiding and looking at ya'll drink the shine. And I heard all of the bad talk. Pi was a bad ass too. Bro Jake and his cousin knew it. Pi told Bro Jake, "You are tough just like me. I want you to remember one thing. You are not as tough and bad as me. You are in the second place." He told him that he could quickly draw faster and could shoot better. Bro Jake said, "That is true, Uncle Jeff." His cousin said, "Yes, sir, Uncle Jeff, you are very good with a knife too." Bro Jake said to Uncle Jeff, "That is the reason everybody call you Uncle Jeff. And the white people too. And they give you utmost respect and don't bother you."

Nig was standing in the front yard. Nervously, she looked down the dirt road. She observed them walking toward the house. She ran back to the house and said, "Mi, they are coming to the house. All of them have a rifle in their hand. And Pi was walking behind Bro Jake and his cousin. Mi said, "It looks like Pi took care of business.

Like always. A job well done. Our Pi is a clever man. Bro Jake should have known that. They are lucky to be alive." When they arrived to the house, Pi made them prop their rifles against the oak tree. The men spoke to the women and were allowed to go indoors. Pi offered them something to eat. They said that they were not hungry. Jake was allowed to talk to his wife, Love. They talked on the back porch. Love told Bro Jake that she was tired of the abuse, and she could not deal with the relationship. "You've been cheating on me with other women for too long." Bro Jake pleaded for her to change her mind. Love had already made up her mind. Bro Jake told her good luck. Love said, "We can be friends instead of enemies. There will not be a relationship between us. I've had it up to my ears." Bro Jake and his cousin decided to leave the house. Pi told them to get their rifles. It was night and dark outside. Pi hitched up his two horse wagon. He took them to their one horse wagon. Nig went with them. He had his pistol and rifle. He took his favorite bloodhound dog with him too. The dog's name is Blackie. He smoked his pipe while transporting the men to their wagon. Afterward, they arrived at their destination.

Bro Jake and his cousin thanked him for his kindness. Pi said, "Ya'll know, sometimes your luck runs out. It is always someone just a little bit smarter than you. Remember, there will not be a second time. The next time, you will not be my son-in-law." They said, "We understand, Uncle Jeff." He said, "You know, Bro Jake, we have been friends for a long time. And we are drinking buddies. We became friends before you met my daughter. You need to stop drinking if it makes you foolish. We've been friends for too long. It would be a sin and shame to have to kill you." Bro Jake concurred and agreed with Uncle Jeff. This incident happened during the late 1920s. Those problems were settled without any police involvement. It was not reported to a law enforcement agency. If a white person was involved, it would be reported.

Bro Jake and his cousin got on their wagon. They entered on the clay road. They went toward the town. That was where they lived. Pi and Nig made the mule turn the wagon around. They went back to the house. Nig was worried that Bro Jake would return and retaliate. Pi said, "Do not worry. He's not going to create any more problems. And that Bro Jake had gotten the message." They went home and joined the rest of the family. All of them sat in chairs near the fireplace. Pi was full of fun most of the time. He was a jovial man. He got some sweet potatoes and cooked them on the ashes. And he grew plenty of them. He ate and drank some of his moonshine. Mi, his wife, and three daughters listened at his jokes. They laughed for a long time. There was no electricity in the woods. They had to use kerosene lamps. Sometimes, they would use candles for light. Shortly, before 10:00 PM, they decided to go to bed. Pi said, "Blackie and the other dogs will warn us about intruders. That is why I taught you to shoot. I have enough guns and ammo to fight a war." He said, "You know I do not start fights. And I don't run from them either. Sometimes, I will run to the trouble. Then he said trouble is easy to get in and hard to get out. You have to be careful. I will die for my family.

It would be Monday morning when they get out of bed. Everybody in the house had chores to do before they eat. After their breakfast, they had to do farmwork. Pi told Love, "You are the oldest. I have a few things for you. I want you to get some wood and start a fire in the stove. Then I want you to help your mother cook for us and bring two buckets of water from the well." Nig and Lil Sis had to split some wood. Nig had to feed the hogs, cows, mules, and other animals. She had to give them water from the well too. Lil Sis had to feed the chickens, ducks, quails, and dogs. She had to give them water. If necessary, they would share getting milk from the cows. While the women were doing their chores, Pi would round up food. Then he would spend a few moments checking his traps in the woods. Sometimes, he would catch rabbits, possums, and raccoons. He would return in time to eat with the family. When they finished eating, it would be early in the morning. They would take a break and rest. Then they would head to the farm. The season of the year dictated their duties on the farm. Sometimes, they would have to gather what was harvested. Other times, they would have to walk behind the mule and plow. Then they would have to put plants in the ground and bury seeds in the ground. It was always something do. Including, hoeing weeds from around the plants. Nig had to go to the well during the day. She had to bring a bucket of water along with the gourd. They would split a gourd in half and let it dry. It was used as a dipper to drink water. The water from the well would be as cold as ice. Pi was an expert well digger. And he dug that well in the yard.

After about six months, Love moved. She rented a house in the town of Leary. She continued to help her father on his farm along with other odd jobs. Bro Jake and Love continued to be friends. It lasted until the mid-1930s.

Ruthie or Rutha got involved into a new relationship with another man. Her boyfriend's name was Charlie Hall. They dated a year or two and got married. During this era, it was rare for a black person to get a divorce. Most of them living in small rural areas had never heard about a divorce. They would leave their husband or wife and marry someone else. She did not get a divorce. She and her second husband continued to live in Leary.

When Jake Phillips ascertained that Love had remarried, he became upset. He knew that she and Charlie Hall were courting. But he never imagined that they would marry. On a weekend, Mr. Zackary decided to visit a few friends in Leary. They were drinking and having fun. Someone said, "You know, Love did the right thing because Bro Jake is a violent man." Another person said, "I think the man is crazy." Zack concurred and said, "I see the point ya'll. Plus he killed his uncle about a bet. And he is real rooty. That is the reason he got away with murder. Another friend told me that Bro Jake said what he was going to do if he could not have his wife, Love. He was going to make sure that nobody else could have her. That included her husband, Charlie Hall." They pleaded with Mr. Zackary to keep their conversation confidential.

On the next day, Nig observed a man on his wagon and mule coming to their house on the dirt road. She could tell it was Mr. Zackary. It was on Sunday, a few hours before darkness. Nig ran to the house. She got the attention of her father. He said, "What's wrong, Nig?" She said, "Your friend is coming to the house on his wagon. He answered and said, "What is his name?" Nig said, "It is your, I get or see the point friend." Pi said it is Mr. Zackary. Nig replied, and he is in a hurry. It was obvious that she couldn't remember his name. However, she did remember, "I see the point."

Pi replied and said he is here now. I can hear the wagon wheels. Mr. Zack pulled up next to his favorite tree. He pulled the reins backward and said, "Wow, there boy, to the mule." He got off of the wagon and tied the reins to the oak tree. Pi told his daughter, "Nig, get some water for the mule." She got plenty of ice cold water from the well. She did it in a hurry. She wanted to hear the news from Zack. Both of them were very nosey and liked to gossip.

Pi sent his other daughter to the barn. She was Little Sis. He told her to get a bottle of his moonshine. Pi said, "Come on in, Zack." He sat down in the chair. She came back with the booze. Before he took a drink, he said, "Uncle Jeff, I have some good news for you. And when I finish, I know I will need a drink." It will settle my nerves. Yesterday, I visited a few of my friends. Everybody had something to contribute, Uncle Jeff. Do you see the point, Uncle Jeff? Uncle Jeff nodded. Several folks had something to say about Bro Jake. One of them said that Jake is upset and pissed off with Love. He became mad when he learned that she had married Charlie Hall. You know those folks. I am not going to tell you their names. I visited them quite often. You've been there with me. The big fat lady in the house said, "That Jake told them that he was going to break up their marriage. And that is guaranteed. And that he is not going to let her keep Charlie Hall." "Uncle Jeff, don't mention my name about this incident. You or your daughter need to get this message to Love." Zack replied, "What do you think he plans to do?" Uncle Jeff said, "I don't know, but I hope it is not something foolish. Zack said maybe he is going to pay his root worker a visit. Mr. Zackary got a few drinks of moonshine. It came from a five-gallon jug. Uncle Jeff gave him the bottle to take home. It was almost nighttime. Zack got on his horse-drawn wagon and took off.

Then Pi and Nig began to talk. He told her that he knew she was going to give her sister, Love, the news. He said it would be permissible to do it. She agreed. He planned to do it too. And plan to confront Jake about it too. The next weekend, Nig and her father made plans to go to town. Nig had made plans to spend the weekend with her sister, Love. She planned to pay Jake a visit. Pi hitched up one of his horses to his double seater buggy. He named the horse Queen. He was able to confront Jake. Jake replied and stated, "Uncle Jeff, we are friends. We go a long way back. I will never harm Love or her husband, Charlie Hall. Both of them are my friends." During the two-day visit, over the weekend, Nig would work in her sisters' garden. She would hoe and, at times, pull the weeds. Sometimes, she would rake the yard. It was clay dirt. The rake was a homemade rake. It was made from the shrubs, which grew in the woods. Other times, Nig would be busy cleaning the house. That was when Love would not be at the house. Love would be working or shopping. On several occasions, Bro Jake stopped when Love was not home. Charlie Hall was at his job. Jake told Nig to tell them he had stopped for a visit. "Tell them that he said hello." On the way back to their home in the country, Nig and her father communicated. They were in the double seater buggy drawn by a horse, and they talked about Bro Jake. She was relieved to know that Jake did not plan to harm his ex-wife or husband. She told her dad that he had stopped by the house. Love was not there. Nig was alone when Jake came to the house.

A month later, Mr. Zackary came to their home in the country. He was greeted, and he entered the house. He said, "Uncle Jeff, I have some more news for you." Jeff replied and told Zack to give it to him. He said that it was not really bad news, but it was bad enough. Jeff asked if he needed a drink to calm his nerves. Zack answered, "No sir. I still have some of the shine from last month." He stated, "You know, Uncle Jeff, Bro Jake continues to visit Love. He is at their house when they are working. Many times, he is there alone. I have seen him inside of the house. I don't know if Jake has a key to the door. Perhaps, she is not locking the doors. Uncle Jeff, you know that he believes in witchcraft. I think it is bad for them to allow Jake to be alone in their house. You know what he said about them. He may be putting something down to harm them." Jeff said, "The three of them are friends. I guess they don't care about his visits. Mr. Zackary was a deacon in the church. He and Nig were very nosey."

Nig continued to spend weekends with Love. She was anxious and eager to tell her about Zack's conversation with her father. She explained what she knew and Love stated, "We are aware of that. He is our friend." Nig didn't like her response. Love said, "Jake is fine He is not going to harm me or my husband, Charlie Hall. Rose was very nosey and continued to observe her sister. Love once stated, "Nig, you look at me the way a hawk looks at a chicken." She was looking to see if her sister was acting abnormal. Nig left and walked to her home in the country. She had to walk about six miles. Later in the day, Love's oldest brother Spudge paid her a visit. He visited her infrequently because he was married. He had to take care of his wife and children.

After greeting each other, they sat down and talked with each other. Spudge said, "I have something that is very important to tell you." It is about Bro Jake. He stated that he was at a house party last week. "Love, you know a lot of people are pissed off with him. They are still mad because he killed Abe Bass and didn't make any time in jail. They are afraid of him because of his reputation. We were drinking and having fun at the party. This was during the winter, and it was cold. Most of the people would burn fires in the backyard. Sometimes, the fires would be in fifty-five gallon drums. The lids would be off the drums.

The drums would turn red because of the fire. People would stand around them to get warm. Spudge said, "Love, They plan to kill Bro Jake to get even with him. I plan to get in contact with him before I leave. I want you to give him the message too. They intend to invite Jake to the party. The party is going to be in Morgan, Georgia. Morgan is not very far away from Leary. The party is going to be at a house just off Couldry Mill Road. People travel on that road to get their corn grounded. They plan to let him park his one horse-drawn buggy. While drinking moonshine around the hot drums, they plan to shoot Jake. They know that he is going to be armed because Jake will never go any place without one of his guns. I heard those folks say that they are going to steal and ambush him. They know he is an expert shooter, and that would be the only way to take Jake out."

Prior to leaving, Bro Jake came to the house. Spudge and his sister, Love, gave Jake the message. They pleaded for him to stay home the next weekend. Spudge said, "Jake, you are going to be invited to a party in Morgan. Please do not go. Those folks plan to shoot and kill you. I know that you are a great shooter, but you will be outnumbered."

Jake replied, "If I'm invited, I intend to go to it. I will encourage Uncle Jeff to go with me. Hell, we are the best shooters in this part of the country." Spudge said, "Jake, I think it would be foolish to go." Jake did not change his mind about the party. He had a big ego and was a fearless man. Spudge left from his sister's house. He got on his one horse drawn wagon and went to visit his parents. He figured that he would overtake his sister walking on the clay road. Nig was young and energetic. She had walked the six mile journey. She had gotten to the house.

After arriving to his parents' home, he parked his wagon and horse. It was parked next to a tree. That was not far away from the well. Spudge took his rifle from the wagon. He was greeted by his mom, Mi, and his dad, Pi. His sisters were happy to see him. All of them sat around the fireplace. It was nice and warm in the wood-framed house. Pi had built it many years ago. Spudge told Nig that he had been to Love's house. He thought he would catch up with her and give her a ride. Nig replied, "I ran and walked to get home. Six miles is nothing for me." Lil Sis was his favorite sister. She went and brought him some tobacco. It was some of the tobacco that their father, Pi, grew on the farm. It had been dried out and ready to smoke.

Spudge smoked it in his pipe. Sometimes, he would chew it. He told his father that he really wanted to talk about Bro Jake. Spudge told Pi about the party in Morgan. He informed him that he had warned Bro Jake to stay home. "I told him if he go there, he might get killed. But Jake is hardheaded. He said he had made plans to go to the party. Pi, he intends to encourage you to go with him. He is your friend. Why don't you discourage him?" Pi responded, "Well, I don't plan to go under those conditions. And Jake had better not go, either." Spudge and his family lived in Morgan, Georgia. He worked on Albert Dozier's farm. They lived in Albert's plantation. All of the houses were painted white. Spudge picked up his rifle. He got on his horse-drawn wagon and went to Morgan.

It was on a Saturday. The party would be held later in the day. It was cold, but the weather was marvelous. Bro Jake visited his friend Uncle Jeff. They chatted and had a few drinks. He told Jake that they would be outnumbered. He was not going to go with him. He said, "Jake, a lot of people are mad because of your uncle. I think you should not go to that party." Jake responded and said, "I will go alone." He got on his horse-drawn buggy and left. "The party probably will be going on when I get to Morgan. Dawson is not far from the party."

On Monday morning, Spudge went to work on his boss' farm. One of his co-workers asked him a question. He said, "Mr. Spudge, did you go to the party which was near Couldry Mill Road?" Spudge said, "I did not care to go. I stayed home with my family. But I had a friend that lived in Leary. He was invited. I was invited but chose to stay home. The man said it was a large crowd of people at the party. Many of them came from the small adjoining towns. There was a lot of booze there. Plenty of single women were there too. Some of the folks were dancing. The singer was very good along with the music. Some of the men were gambling. They were playing Georgia Skin card game. Others were gambling with their dice. It was very cold, but the weather was nice.

The co-worker asked Spudge, "Did you hear about the trouble at the party?" Spudge said, "No, and please explain it to me." "The fella who came from Leary got killed. I'm talking about your friend Bro Jake." Spudge asked, "How did he get killed?" The man told Spudge that some gangsters were at the party. "I understand that he got into an argument with them. They got into a fight. Jake was shot and killed. I do not know if he had a chance to get his gun. But he had one on him. After the shooting, everybody got the hell out of there. The sheriff came there, and the folks advised them that it was self-defense.

Spudge told the co-worker that it would happen to people like Jake. "I warned him that those people were having this party to kill him. He didn't believe me. Now he is dead. His ego was too big. He had to have a lot of courage to go there." The man said, "Nobody knows who killed him." He said, "You know, Jake killed his uncle. He got what he deserved. You live by the sword, and you die by it. Karma is a bitch."

All of the farmworkers worked very long hours. They worked from sunset to sundown. They would be tired when they go home. When Spudge arrived at his home, he told his wife about the incident. His wife's name is Fannie Ivy. Fannie Ivy told him, "I'm quite sure that all of the folks in Leary is aware that Jake is dead. They couldn't call because telephones did not exist." Spudge asked her, "Do you believe that one of the Colley's had something to do with it?" Fannie Ivy said that it could have been someone else. It could have been some of Abe's kinfolks. "All we know is that he was killed by somebody."

Just like Spudge and his wife had said, "The news had spread into all of the small towns. The gossip was cancerous!" Jake Philips shot and killed his uncle, Abe Bass. Someone shot and killed him. It was in Morgan. He got what he deserved. Those folks told the police, "It was self-defense." Spudge said he was ambushed by some gangsters. It was another unsolved murder. According to Ancestry. com, he was killed in 1935 in Morgan and was fifty years old. Based on that information, he was born on 1885. Jake had a son who was five or six years younger than Love. His name was Johnny Phillips.

Charlie Hall noticed that his wife was not acting normal. This was a few weeks before Jake's death. Shortly after that, he decided to get a separation. He decided to visit his father-in-law, Uncle Jeff. Mr. Hall told him that something was wrong with Love. He told him about her strange, bizarre personality. He said, "My wife is not taking care of herself. This started a few weeks before Jake's death. So she is not grieving over him. I moved, and she is living alone."

Nig said, "We had warned her that Bro Jake was dealing with a real good root worker. She should have stopped him from coming to y'all house. He never should have been there alone. He probably was putting down some ' hoobie-doobie' dust." Hall said, "Y'all know that Love is a very clean person. She likes to wear makeup and take care of her skin and hair. That included wearing clean starch-ironed clothes. The house is a mess. I couldn't take it so I moved," Nig concurred with Hall. She had noticed that Love was not taking care of herself.

Pi asked Nig to move in the house with Love. She was eager to go. When she got there the house was in disarray. It was exactly the way her husband had described it. Love was at her job when she arrived at the house. A few hours later, her sister arrived from work. She was happy to see Nig. Love said that she and her husband had quit. "It would be nice if you stay for a while." Nig agreed with her. The house needed to be cleaned. Love's appearance was not that bad. Nig cleaned the house for her sister.

While at the house, Nig would hide and observe Love. Sometimes, she would pretend that she was asleep. It was referred as playing the possum. Rose, who was Nig, had always told me, "Every shut-eye does not mean you are asleep. That means that their ears are open, but their eyes are closed."

One day on the weekend, Nig hid from around the corner of the house. She had told her sister that she was walking to the store.

Instead, she chose to hide and watch her. Nig said that Love was in the house. She could not see Nig. She noticed that Love had a pair of scissors in her hand. She said that Love proceeded to start a fire in the fireplace. Then her sister begun to cut her hair and throw it on the fire. After that, she threw two beautiful dresses on it. Nig knew that something was wrong with her. And that she was acting strange. Nig did not tell anyone about her strange mannerisms. She kept it as a secret. She intended to continue to observe Love.

The next time, Love was walking in the yard completely naked. She did not have any clothes on. Of course, Nig got her some clothes. She encouraged Love to put them on. All of this had transpired before Jake's death. Shortly, after his death, she was observed catching and eating toads, frogs, and snakes. She even pulled hair from her head and ate it. She burned up most of her clothes in the fireplace. She was depressed and speaking very irrational. She continued to talk to herself. Then she would laugh. Nig was able to get a message to her oldest brother, Spudge. He came to the house on his one horse-drawn wagon. When he noticed Love's disposition, he got on his wagon immediately. He told Nig, "You stay here and take care of her. I am going in the country and get our parents. They returned to Love's house. Pi noticed that Love was not acting normal. The first thing he said, "Bro Jake had messed her up before he died. He said that she had voodoo and witchcraft on her. That is the reason Jake went to Ray City, Georgia. It is near Albany. The woman was supposed to be a real good root worker."

Pi left all of them at the house with Love. He went and got one of the Colleys. When Mr. Colley saw her, he said, "It is scandalous and a shame because Love have lost her mind. It is terrible. She is such a nice, classy black lady. Then he told Pi and his family that he would report it to the Sheriff Department. A few hours later, the sheriff arrived. Love was evaluated and assessed by the law enforcement officials. They concluded that she was mentally incapacitated and insane. She was taken into custody and transported to the county jail. Subsequently, Love was admitted into Central State Hospital in Georgia. I do not know whether they had branches located throughout Georgia. I know that she ended up in Milledgeville, Georgia. Records revealed that she was admitted at the hospital on September 28, 1939. They documented that she had Epilepsy. It alleged that she destroys clothes, leaves home at night, burns up her trunk at night and all of her clothes, and delusional. The records indicated that she was born on 1907 with her name as Ruthie Hall. It lists her husband as Charlie Hall in Leary, Georgia. She was discharged on May 10, 1972. The hospital stamped, "Transferred to Thomasville." They scratched it out. Love was admitted into the Central State Hospital, and her family members did not have any more contact with her. However, her sister, who is my mother, did send some letters. She was living in Pompano Beach, Florida. They were mailed in the 1960s thru the early 1970s. As of this date, Love's whereabouts is unknown. I was unable to get any information from the Social Security Administration. I used some numbers from the hospital record. I believed they were her social security number. I was unable to get a copy of a death certificate in Georgia. I was told by a representative that they cannot find any record of her death However, the Internet revealed that she died on July 1, 1987. She was eighty-seven years old. Her last residence was in Glenwood, Georgia. It was shameful, but her legacy was a sad story. I would love to know if she is dead or possibly still alive. If she is dead, I would like to know whether she was buried or cremated. She was admitted in 1939, and I was born on 1941. I never got a chance to see or know my aunt. That is painful, and it hurts. Love did not have any children.

BAY

Charley Anderson's nickname was Bay. According to the 1910 U.S. Census Bureau, he was nine years old. He would have been born on 1901. His name was listed as, Charlie. Jeff was his father and it showed that he was 45 years old. He would have been born on 1865. The report indicated that his mother was Phenora Anderson. She was thirty years old. She would have been born on 1880. The 1920 report wrote her name as Fennie Anderson. She was shown to be thirty-eight years old. Based upon that information, she would have been born on 1882. Jeff told his family that he was born at the end of the Civil War. It ended in 1865. Birth certificates did not exist. They based their records written in a bible or by word of mouth.

My mother, Rose, referred as Nig did not grow up with her brothers. They are Spudge and Bay. They moved when they were young. They were about twelve years old that time. Spudge was the first one to move. He refused to take a spanking from his father. They got into an argument while working on the farm. Spudge walked away from the farm. He went to the house and packed up a few clothes. He hitched up a horse to the buggy. A few years later, he was married.

A year or two later, Bay got mad and walked away. Pi always told his children, "If y'all are too old to take a beating, you better leave. Because if any of you raise your hand to hit me, you will die. If

I don't shoot you, I will cut your head off with my knife." He would spank the boys in one of the barns. They had to get naked in the barn prior to the spanking. A wide leather belt was used to beat them. Those belts were used by barbers to sharpen their razors.

When the boys became older, they would visit infrequently. Bay migrated to different towns in Georgia. He migrated to different states. He did farm labor. He was illiterate because he had no formal education. He ended up in West Virginia or Virginia. It was one of those states.

Nig told me that her brother, Bay, and another man were roommates. They rented a room together to reduce their expenses. Both of them did some sort of work as laborers. She said that Charley went out on the weekend with his girlfriend. After a little fun and a few drinks, they went home. Charley alleged that when he entered his room, his roommate was asleep in his bed. Nig said that Charley told her, "I placed a few dollars in my dresser drawer along with a gold pocket watch and gold chain." The door was locked and the windows were closed. "I got in my bed and went to sleep." He told his sister that when he woke up the next morning, his belongings were missing. The door was locked, and the windows were closed. Charley woke his roommate up and confronted him about the property. The man denied taking the property and refused to give it up. A fight ensued between them. He knocked his roommate down on the floor. Then he got on top of him. He took his very sharp knife from his overall pants' pocket. Charley killed the man with his knife. A policeman was sent to the crime scene. Charley was arrested and taken to jail. He was convicted and sent to prison. During that time in those states, the prisoners had to work in the coal mines. Many of them died from breathing ailments or lung cancer. A lot of them died from explosions and toxic fumes. Sometimes, the mines would cave in on them. He served his time and was discharged from prison. Someone got in contact with him a few days after his release from prison. Charley was told, "You are a lucky man. All of your friends were dead. They were killed in the coal mine the next day." All of those prisoners were his friends. The prisoners worked as crews in the coal mines. Sometime after his release from prison, he migrated to Florida.

While working as a farm laborer in or near Satsuma, Florida, he got married. His wife's name was Rosa Lee Drive. She must have been a spiritual or religious lady. All of the folks called her, "Mother Drive." They separated after a few years. After that, he moved to Pompano Beach, Florida, where he worked on farms. My mother, Nig, and my grandmother, Mi, migrated to Pompano Beach, shortly after Pi's, death. My granddad, Jeff, referred as Pi died in 1939. In Pompano Beach, they rented a room from some rich white farmers. The rooms were made from wood. In those days, majority of the buildings were made from wood. The buildings were named after the farmers. They used the word "quarters" after their last name. They rented a room from Lynn Walton and Ogden Brothers. All of the folks referred to the rooms as Lynn Walton Quarters. His whole name was used. The other one was called the Ogden Brothers Quarters. When a person rented from them, they had to work on their farms. Those were not the only quarters in Pompano. There were Buck Lyon Quarters, Blount Quarters, Peg Leg Jones Quarters, and Ghost Town Quarters. My mother, uncle, and grandmother did not like the idea of renting and having to work on that persons' farm. It was seven days a week. They saved up enough money and bought a lot in the subdivision of New-Town in Pompano. They bought the land from a successful black farmer. His name was Mr. Tony Mitchell. Mr. Tony and his wife, Miss Mercy, lived in front of a vacant lot. They lived in Northwest 10th Avenue. The vacant lot was directly behind their house. It was situated in Northwest 11th Avenue. There were three avenues in the New-Town subdivision. They were 9th, 10th, and 11th Avenue. Mr. Tony farmed on a large scale similar to the white farmers. He owned plenty of real estate. He became the first black millionaire in Broward County. I believe he became rich in the early 1950s. He sold the lot during the 1940s, for fifty or five hundred dollars. The size of the lot was 100 by 150 feet. My mother, her brother, and mother subsequently saved enough money to build their home. When they were not working on the farm, they would work with the builder. The address was 104 Northwest 11th Avenue, New-Town. All of the roads were dirt without any streetlights. The house was built in the mid 1940s. They didn't have any electric lights. Candles and kerosene lamps were used in the house. The stove was called a wood stove. Wood was used to cook and heat food. Refrigerators had not been invented. Food was stored in an ice box. Blocks of ice would be bought to keep in the ice box. Ice picks were used to break the blocks of ice to make cold drinking water. The bathroom was not attached to the wooden house. It was about fifty feet away from the house. It was called an outdoor toilet. It was built with two seats. Two people could use it at the same time. The house had a front and rear porch, two bed rooms, a dining room, and a living room. Now they were free to work on a farm of their choice.

When the house was built they moved out of Lynn Walton's Quarters. It was in New-Town. They were sharecroppers on his farm. He refused to pay them their share. Rose stated that Lynn Walton said, "The harvest is too good to pay y'all." He beat them out of their money. He probably retaliated because of moving out of his Quarters.

Rose told her mother to stop working and stay at the house. She had to take care of me. Rose and Uncle Charley worked on many different farms in Broward and Palm Beach counties. The farmers used large flat-bed trucks with side boards. The workers would board the trucks. They stood in rows until the trucks were filled with the laborers. There were not any laws against it. Sometimes, they would sharecrop with white farmers. A few times, they would rent an acre of farmland. They were not successful farmers but did make enough to take care of their basic needs.

During the early 1950s, Charley was able to buy him a used T-model truck. He was a quiet man. He did not talk that much. It seemed as if he was in a deep thought. He was a very good man. He kept a square of chewing tobacco. It had the picture of a bull on it. He would sat on one of the porches and chew it. He would cut a plug with his knife to chew. When he was not using tobacco, he would smoke his pipe. His choice of alcohol was moonshine or Gordon's gin. The gin had the picture of a wild boar hog on the bottle. His girlfriend lived across town not far away from the Grishams and Adderleys. She had a house situated around plenty of dirt. Her name was Miss May Bell. One of her daughter's name was Anna. Her husband's name was Paul. She had a grandson by the name of Gordon. We attended the same school. He was a few years my junior. He had another girlfriend who lived in a house next to Mother Jones' property. Miss Doanie was her name. I rode with my uncle a few times to visit his girlfriends. There were kids at both homes. I would play with them.

Until the early 1950s, Pompano was one of the leading cities in the nation that farmed. The farmer's market is the largest in the state of Florida. People migrated from many states to work here. However, in the early 1970's, most of the farm land was sold for the development of homes and business. The migrant workers had to travel to other areas to work on farms.

Charley decided to work as a construction laborer. Rose would do domestic work for different white folks. I remember his last construction job. It was on Powerline Road, which was almost to Deerfield, Florida. The company built large concrete pilings. "Doran and Doran was the name of the company. On Charley's days off, he worked at Mr. Doran's house. He would cut their grass and clean the swimming pool. Sometimes, he would take me with him. When nobody was home, we would sneak and swim in their pool. The house was in Pompano. It was a waterfront home and was not far from the ocean. This was during the 1950s when I was young. I was very strong and one of the best wrestlers in Pompano. I remember throwing my uncle on the ground. Man, did he get mad. Mrs. Doran had a son who was a few years younger than me. He loved to play with me indoors. We would eat lunch with them on the dining table. Her husband would rarely be home when we were there. The young white kid would ask his mother to let me swim with him. This was in the segregation era. She told her son, "We can't do it because of our neighbors." He begged his mother so much about it. They bought some tall plants to help block the view of the pool. Then they installed something to prevent their neighbors from seeing the pool. Afterward, I was allowed to swim in the pool with her son. His mother told us not to make any loud noises while in the pool. We had fun in the pool and did not make too much noise.

On the construction job, when Charley became older, he was transferred from the field to work in the yard with the pilings. The young black workers called him Old Pop. Two of the men lived in the projects. Their apartment was in front of Northwest 6th Avenue. All of them have been demolished because of a revitalization program by the city. The lots are currently vacant. They are between Sanders Park and the Liberty Park, subdivisions in Pompano. All of them rode to work together. They came to our house to transport him to work with them. Sometimes, they would go fishing together on their days off. Charley loved to go fishing. I was young, and I do not remember the names of the co-workers. Charley was eventually laid off. The co-workers came to our house and stated, "Charley's supervisor said that he is too old to do the hard construction work." I remember them saying, "We are going to strike and picket until they hire him back." They said, "Charley have worked for them for a long time. They need to look out for him. He had been dedicated and loyal to this company." Charley was rehired within a week. He was given less strenuous work. He remained with the firm until his illness in 1958.

I remember when the city made all of the homeowners get rid of the outdoor toilets. They were given a deadline. A bathroom had to be built inside their house. They had to be on a septic tank. Safe sanitation was the reason for it. Charley was the man of the home. Therefore, my mother chose to put the deed in his name. That turned out to be a crucial mistake. The reason is that he was illiterate. He could not read or write.

They did not have enough money for the plumbing and addition. A list of mortgage companies and banks were provided by the city. Rose could read and write. She made contact with one of the lenders. Their office was in Ft. Lauderdale, Florida. I think it was Barnett Bank in Broward Boulevard. I remember when the lender came to our home. He spoke with both of them. I remember some of the conversation. The lender, who was a white man, told my mother and uncle that he could add another bedroom, bathroom, and rear porch to the house for about $3,000. Rose could not enter into the contract. Her name was not on the deed. The lender ascertained that her brother could not read or write. He asked him, "Are you a Masonic Brother?" Charley did not tell the truth and replied, "Yes." In those days, many blacks were in the Mason Lodge. It was considered as a big accomplishment. The lender knew it. He advised Charley to go and sit in his car. Then they could enter into the contract. He told Rose that he did not need her. After learning that she had some education is the reason he took Charley to the car. When my uncle was in the car, he marked an X on the contract for his signature. I was in elementary school when that happened. I had taught my uncle how to mark an X. The lender stuck it to him. He must

have given him thirty-six inches in the rear. It was a balloon mortgage for two years. It was approved for the addition to the house. It
excluded the plumbing work. Rose had to hire a plumber prior to the
construction work. A plumber, who was a black man, did the plumbing for $600. The pipes for the sink, toilet, and bathtub were at the
wrong place. That was learned when the addition to the house was
finished. If my mother had read the contract, it would not have been
understood. She knew that she had two years to pay $3,000. But she
did not understand the balloon mortgage. After making payments
for two years, she thought the mortgage had been paid. The lender
contacted them and demanded the $3,000. She went to their office.
They explained the meaning of the loan to her. Then she remembered that the prior lender was a crook. Most of the folks in our community were not aware of lawyers in those days. We did not have any
lawyers in the black community. The banker told my mother that he
could finance the original $3,000 at a fixed rate. He told her that it
would not be a balloon mortgage. Between the two mortgages, she
ended up paying $6,000 plus interest. An example when a borrower
contracts for a balloon mortgage, you are only paying for the interest
for the amount of years on it. The principal is not reduced. It remains
the same. When time is up, the borrower owe the amount that was
borrowed. My mother was able to pay the debt. The banker was not
a crook.

In 1958, I was a member of the varsity basketball team at
Blanche Ely High School. About 5:00 or 6:00 PM, I walked home
after practice on the dirt road. When I arrived, Charley was sitting
in a chair on the front porch. I spoke to him. He was unrespon-
sive. I could see foam around the corners of his mouth. I ran to
Freeman's Funeral Home. Clinton Freeman was the director. I rode
with them to our house. Charley was transported to the small hospital in Atlantic Boulevard. The physician's name was Dr. Millman.
A Baptist Church is in the building today. My uncle was admitted
to the hospital for a week or two. He probably had a stroke. At that
time, Freeman was the only funeral home in our neighborhood.

About a year before my uncle's illness, my mother had moved to
Glenn Cove, New York on Long Island. She did domestic work for a
wealthy Jewish family. They wanted me to move in with them. Rose
said that they told her they would pay for my education. A couple

rented our vacant room. I was not alone while my uncle was in the hospital. I do not remember their names. The man was called Shorty, whereas the lady was called Little Bit.

I had spoken to Rose on the telephone about her brother. He was discharged and came home. Boy, I was happy to see him. I was a seventeen-year-old teenager. Shorty and Little Bit told Charley that he was messed up with witchcraft. I heard them say, "There are two spiritual healers in Ft. Lauderdale. We can take you there to get healed." One of them was called Dr. Sweeting. A street was named after him. The other spiritual healer was Hollis. He lived in Northwest 27th Avenue near Dillard High School. All of us got in Shorty's car and went to Ft. Lauderdale. We visited Dr. Sweeting a few weeks. Afterward, contact was made with Hollis. He was visited a few times. Charley's condition did not improve. He was readmitted into the hospital. He died after four days. Rose returned from New York. Freeman received his body. It was sent to Leary, Georgia, in the Florida East Coast train. He was buried at Mt. Zion Missionary Baptist Church. That is where both of his parents are buried. My mother refused to return to her job. She told me that it was the best job she ever had. Charley did not have any children.

He was a casual weekend drinker. I have never seen him drunk. I remember a few of his drinking friends. One of them stuttered in his speech. His last name was McHenry. Sometimes, he would come to our house. After a few drinks, he would stutter. I mean it was real bad. He never could finish the word. I was young. I thought Mr. McHenry was crazy. He was the first person I had heard to stutter. Charley would transport him home in the truck. I wouldn't go with them. I remember a few more of my uncle's friends. I will list their names below.

(1) Joe and Ruth Oliver, husband and wife, lived across from Mt. Zion Baptist Church in Pompano.
(2) Jew Baby, the shoeshiner.
(3) Mr. Jim Benefield and daughter Sister Benefield lived in New-Town.
(4) Little-Shorty lived next to The Oat Field.
(5) Danny Gates lived across the street from our house.

He played the illegal Cuba numbers too. Some people called it bolita. In those days, some of the police officers played it too. The laws were not enforced. Many players thought that it was legal. If the banker of the numbers refused to pay, they would be put in jail. The numbers were announced on the radio. They came from the Island of Cuba. When Fidel Castro became their leader, it ended. In Florida, a system was designed from the winning numbers at the Dog Tracks. It continues to exist.

SPUDGE

Edmond Anderson is Spudge. I had two maternal uncles. He was the oldest. According to the 1910 U.S. Census Bureau Report, he was a year older than Charley. It showed that he was ten years old. According to the report, he was born on 1900. On the Report, Leary was in the Militia District 626 in Calhoun County. He was the first child to move away from his parents at an early age. He was about twelve years old. He was short but very strong. His father was a very strong tall man. Except for their height, they looked alike. Rose told me that Spudge was a perfect picture of their father, Pi. They could not read or write. Charley learned how to mark an X for his signature. I do not know if Spudge marked an X.

He was delivered by the midwife without any complications. He was born with his fist clenched like a prize fighter. She washed and cleansed him up. There was an extraordinary, special characteristic about him. He was born with a veil across both eyes. She carefully removed the veils. Then the midwife had a few words with his mom and dad. She said, "This is a rare baby. He was born with a veil over both eyes!"

"I have seen a few with it across one eye. He is a rarity and special. Remember to give him special care," Jeff, his father, answered, "It means that he was born to see spirits and ghosts. She agreed with Jeff. The nurse jotted his name down and left the house. Jeff made his wife comfortable. She held her son and smiled. This was their first child, and they were happy.

Mrs. Fennie said to her husband, Jeff, "He looks like you. I believe that he will be strong and smart just like you. Do you think he will see something to scare us?" Jeff chuckled for a while. Then she asked whether he had seen any ghosts. "And I know you are not afraid of them. You are not afraid to sleep at the graveyard during the night." He nodded. "Well, my father taught me a few things." He said, "Old Pop told me a few things to do:"

(1) Most people are too scared to see a ghost or spirit.
(2) If you were born to see them, it is different.
(3) Most mean people are not afraid to see them.
(4) If you have had a few drinks and it is night or the weather is bad, it is safe to go to a graveyard.
(5) Most people are too afraid to go to one because plenty of ghosts are there.
(6) Remember to have some whiskey in a bottle with you.
(7) If you do not have any booze, the alcoholic ghosts will worry you all night. They can smell it when you are drinking.
(8) When you find a spot to sleep, pour half of it on the ground and leave the half bottle standing on the ground.
(9) Then they will let you sleep in peace.
(10) Do not be afraid to talk with them. You will learn a few things.
(11) The police is afraid to go to the graveyard.

Jeff said, "This kid will be fine. I will teach him all of my tricks and secrets. I was not born with a veil, but Poppy had one over his eye. He could see them often. Sometimes, he would really scare us with some of his stories." His wife stated, "I don't need to hear about them." Pi spoke again. "You know, there are two types of them. There are mean, evil ghosts. Those are the bad ones. And you have the good spirits. They will not bother you."

When Spudge was eleven or twelve years old, he was strong. He was short and could really fight. He was tough and hard to handle. My grandmother said that he became angry with the mule on the farm. She said, "Spudge balled his fist and hit the animal on the head. The mule was unconscious. They chastised him for hitting the mule."

When he was twelve or thirteen years old, he ran away. His father wanted to chastise him. He refused to take a beating. Rose said he left to keep from killing their father. After a few years, he got married to Fannie Ivy Williams. They had three children, which are my first cousins. All of them were born in Leary, Georgia. Their names are as follows: (1) Charlie Anderson; (2) James Willie Anderson; and (3) Fannie Bell Anderson-Crittenton. Charlie and James Willie resided in Orlando, Florida. Charlie was a taxi driver. James Willie was a veteran in the U.S. Army. He was a member of the Seventh Day Adventist Church. He did work as a security officer at a hospital in Orlando. Both of them died in Orlando. Their sister, Fannie Bell, lived in Orlando. I will list the names of their children. The names of Charlie's children are as follows:

(1) Nellie, a resident of Orlando. I understand that she enjoys bowling.
(2) Charlie Will, a perfect picture of his dad.
(3) Zelma
(4) Ozzie

Cousin Charlie was a quiet man. He was very strong and mean. He was double-jointed. His father, grandfather, and maternal grandmother were double-jointed. All of them were very strong. He kept a very sharp switch blade knife in his pants' pocket. Sometimes, Spudge and his wife would go out on the weekends. That is when they lived in Leary. The boys were eleven or twelve years old. Rose said that Charlie kept a sharp knife in his overall pants. She said that he was a good fighter and could hit very hard. And he would not hesitate to cut a person with his knife.

He had a tremendous amount of love for his brother. He named him Honey. They got into an argument. Charlie continued to tell his brother. "Leave me alone, Honey!" Honey continued to bother him. Rose said that suddenly, Charlie hit his bother in the chest with a thunderous blow. He was knocked out. Rose said that the blow was very loud. She thought that her nephew was dead. He was bleeding from his ears, mouth, and nose. Rose spanked Charlie. He became angry because he did not start the fight. He attempted to cut her with his knife. The boys grew up and really loved their aunt.

My mother's last husband was Willie Lee Dunlap. They got into an argument and a fight. Rose told him, "If you continue to bother me, I will make a phone call to my nephews." He did a lot of bad talk. Rose telephoned her nephews. They got on the turnpike and were at our house in a few hours. Charlie asked Willie Lee if he did all of that bad talk. Willie Lee was batting his eyes and shaking his head. He said, "Yes, I said it." We were on our front porch. Charlie said, "You crazy ass punk! I am going to teach you a lesson. I am a real man." Then he grabbed Willie Lee with his left hand and lifted him off the floor." He said, "I am going to get my knife and cut your throat." When he was reaching for his knife, his brother and father grabbed him. They prevented him from killing Willie Lee. Then Charlie made him move out of the house. Both of them were about the same size. Each one of them weighed about 220 pounds.

When I was in the sixth grade, Spudge and his family visited us. It was on a Sunday when they drove from Orlando. A few days prior to their arrival, I had been on a farm to pick beans. It was the plant's first crop. We were paid fifty cents per hamper for the first crop. The farmers would pay one dollar per hamper for seconds. I would pick five or six hampers of beans per day. I was not a very good bean picker. Another farmworker who was two years ahead of me in school was at the farm. He was a very good bean picker. Dupree is his name. He became the quarterback for our football team. Dupree was left-handed. He wore a pair of short pants at the bean field. When he finished picking beans, he ran and played. He would run and flip over. He apparently lost his money from the beans. He was not aware of losing his money. No one was aware of it. I decided to take a short walk. Then I saw some money on the ground. I picked it up and put it in my pocket. Boy that was a real good day for me! It was a combination of fifty cent and silver dollar coins. It was between six to eight dollars. Man, was I happy. I told a few people about the money.

My cousin, Charlie, asked me to walk with him to the small family grocery store. The name of the store was Harden's. A white lady named Miss Harden owned it. At that time, supermarkets did not exist. We walked by a few businesses before reaching the store.

Dupree was leaving the Loveland Theatre. He lived in Jones Quarters, which was behind the grocery store. He ran and confronted me. He said, "Charlee, someone told me you got my money." I replied by saying, "Dupree, I found some money when I took a short walk in the bean field. It is my money, and I ain't giving it up."

Dupree said, "Well, I am going to have to beat you and take it." I told him that I was not afraid of him. I told Dupree that we would beat each other up. And he was going to have a hard time taking the money. We were getting ready to fight. Cousin, Charlie, stopped it. He told Dupree that he was visiting from Orlando. And no one living in Pompano could beat him. He said, "Charlee found the money, and it belongs to him. Founders are keepers and losers are reapers. He grabbed Dupree and said, "You better not touch him even when I return to Orlando." Dupree ran home and forgot about the money. I joked with him about the money after we finished high school. We were young adults. We've been friends for a long time. Charlie was cremated or buried in Orlando. I was unable to attend his funeral. When he died, we were not notified.

James Willie Anderson is his brother and another first cousin. All of us called him Willie James, except his brother. Charlie called him Honey. He went into the military and was an army veteran. I was unable to pull his name up on the Internet under Willie James Anderson. However, an obituary was located with his name as James W. Anderson. We attended his funeral. The Seventh Day Adventist Church concluded his funeral. I was really impressed when I learned that he was loyal and faithful to the church. He and his family attended church on a regular basis. He was a role model for many young people. He inspired several members to become law enforcement officers in Orlando. So many kind words were said about him. His body was transported to a military cemetery in a city north of Orlando. I went to it. It was a long drive. According to the Internet, he was buried in Bushnell, Sumter City, Florida. He was born on July 14, 1920. He died on August 5, 1990, at seventy years of age. He was an educated man and a hard worker. His name was recorded as James W. Anderson. He and his wife lived with us in Pompano about a year or two, shortly after their marriage. He had a job in Homestead, at the military base. His wife and children are listed below.

(1) Mrs. Bernice Anderson
(2) Frank Anderson, oldest sibling, and a perfect picture of his father
(3) Minnie Anderson
(4) Sherry Anderson
(5) Gloria Anderson-Jackson
(6) Mary Anderson-Callahan
(7) Leola Anderson-Davenport
(8) Juanita Anderson

Their sister resides in Orlando. Her name is Fannie Bell Anderson-Crittenton. I am a few years her senior. When I was six or seven years, I remembered visiting them when they lived in Georgia. I would travel with my grandmother, Fennie. I gave my cousin the nickname Bay. I loved her the way I would love a sister. I am the only child. Her children are listed below.

(1) Terry Murphy, male
(2) Jamie Murphy, female
(3) Rodney Crittenton or Anderson, male, a U.S. Navy veteran. Living in Atlanta, Georgia, and married to a white lawyer.

My uncle was married to Fannie Ivy Williams-Anderson. My uncle was 91 years old when she died. His wife was one hundred eight years old when she died. Both were buried in Orlando. I did not attend her funeral. I was not notified about her death. Her parents and siblings are listed.

(1) Frank Williams, father
(2) Fronnie Williams, mother
(3) Fannie Ivy, daughter
(4) Rose Ida Williams, daughter
(5) Willie Lee Williams, daughter
(6) Annie Williams, daughter
(7) Charlie Williams, son
(8) Buddy Williams, son

In Morgan, Georgia, Spudge worked for Albert Dozier. He and his wife, Fannie Ivy, lived in Dozier's Plantation. He did farm labor for Albert. He painted all of the houses white. Spudge had a friend who lived in the plantation. His last name was Page. They lived in Morgan, Georgia. One day, my uncle got into an argument on the farm with his boss, Albert. When he quit the job, Albert became upset. Spudge had a reputation among the black farmworkers. He had beaten the ones he fought. My uncle told the white man he was going to kick his white ass. When he went for his knife, all of the workers grabbed him.

Albert walked back to his house. Spudge moved to his parent's home in Leary. His wife refused to move. Spudge and his father, Pi, got on their horse-drawn wagon and went to Morgan. They brought their rifles with them. When they got there, Albert was gone. They could not find him. Spudge told his father that the white man wouldn't forget him. Pi told his son not to worry, and he will be fine. "All of the white folks respect me. That is the reason they call me Uncle Jeff." Then they encouraged his wife and children to come to Leary. All of them got on the wagon and left the plantation. He did not have any more contact with Albert Dozier.

While living with his father and mother, he worked on Albert Jordan's farm. Sometimes, he would work for George Colley on his farm. The Jordans and Colleys were wealthy white people. They were farmers. Some of them were entrepreneurs.

Marshal Jordan owned a store in Leary. Albert Jordan was one of his brothers. Willie Jordan and Albert Jordan owned a peanut mill. A major problem happened at the mill. They got into a serious argument in front of the workers. They almost got into a fight. One of them was not allowed to work there anymore.

One of George Colley's sons rode a bicycle. He carried a rifle on it. His name was John Colley. All of the black folks thought that John was mentally ill. He could function. Some of the white folks said, "John had learned too fast in school. The education messed up his mind." One Sunday, John rode his bicycle to my granddad's place. His rifle was attached to his bike. He said, "Uncle Jeff, all of the other black folks work on Sunday. And I want to know why you all are not working." Pi told the young white boy, "I do not care anything about that little rifle on your bike. As a matter of fact, I have many of them in the house." He said, "Son, that is the reason I do not sharecrop. I rent this land from your daddy. Boy, let me tell you something, we rest on Sundays. We work six days a week. We go to church and rest on Sunday. And you had better get your ass on that bicycle and get the hell out of here." Rose said that his dad probably told him not to bother with my grandpa. John did not come to the property anymore.

George Colley's youngest son lived in Atlanta. When George died, his oldest son returned to Leary from Atlanta. He took over his father's business. His name was Dewey Colley. He had another son whose name was Morgan Colley.

Thomas Colley was George's nephew. He was half black and white. Thomas got married to one of my granddad's daughters. She was (Anna) Fannie Anderson. They lived in a plantation in Leary. It was in the country.

Prior to moving to Orlando, Florida, Spudge worked for Bozzie Keel. He worked on the farm and lived in Keel's plantation. He had a friend who lived in the plantation. Clark Smart was his name.

Subsequently, my mother added a few more stories about her brother, Spudge. She said, "He would visit them in the country. That was a while after his marriage." Rose further said that he told them about his first experience with a ghost. He cleared his throat by grunting. Then he told them about it.

Spudge said, "It happened after I moved. I had Fannie Ivy as my girlfriend. It was on the very first visit to her house. I had to walk about six miles on the clay road. Her parents had a nice house on a few acres of land. It was about five or ten acres. I introduced myself to her parents. Then we stood and talked in the yard. After that, we sat and talked on the front porch. They had a wood fence around the property, typically the type used by ranchers. I had to open the gate to enter the property. After a few hours, the sun began to set. I could see a man sitting on a post. The post was next to the gate. He was wearing a pair of overalls. I could not see his head. His body did not have a head on it. My parents had informed me about the veil over my eyes. Pi had told me to be prepared for my first encounter with ghosts. And it was here at my girlfriend's house. You will be the only one to see it. Ghosts are very clever. They will allow you to see them if they want you to see them. You don't have to be born with a veil to see them. But a person born with one can see them frequently.

"Spudge did not want to walk through the gate to go home. That was the only way to leave the property. Fannie Ivy would look into that direction. She did not mention seeing the man. Apparently, she could not see him. It was a beautiful sunset. He figured the man would be gone with darkness. Each time he looked into that direction, he could see the man. It was night, and he knew the road would be very dark. He made up his mind to walk through the gate and go home. He kissed Fannie Ivy good-bye, and she went indoors."

"Then he said that he looked at the headless man. He walked through the gate and told the man, "Sir, I do not know you. I ain't done nothing to you. You ain't gonna do nothing to me. The man was quiet. He said that the man followed him on the dark clay road. He walked behind Spudge. It was pitch-dark night. The man walked behind him for nearly six miles. I would turn and look behind me. There he was! I continued to say things to the ghost. That he was not gonna do anything to me. And I was not gonna do anything to him. When he could see where he lived, the man disappeared. The first experience was not bad. It was a little scary. It showed me how tough I am.

Rose told another story concerning her brother. It was when she was about thirteen years old. Spudge gave them a visit. Rose and Little Sis decided to go with him to town. He was more than twenty years old. It was a long walk. Shortly afterward, it was night. It was dark while walking on the clay road. It was wide enough to have one lane in either direction. They chatted while walking. He had his flashlight in one hand. It helped them to see the road. They walked on the left side. His sisters walked next to him on his right side.

Then their brother grunted a couple of times to clear his throat. He walked to the opposite side of the clay road. It scared Rose and made her a bit nervous. She walked as close as she could to Spudge. If he grunted, it meant that he was seeing a ghost. His sister, Nig, questioned him about the grunts. He said, "Oh, I just wanted to change and walk on the other side of the road. She really did not believe him. When they arrived at the house, he told the truth. He said, "I did not want to scare the two of you. I did not want y'all to see it." He said, "Two horses were coming into our direction on the clay road. They were pulling a wagon. An old man and woman were steering them. I moved over to let them pass by us. On the rear of the wagon was a casket. I guess they were taking it to the cemetery." Nig said, "When you grunted and cleared your throat, I knew it was a ghost." She went on to say, "I do not plan to walk at night with you anymore." Spudge smiled and stuttered a little in his speech and replied, "Those were good ghosts." Nig said, "I do not want to see the good or bad ghosts." My mother shared a few more stories concerning ghosts with her brother. But those are the only ones I will mention.

I enjoyed visiting Spudge during the summer when the elementary schools were closed. I rode on the FEC train with my grandmother. I think I was in the first and second grade. I remember getting water from his well. He had a few peach trees. The peaches on the trees resembled guavas. I lived in South Florida, and we have guava trees. I would ask my grandmother to pull some peaches off the tree for me. I thought they were guavas. I would say, "Grandma, pick some of those guavas for me to eat."

One day, I remember riding on the wagon with him. He had to purchase a few things from a hardware store. It was the season for the wild bullet grapes. A vine grew on a large tree near the edge of the clay road. Spudge made the mules stop pulling the wagon. He got me a bag full of bullets. Oh boy, they were sweet and delicious!

LITTLE SISTER

Anna Anderson was her birth name. Informally, she changed it to Fannie. The reason was because she did not like the name Anna. According to the 1910 U.S. Census Bureau Report, she was two years old, which meant she was born on 1908. Her nickname was Little Sis. She attended school until the sixth grade. She had to work on her father's farm. He did not like education and made it difficult to attend school. When it came to making money, she was the slick one. On Sundays, her father would get some rest. He would leave her in charge of his moonshine business. She would steal some of the money. Sometimes, her baby sister, Nig, would see her steal some of the money.

Nig told her, "When Pi wake up, I am going to tell on you." Nig had a sweet tongue, and Lil Sis knew it. She would tell Nig, "If you keep it a secret, I will buy you a large bag of candy on the week-end." Then she would mix the balance of the moonshine with some water. Pi would awaken and get his money. He would make a drink for himself. Then he would say, "Lil Sis, did you mix my moonshine with water?" She would say, "No." Pi replied, "My moonshine taste like it has been watered down. The strength is weak. It is not as strong as it was when I left it with you." Little Sis, would not tell the truth. But she would buy the large bag of candy for Nig. She would be so happy after getting the candy.

Some years passed and Little Sis decided to get married to a much older man. He was half white and black. Thomas Colley was his name. According to my research on the Internet, in 1901, he was twenty-three years old. Therefore, he was born on 1878. When I was young, I thought that he was a white man. He was a mulatto and owned a very large ranch in the country of Leary. It was many acres of land. The house was huge. On the property, there were many storage barns—one to store hay and another one to store corn. They had cows, hogs, chickens, mules, and horses. They made their syrup. There were beehives. They had just about all of the necessities in that era. There were several wagons and buggies. The only thing missing was an automobile. Their house faced the hard clay road. You would have had to travel some miles to view another home. No homes were in sight or near their ranch.

Prior to and during the first grade, my grandmom and I would visit them. We rode on the passenger train. The station was parallel to Dixie Highway in Pompano. In those days, to travel on a train was very popular. Train stations were all over the United States. It was the Florida East Coast (FEC) train. Many blacks had jobs on the train, especially the Pullmans. They were really waiters on it. A movie was made about them. The Pullmans were very popular in the black communities. People looked up to them including white folks. They were given a gold pocket watch as a gift. I forget the number of years they had to work to get it. The watch had the picture of the FEC train engraved on it. Many years ago, someone gave one to my mother. It had the FEC logo. She gave it to me when I was with my first wife. But it is not made with gold. It is a brass one. Obviously, the FEC must have stopped making them with gold. Sometimes, we would spend the whole summer in Georgia. I learned a lot about wildlife in the woods. We would visit all of our relatives in the small towns near Leary. I had a lot of fun at Aunt Lil Sis' house. Some of our relatives lived in Dawson and Arlington. We spent about a week at each house.

Little Sis taught me how to make butter in the churn. She was a great cook. Sometimes, she cooked preservatives. I would help her put them in glass jars for storage. It was made from a wide variety of fruits. I remember the metal connected to each lid. It snapped on the jar. On few occasions, she made moonshine inside the house. The still had copper pipes inside it. The pipes were inside of a trough. She made a fire in the fireplace, and the still was in front of it. When the pipes were hot, I had to cool them off with water. Then the moonshine would start running out of the pipes. And it tasted real good. I would mix my drink with plenty of sugar. I did not drink enough to get drunk. Once a month, she would brew about twenty gallons.

Sometimes, I helped squeeze milk from the heifer cows. Then I would beat it up in the churn to make butter. We made cheese, buttermilk, and other items. My grandmom and I picked wild berries and wild garlic for the house. All of that stuff was plentiful in the woods. When it was time to harvest the peanuts, I helped them. I remember having to grab the peanut bush. Then it would be pulled out of the ground. The next step was to shake the soil from around the nuts. Real tall wooden poles stood in the ground. After shaking the dirt away, we had to stack them around the posts. They would be stacked as high as you could stack them. The sun would make the peanuts dry.

We would gather pecans and walnuts from their trees. It was always something to do. I was excited about it. It was enjoyable. I remember when I helped Uncle Thomas make syrup from cane juice. He grew plenty of cane. Plenty of cane stalks were on the ground. They were about twenty feet away from a large black pot. Some sort of shed was built near it. I remember that one or two mules were in their harness. They had to walk around in a circle to squeeze juice from cane stalks. The cane was between six to eight feet long. I think they had to strain the juice. It would be cooked until it became syrup. I enjoyed helping them make it. The juice was delicious! At times, we had to watch out for honey bees and wasps. The juice would attract them.

Once, we robbed his beehives for honey. My uncle had to build a fire. Then he would make it turn to a smoke. That would prevent them from stinging us. Mr. Thomas told me, "Charlee, when you get honey, you must leave some for them. If you get all of it, they will leave and never return." One time, he gave me some wax with honey. Wow, that was real delicious when I chewed it. They had a few peach trees along with walnut and pecan ones. I helped pick cotton. I remember getting my fingers stuck when picking it. That would piss me off.

They had an old-fashioned swing on their front porch. It was a man-made swing. On my free time, I had a lot of fun on that swing. Three to four people could ride on it. Since there were not any stores nearby, a catering truck would come in the country. It was called The Rolling Store. It came in our area on Thursdays, at the same time. The driver would blow the horn when he was in our area. The driver sold just about everything you could buy from a store. On Thursdays, I would rock back and forth on the swing and looking out for The Rolling Store. I made sure that they would buy me some sweet goodies, such as candies and so forth. I did so many exciting things, but that is all I can remember. The reason is because I was a young boy. I remember fishing in the creek. They had a well in the yard. The water was delicious and cold as ice. A small building was built, which covered the well. At the top of the building was a pulley. A metal chain went across the pulley. Then a bucket was connected to the two ends of the chain. We had to pull one end of the chain down to the water. Then we would pull the other side of it to bring the water to the surface.

On one occasion, my grandmother and I were sitting at the dinette table. My aunt was cooking breakfast for us. Mr. Thomas took a seat with us. Fannie was cooking those large homemade biscuits. He picked up the syrup bottle and put it to his mouth. He drank some from the bottle. My grandmom told me, "Mr. Thomas was stingy and selfish. He did that to prevent us from getting some syrup." She refused to use that bottle.

As farming became less popular, Mr. Thomas sold the ranch. They moved to Albany, Georgia, and bought a house. The house was on Van Buren Street. A cemetery was not far from the house. There was a swimming pool within walking distance. It was at the City Park. Around 1950, my mother and I went to Leary to bury her mother. After the funeral, we stayed with Fannie and her husband for several days in Albany. My aunt tried to be a classy woman. The country never left my mother. One day, Fannie prepared a tuna fish meal. That was my first time eating tuna. It was delicious. I observed her cut some celery to put in it. That was my first time eating celery.

She didn't have any children. One of her friends asked Fannie to raise their daughter. The girl was eleven or twelve years old. Her name was Rosa Lee. All of the folks called her Dixie Lee. One day, she did something that was not approved by Fannie. Dixie Lee refused to allow Fannie to chastise her. Fannie returned her to her mother. She lived with her mother until adulthood and got married.

After married for many years, they decided to get a divorce. The house was given to Fannie. After a few years, her husband died. She did domestic work for a white family in Albany until the Civil Rights Movement. Martin Luther King was picketing and boycotting businesses. That was during mid-1960's. Most of the white folks fired or laid off the black workers. Little Sis called her sister who was living in Pompano. She told my mother, "The white folks are firing and laying us off. I cannot get any work." My mother bought a Greyhound bus ticket for her. She rented the house in Albany and moved to Pompano. She sold the house to a friend around 1970.

Some of Thomas Colley's children are stated below:

(1) Sam Colley, son
(2) Goot Colley, son. Elbert Colley was his son and he had a waterhead. He had three daughters: Fannie Mae Colley, Sally Lou Colley, and Tee-Tie Colley. I am not sure about Tee-Tie's gender.
(3) Dewey Colley was the youngest.

Elbert and his mother moved from Leary to Albany. They lived in the projects. It was not very far from Fannie's house. When I was young, I would talk and have fun with him. That was in Leary. He was happy to see me when I came to Albany. He remembered my name and was intelligent. He died many years ago.

In New-Town, we lived in Northwest 11th Avenue. It intersected with Atlantic Boulevard. We had to sell our property for the development of 1-95. Both sides of our street were taken but only one side of 10th Avenue was taken. In 1968, the property was sold for about $5,800. My mother said that the government had ripped her off and beat her out of the property. I grew up near the north bound lane of 1-95 and Atlantic Boulevard. Prior to the expressway, Atlantic Boulevard was a dirt road. It ran near the State Farmers Market.

Fannie got a domestic job in Pompano. On the weekends, she would drink and dance at the local bars. She kept her some snuff to dip in her mouth. She did not pay rent or help with the bills. Many folks said she was a lesbian. Her brother-in-law accused her of one. His name was Willie Lee Dunlap. They were drinking partners. He alleged that Fannie said, "If I cannot get a man I earn enough money to buy plenty of pussy."

A man we called Shorty mentioned something about her. He lived in the Collier City subdivision. This man is not Little Shorty, who lived on 9th Avenue. He said that he knocked on her door without a response. Then he went to the bedroom window and looked into the house. Shorty said that a neighbor was in the room with Fannie. Her neighbor is named Virginia. Fannie was on top of her. Both of them were naked. They were bumping and bumping each other. They were busy and did not see me."

For some reason, Fannie was jealous of her sister, Rose. However, Rose loved her dearly. She wanted Rose to be down and under her. That meant she wanted to possess better things, which included money. When she got a chance, she would steal some of her money. But she would help out with an argument or fight. So she did have some love for Rose. I always thought it was a sibling rivalry. Fannie is a few years older and had to help take care of her sister. When they were young, she would take her food and make her cry. Fannie told her parents, "She ate all of her food. She is greedy." That is the reason for crying. Sometimes, she would hit Rose and make her cry. Their father would tell her that he did not believe her. He said, "Just keep picking on your sister. She is going to get larger and older. She will pay you back." It happened that way. After that, Rose won every fight between them. Fannie never liked losing to her sister. They fought a few times as adults. You know who won.

Fannie had a friend in New-Town who was married. Her name was Mamie Rainey. She was married to Bud Rainey. Mamie and Fannie were drinking friends. They spent a lot of time together. Most of the time, Bud would be at his job. Fannie had a boyfriend whose name was Bill Ross. They would drink at home and at the bars. Sometimes, they would get into an argument. After a heated argument and a threat, he was advised to leave our house. He had a reputation in Pompano. He was usually armed with a pistol. A white policeman had told my mother and aunt that he was a dangerous man. He was accused of killing a former wife. They told the officer that they owned guns too. They said, "We carry one in our pocket books." The officer responded, "Use it if you have to use it. In my eyes, it will be self-defense."

They went and got their pistols and told Bill Ross to leave the house. When he saw their pistols, he ran out of the house. While running, he pulled out his pistol and got off a shot. Then they shot at him a couple of times. He got into his car. Then they ran to the dirt road and stood in the center of it. A few more rounds were fired from the pistols. One of them blew out the rear window of the car. That was the last time ever coming to our house. Bill told a friend, "A bullet had grazed his right ear. Those women are crazy. They will kill you. Be prepared to fight both of them." The police was not aware of it and had no involvement into the shooting.

After the house was sold for the expressway, Fannie rented a room. It was with one of her friends. Rose rented an apartment in the subdivision of Collier City. It is in Pompano. Some vacant land adjacent to Collier City was under construction. Homes were being built. The subdivision was named Esquire Lakes. They signed a contract jointly to purchase one of them. Fannie changed her mind and bought a house in Collier City. Rose did not qualify alone as a farmworker. She did not earn enough money. She had been tricked by her sister. I was married to my first wife. We signed the contract and got the house for my mother. She was able to get the house in Esquire Lakes.

Fannie was an outgoing woman. She was more or less an extrovert. Friends would visit her frequently. Most of them would be women. She enjoyed cooking and would have parties at her home. Fannie was active in the church. She purchased nice clothes to wear.

Rose was an introvert. She will do a lot of talking after getting into a conversation. She and her sister, Fannie, would argue and fight a few times per year. Fannie would lose the fight and didn't like it. It was probably because she was a few years older than Rose. They did not get along with each other. If one of them got into a fight, you would have to fight both of them. Fannie liked to drink booze, dance, and party. Rose did not indulge into those things. Rose's former husband, Willie Lee Dunlap, would drink and dance. All of her boyfriends consumed alcohol. Fannie called her sister a square because she did not socialize with other people. Fannie would hang out with her sister's former husband and boyfriends. They would drink, dance, and entertain together. Rose did not do those things. The majority of times, she would be home while they would be at the barrooms. Rose was not a cheater. She would have only one man at a time. After quitting and breaking up for a while, she would get another man. Rose accused Fannie of having sex with all of them. She would deny it.

While residing in Collier City, Fannie became ill for about three years. She was unable to work. Rose paid her mortgage payment and all of her bills. She bought food for her to eat. Fannie recovered and returned to her job. Fannie told Rose, "I am going to make out a will. I am going to give you the house and all of my personal property. It did not happen like that. That was very nice for paying all of my bills."

She was active at the community center for seniors. A bus would come to their residence. It took them to the center. Rose never went there. The seniors played games and would have group discussions. Sometimes, they would get lectures or taught how to read and write. One day, I remember when Fannie thought that she was speaking correctly. She had planned to go to the store. She said, "I are going to the store." I told her the correct way to speak.

* * * * *

At the community center, she made a few friends. One of them was Willie Gilbert. He could not read or write and lived with his son and daughter-in-law. They lived across town. One day when the activities were over at the center, he went home with Fannie. He got off the bus with her. I do not know how often it happened. He would get Fannie to call his son when he was ready to go home. All of the neighbors were her friends. The main one was a lady named Gwen. She lived in the opposite side of the street.

Gwen encouraged Fannie and Willie to get married. He was receiving a social security and retirement check from Chrysler Corporation. He was a janitor for many years with them. He refused to go home with his son. Fannie would not allow him in the house to talk with his father. She basically kidnapped Willie. They stopped going to the center and got married at the courthouse. Fannie probably married him for his money. His son was married to my classmate whose name is Annie Pearl Barr. She grew up in New-Town too.

Willie's son was unable to encourage him to move back with him. Fannie told his son that they were married. She showed the marriage license to him. Fannie's house had two bedrooms. They did not sleep in the same bedroom. Willie was illiterate and not very bright. He seemed to be retarded. He loved his wife. He would drink alcohol with her.

Fannie kept a shotgun on the floor underneath her bed. Willie was unaware of it. One night, Willie got out of his bed. He went into Fannie's bedroom and got into her bed. It awakened Fannie. Fannie told Willie to let her know when he is coming to her room. She said, "Willie, I have a gun under the bed. I don't want to shoot you by mistake." I don't believe they ever had any sex. He kissed her a couple of times.

She would cash his checks. Some of the money were spent and the other saved. Fannie gave him five dollars per month out of his money. He would walk and pick up aluminum cans to sell. Fannie would end up spending the five dollars prior to receiving his next check.

Fannie did not learn to drive an automobile. She decided to purchase a car. Willie had retired with Chrysler. It was a brand-new station-wagon automobile. Chrysler gave them a discount on it. She didn't know how to drive it. Fannie asked Gwen, her friend and neighbor, to drive it home. From time to time, Gwen attempted to teach her how to drive. She did not have a driver's license. Fannie bought an illegal one to drive. She paid a Cuban five hundred dollars to make the license. It looked as if it was genuine.

One day, she decided to drive the car to the store. It was parked into her driveway. She had to back it out. The engine was started, and the gear was placed into reverse. She was able to back it out of her yard. When she attempted to stop the car, her foot went on the gas pedal. She destroyed a neighbor's fence. Another neighbor had an abandoned car parked alongside the road. It was not worth much money. That incident stopped Fannie from using her car.

The neighbors knew that she had a phony license. They threatened to call the police unless she paid them money. She paid both of them around one thousand dollars each. Fannie destroyed the license and never drove again. The car was parked in the driveway after getting it repaired. She would loan the car to her friends. Sometimes, they would drive with her in it. The only thing she could drive was to steer a mule or horse.

I did not get along with my aunt. I did not take spankings from nobody. That was after I was big enough to take care of myself. In New-Town, I picked her up and slam dunked her on the floor. She had spit some snuff in my face because I wouldn't let her beat me. She wanted me to wash the dishes. I told her to wash them. That is when the fight started. She was bruised and bled. The city police responded after she made a phone call. We had one black policeman for our community. His name was Criswell. All of the boys called him Sugar Criss. Fannie had been drinking that day. I told officer Criswell that she was drinking whiskey. That we got into an argument. She spit snuff in my face, and I threw her ass down on the floor. He made a report and left the house. I was around twelve or thirteen year old.

Over the years we frequently were involved with verbal altercations. The last time, I told her that she was no damn good. "You are a snake in our family". Whenever she had a chance she would steal her sister's money.

My aunt's friend, Gwen was a spiritual root worker and healer. She worked for the police department. She drove one of their cars in the black community. The car was a marked police car but it had "Community Watch Officer" on it. She was a volunteer and not a paid job. She would report crimes to the police. I heard that she was paid a percentage of the take from drug raids. Sometimes she would ride in the police car with Gwen. They were buddy, buddy. Gwen's husband and boyfriend lived in the house with her. All of the folks said that she must have had some real good roots. The reason was from having both men living with her.

I remember another argument between Fannie and Rose. We were visiting Fannie. After the argument Fannie told my mother to leave from her house. As we were leaving, Fannie used some profanities. She cursed her out. She yelled, "That is the reason you are not in my will·. Rose told her that she could care less about it.

My mother believed that Fannie and Gwen were intimate with each other. She believes that Gwen beat her out of money. Willie received dividends at the end of year from his pension. Chrysler sent a Christmas bonus, too. Fannie thought they were worthless. Gwen had told her to throw them away. When Fannie was not around she would get the check from the garbage. Gwen would endorse the check and put it in her bank account. She ripped Fannie off for years. Fannie borrowed money on her house about four times. It totaled to about $60,000. There was nothing to show how the money was spent. She paid the loans *off*. My mother, Rose, believed Gwen beat her out of the money.

Fannie, Willie, and Gwen have died. One day before her death, Fannie became ill while working in her garden. She was transported to the Emergency Room. After a few days she was discharged and sent home. Several weeks later she was in the hospital. She was diagnosed with gangrene in both feet. The doctor told me that it was two different types. He said, "There is a dry and wet gangrene. She had both of them. One foot had dry gangrene and the other one was wet. She needed an amputation to try and save her life·. I forgot which type was amputated.

The lady referred to as "Dixie Lee" was granted all of her property in the will along with a "Durable Power of Attorney. We could not make any medical decisions for her. Dixie Lee lived in southwest Georgia, with her husband. She took her time in contacting the hospital. Fannie was suffering but unable to talk. She realized that she had made a mistake with the will and Power of Attorney, decision. She murmured some words to me. I think she said, "I am sorry". That was too late. After a week or so, Dixie Lee, arrived and produced the legal documentation to the physician. Afterwards one of Fannie's legs was amputated. She died within a month.

When Fannie, first entered the hospital she was able to talk. She realized her mistake with Dixie Lee. She did not call or visit Fannie. Fannie told her sister to get some valuables from the house. The only thing I wanted was a couple of small trees in the yard. I wouldn't allow my mother to remove anything from the house. Gwen and Dixie Lee, had been communicating on the phone. They became friends. Gwen wanted to buy Fannie's house.

One day we went to Fannie's house to get two small trees. Gwen saw us at the house. She called Dixie Lee, and told her what we were doing. The police was dispatched to Fannie's house. Dixie Lee had made a complaint against us. The police arrived and made us leave the yard. We were threatened by the officer. He told us that we would be arrested if we returned to the property.

Fannie died and we did not go to her funeral. My mother was hurt badly by the incident with the police. She was pissed off with Gwen and Dixie Lee. I knew my mother was hot-headed. I refused to take her to the services. She would have gotten into a fight. She did not want to go either

My mother had these words to say about her sister. "*God* made her suffer. I did so much for her. I paid her mortgage note and bills for three years. I bought food to eat. I paid for her bus fare from Georgia to Pompano. She lived with me for many years and did not give me a penny. She lied about the will. She gave away everything to Dixie Lee. She was not even kin to her. She didn't visit Fannie and took her time to report to the doctor. That is why my sister suffered. *God* doesn't like what's ugly. You reap what you sow."

Gwen bought the house. We believed it was purchased with some of Fannie's money. Now all of them are dead. My mother is alive and fairly healthy. She is one hundred years old in 2014. I forgave my aunt for her misdeeds toward us. I prayed for her when she was in the hospital.

NIG

Rosa Lee Anderson is my mother. She was the last sibling. Her nickname was Nigger. All of the folks called her Nig. I hate the word "nigger" with a passion. To me, it is highly offensive. It is a fighting word to me. As a young adult, I didn't allow her family or friends to use it. We were at a funeral in Orlando. I overheard a second cousin call her Nig. Her name was Tom or Hattie. I told her to refrain from using that word with my mother. That was the last time any family member would use it.

Her father decided to give his last child the nickname Nigger. He hated that word because he knew it was a hateful word. Pi told his family members, "I would like to know what happened to my parents. I would like to see Lela, my sister. I made a promise to myself to stay out of Alabama. The white folks are the reason. He said the white folks have always treated us wrong. I would be living in Alabama, had I not met those white thugs. I was alone in the woods and minding my own business. They approached me in the woods and wanted to kill me. They said we are going to kill a nigger today. I had to protect myself and kill all of them. That is why I gave my daughter an awful nickname. It reminds me of that incident."

"With that nickname, I will not slip up and return to Alabama. You will never get a chance to meet my kinfolks. If we should decide to go to Alabama, those white folks will kill us. I know what the Klan would do. I hope that my people were not killed because of me. But if they found out I killed those thugs, they are dead."

Rose and her sister Fannie were the last two of the siblings to live with their parents. Fannie was about five years older and had to help take care of Rose. When Rose was small, her sister would make her cry frequently. She would eat her food. Then she would rub some crumbs around her mouth. Their mother, Mi, would inquire about the crying. Then Fannie would tell her, "Mi, this child is greedy. Look at all of the crumbs around her mouth." Fannie would pick at Rose and beat her. One day, her father told her, "Just keep on picking on your sister and making her cry. One day, when she becomes older, she is going to whip your butt." It turned out to be true. When Rose became bigger and older, she gave her sister a good old-fashion butt whipping. Fannie never won another fight with her. When it came to eating food, Rose was gluttonous with a great appetite.

Jeff told his wife and children a few more things about white folks. My parents were free slaves and owned their land. They had a house on it. They were farmers and even grew rice. Some of the white folks were jealous of them. The white folks have done so many bad things against black people. They don't go to jail for it. He said, "My folks were kidnapped from Africa. They were kidnapped and brought to this country. I don't know anybody in Africa. I would like to know my kinfolks in Africa. I blame the white folks because I cannot trace my descendants in Africa. I would love to know my tribal descendants."

Jeff apologized to his daughter because of the terrible nickname. He said that will help her understand it. Then Jeff said, "Not only did they kidnap my folks, many other bad things were done to them. They worked in this country for nothing. If they refused, they would be beaten, maimed, or killed. My mother was beaten and raped by her boss. She became pregnant and had a half-white child whose name was Lela."

Rose said that her dad was in a talkative mood. They were sitting around the fireplace. It was during the winter. The conversation was sensitive and painful to them. Jeff said, "Based upon what I told you, I do not trust white folks. I mean, no further than I can see them. You had better be like me. Look at the evil things they have done to us. They have destroyed our families. All white folks should be rich. I can prove it to you. If I could get between twenty to one hundred white slaves, I would get rich. They would be my slaves and made to work on my farm for many years. They would not be paid. I would become a rich man."

Jeff told them a few things his parents shared with him. He said that his parents were hard workers. They told him that white folks could not be trusted. The Indians told my folks, "When the white man talks, I want you to listen to them closely. They are great liars and deceivers. Their words are like the teeth on a fork. When they talk, their words are like the spaces between a folk. Their words go into many different directions. You cannot believe a damn thing they say. He said, "I know that some white folks are good. Hell, George Colley is white. He is my friend."

Rose was born in Leary, Georgia, on January 15, 1914. Martin Luther King was born on the same day. My best friend was born on the 14th day of January. His name is Sammie Lee Wells. His mother was named Zula Wells. When my mother migrated to Pompano, she lived near Zula. Zula lived in Ogden Brothers Quarters. My mother and Zula became friends.

She was not as outgoing as Fannie. But she liked to wear nice clothes. Rose is a few inches taller than five feet. Her weight is in proportion with her height. She lived with her parents in Leary, until her father's death.

She believed everything her parents told her. It made her naive and gullible. Her parents told her that Santa Claus came down the chimney with her gifts. She believed that was true. Around Christmas, her parents would make some scratches on the smut in the chimney. On Christmas Day, they would show her the scratches on the chimney. They would smile and say, "Santa Claus made those marks when he came down the chimney."

A pregnant lady visited her mother. The lady had a large stomach. It was her mother's friend. They chatted for a few hours, and the lady went home. Rose said to her mother, "Mi, what is wrong with your friend. Why is her stomach so large?" She answered, "She loves to eat a lot of peas, beans mixed with rice. She eats it every day. I have told her to stop eating like that. It gave her a swollen stomach. That is the reason it is sticking out." Rose believed her mother.

Rose was short and very strong. She could fight like a champion. It would take more than two boys to handle her. She would ball her fists and fight like a prize fighter. She was good at wrestling too. A few days after Christmas, she played with some friends. Some of the kids said that Santa did not exist. They told Rose, "Your mom and dad are Santa. They bought the gifts and put them under the tree." Rose told them that they were not telling the truth. My parents told me that Santa came down the chimney. The children laughed and ridiculed her. She became upset. She got into a fight with two of them. Rose beat them. The other kids ran home. If her friends disputed her parents, it was going to be a fight.

Rose and Fannie were the only siblings living with their parent's permanently. The oldest female was married. She was called Love. Her brothers ran away at an early age. They refused to be chastised by their father. Love worked on the farm with her sister and parents. They worked from sunup to sundown. The days were long, and the work was hard. It was not easy. The girls worked like men and boys.

It was always something to do six days per week. Their father took Sundays off from work. He rented his land and was not a sharecropper. They went to church on Sundays. Rose and Fannie were taught about wildlife. They did not know how to hunt large animals like a bear nor were they taught how to trap and gig alligators and crocodiles. They were taught how to use weapons. They were pretty good with a rifle and shotgun and would have been able to protect themselves. The girls did not learn how to swim. Their father and brothers were excellent swimmers.

In the woods, Rose and Fannie had to cut timber with the axe. After that, it had to be cut into logs. The logs had to be hauled to the house. It was used to make heat to get warm in the winter. They were burned in the fireplace. Some of them were used in the stove to cook food. The other logs were stored for daily use during the year. The girls were as strong as an ox. The boys would say, "Those are Uncle Jeff's girls. You better not bother them. They will beat your butt."

They had to pay tuition to attend school. Most of the schools were at local churches. They attended school at Mt. Zion Missionary Baptist Church. The teacher was Emma Simmons. They were members of that church too. Another school was free. There was no tuition fee. The teacher was Mary E. Anderson. She was not related to them. Rose told me that she was one of the top students. She is an excellent speller, and I can vouch for that. The teacher would ask her to assist with the slow-learning students. Basically, she was a teacher's aide. She said that Fannie was not that bright. Fannie had to cheat and copy from Rose's paper. Their father did not like education. He made it difficult for them to attend school. They quit in the sixth grade.

One day, she and a friend played with marbles. The marbles belonged to her friend. Rose did not own any marbles. They finished playing with the marbles. One of the marbles was not picked up. The boy failed to see it. The boy went home. Rose picked it up and took it to her house. Rose was playing with the marble indoors. Her mother, Mi, knew she did not have any marbles. She asked Rose where did she get the marble. Rose told her that she found it on the ground. Her friend had forgotten to pick it up. Rose's mother became upset. She said, "That is stealing. You stole the marble." She chastised Rose with a real good spanking. Then she made Rose return the marble to her friend. Rose took the marble to the boy. She stopped playing with them. After that whipping, she was afraid to take anything.

Their mother used powdered snuff in her mouth. Their father chewed tobacco and smoked a pipe. Rose started dipping snuff when she was three years old. All of her sisters dipped it too. Sometimes, her mother would give out of snuff. She would send Rose to her mother-in-law to get some of her snuff. Her name was Fronnie Williams. Spudge was married to her daughter. Rose was afraid of Miss Fronnie. She was large, tall, and double-jointed. Rose said that she saw her beat a man. Miss Fronnie lifted the man up in the air with one hand. He was not a small man. She held him with one hand and whipped him with her other hand. Rose was afraid of her. She didn't want to go to her house. She had no choice. She would get the snuff and run home. Once, she had to go and get some snuff from her. Miss Fronnie had a young baby. Rose said, "The baby was a pretty one." She rushed home and gave her mother the snuff. Then she asked her mother, "Mi, where did Miss Fronnie get that pretty baby?" She answered, "She went in the woods and got the baby out of a cypress tree. Inside them is hollowed. All of them don't have a baby in them." Then Rose asked her mother, "I want you to go in the woods and get me one. I want to play with a pretty baby.". Her mother answered, "When the time is right, I will get you one."

Rose and Fannie were agile and fast. I was told that they could really run fast. A few of the local baseball teams would use them as runners to the base. Rose told me that they were the fastest runners at the school. They would go in the woods to hunt wild rabbits to eat. Instead of shooting the rabbits, they would run and chase them. They would chase them until the rabbits became tired. Then the rabbits would be caught. Rose said that she was very energetic. She was athletic and good at all of the games played. When she was young, she enjoyed playing on the swing. It was homemade by their father. She liked to jump the ropes or play hopscotch. One of her favorite games was jumping jacks.

They wore nice clothes to school. Their clothes were not the same as the other girls. Rose wouldn't tell them where their clothes were purchased. However, they were bought from Sears and Montgomery Ward by mail order. They would use some of their father's money to buy them.

They were given a message by their father, Pi. He told his daughters, "It is alright to play with the boys. You can get a boyfriend, and I will let you go out with him. He will be allowed to come to the house. One thing you better remember is to keep your clothes on. I dare you to let the boys pull your dress or skirt tails up. If you do that, I will kill you." Rose said that really put a lot of fear in her heart. She was already scared of him. She was afraid of that big, tall, and muscular man. "That jet-black red-eyed man was the meanest man on earth." She really believed that was true.

Rose would have fun with some boys. They would laugh and talk. She was afraid to kiss or hug them. She wouldn't even hold their hands. She remembered what her father had told them. Her first boyfriend was named J.B. Johnson. His parents owned a 1925 and a 1926 Ford cars. He took her out in them. Rose was a virgin. She was too afraid to hug or kiss him. They would ride in the country or go to town in the car. He would take Rose home. Rose was unaware that her boyfriend was cheating with an older woman. She was single and had a couple of children. He would take Rose home and go to the woman's house. All of the folks called the lady May Lee. He was spending some nights with May Lee. She was giving it up. Rose was not doing that. Someone told Rose that May Lee had gotten pregnant. It was by J.B. Johnson. Rose said that she separated him. Her father warned him not to come to their house. Years later, he moved to Orlando, Florida. Rose remembered two of his brothers. One was named C-Johnson. The other one was called Bubble Johnson. Their parents were well-off and had plenty of money.

She told me that a boy whose name was Bo-Weaver Barnes really liked her. He tried to get her to be his girlfriend. Rose said that he was too ugly for her. She didn't give him the time of day. When he became an adult, he became wealthy.

Rose had some friends in the Carter's family. Their parents were Ned and Gussie Carter. Their children, who were her friends, are listed below.

(1) Mel Carter
(2) Buddy Carter
(3) Richard Carter
(4) Barbara Carter
(5) Rosa Lee Carter

In Leary, there were many creeks and spring water. There was quite a few swamps. They had a creek on their land. It was rented from George Colley. Rose and Fannie did not know how to swim. They liked to fish in the creeks. Their father had a boat in the creek. The creek was not small. The water was deep. Sometimes, the girls would ride in the boat. They had to use the oars. There were times when only one would be in the boat. They would do it without their father's permission. Sometimes, he was not at the house. Something happened the last time they got into the boat. When they were riding in it, they saw a log in the water. It had a snake on its top. Fannie steered the boat into the log. Luckily, the snake went into the water. They stood up in the boat. It nearly turned over. Luckily, it did not because they could not swim. That was the last time getting in the boat without their father. The snake was poisonous, and they did not know it. It was a water moccasin snake. Their father explained it to them.

My mother told me a few things about the Great Depression. She was fourteen or fifteen years old when it happened. I was told that the economy had gotten real bad. All of the folks called it Hoover Days. Hoover was the president of the United States. He was blamed for the terrible conditions. Rose told me that no one could get any work to earn money. Some folks were able to work for food or clothes to wear. They had plenty of food to eat. When their trees would bear fruits, Rose would gather them. The fruits were bartered for used clothes. The white folks in the town were happy to get the fruits. They really liked the plums. She would get enough for the whole family.

Rose said that she saw her fair share of poor people. The hobos would walk and beg for food and clothes. They fed plenty of them. Some would work for it. Hardly any money was in circulation. She said that a lot of people had walked the soles from their shoes. Some of them would put cardboard in their shoes. It was used for soles in their shoes. Some of the folks were unable to get clothes. They covered the holes on them with patches. My mother said, "That is the reason I don't like patches today. I saw too many of them during Hoover Days. There was a ton of people who were impecuniously poor.

When the economy began to rebound, she landed her first job at the peanut mill. It was in the town of Leary. The name of it was Jordan's Peanut Mill. She told me that it was owned by Willie Jordan. The vacant peanut mill continues to stand. The buildings are made of wood and dilapidated and uninhabitable. At the mill she got her social security card. You can read the writing on it. Today, only one business exist. It is a small mom and pop grocery store.

Before the Great Depression, Leary was booming with farmers and sharecroppers. A train station was in the town. There were stores in the business district. All of them would ride on a wagon drawn by a mule or horse to town. She said, "An artesian well was in the town section. It made a loud roaring noise. All of the folks in town would drink water from it." Rose said, "They thought the well was made by *God* through one of the springs." However, artesian wells were made by man.

In the late 1930s, her father, Jeff, injured his foot. He was riding in his horse-drawn buggy. He was drunk and had passed out. His foot got between the spokes on a wheel. He had to go to the hospital in Albany, Georgia. When he was discharged he had an outstanding bill. Fannie was married and doing well. Rose said that she went to her house. She stated, "I asked Fannie to help me pay the hospital bill."

Fannie agreed to help pay the hospital bill. She lied and did not keep the promise. Rose worked and paid the debt in full.

Rose was an obedient child. She believed everything they told her. Sometimes, it would not be true. She gave them utmost respect. Elderly people were given the same respect. She remembered everything they told her. She was afraid of her father. When he died in 1939 or 1940, she was twenty-six years old and a virgin. She knew nothing about sex. She migrated to Pompano Beach, Florida, to work on the farm. Her brother Charley was living in Pompano, in Ogden Brother's Quarters. She moved in with him. Her mother remained in Georgia. She lived with her sister in Arlington, Georgia.

After a few months in Florida, she moved and shared a room with her friend. Her name was either Annie Mae or Annie Bell. They lived in one of the quarters, which was owned by a white farmer. All of them worked on the farms to pick beans by crawling on their knees. The workers were paid by the hamper. A variety of vegetables were picked. The beans were the only ones they had to crawl on their knees. The farmers used large flatbed trucks with tall side gates. The farmworkers got on the trucks and stood in rolls. They would be very close to each other. That was done until the trucks were filled with them. Most of the women wore straw hats and a long pair of pants. They would wear a dress on top of the pants. The length of the dresses would stop at their knees.

In 1940, there were many farms in Pompano. Farming was very good. A lot of white farmers became rich. It was during the segregation era where black and white folks had very little interaction among themselves. At the black community, the business district side was alongside Hammondville Road. About half of them were owned by black folks. The businesses were between two railroad tracks. One of the train tracks was The Florida East Coast. The second one was The Seaboard Railway tracks. On the weekends, Rose's roommate would go to the theatre. It was in the black community. The majority of times, she went with her boyfriend. He worked at a shoe shine shop in the business district. All of the folks called him Jew-Baby. Rose did not have a boyfriend. A few times, she went with them to the Loveland Theatre. My father and Jew-Baby were friends. He was named Alonzo Williams, and his nickname was Par-Gross. He was a fair-skinned young man. Sometimes, he would come to the apartment with Jew-Baby. While Annie Mae was working on the farm, they would chat with each other. She told Rose, "You know, Jew- Baby's friend said that he likes you." Rose thought that he was a white man. She replied, "We are not allowed to go with white people, and I don't want a white man." Annie explained to her that he was not white. She told Rose that he was one half Indian and black. My mother appeared to be younger than her age. She was twenty-six years old and a virgin; Par-Gross was sixteen years old. He had a mustache and had to shave. Rose thought that he was about her age or older. She had heard her father say that men had to shave. She was a virgin and didn't know anything about sex. She hadn't kissed a man. She would sit and talk with Par-Gross. She was encouraged to drink a little whiskey with them. Annie Mae and Jew-Baby would take off their clothes and get in the bed. They were having sex. Rose was a square, lame and green as grass. One day, she was encouraged to get in the bed with her boyfriend. They took their clothes off and managed to engage into sex. Annie Mae and Jew-Baby were in their bed. After about six months into her relationship, she became ill. She hadn't ever gone to a medical doctor. She and her friend walked across the tracks to visit Dr. George. Rose was examined, and the doctor said she was five months pregnant. She did not know what it meant and continued to work. Her friend was unable to make her understand what it meant to be pregnant. Rose thought that babies were taken from a tree trunk. She was ten years older than her boyfriend. In those days, a person became an adult when they were twenty one years old. There was not any statutory rape laws. If so, they were unenforceable.

Rose did not show any signs of pregnancy. Her skin complexion was a few shades lighter. She was about seven months pregnant when she stopped working. Rose did not get any prenatal care. Her brother, Charley, had moved back to Georgia. Their mother had moved from Arlington to Leary. Rose returned to Leary and moved in with her mother. Charley decided to visit them on a weekend. He noticed that his sister's skin color was getting lighter. Rose's stomach was small but protruded slightly outward. Charley told their mother, "I believe that Nig is carrying a baby. That is the way she looks to me. She had a boyfriend in Pompano." Mi said, "Charley, she is a big eater. It looks like she is gaining a little weight to me. I think she is still a virgin." Rose was into her eighth month of pregnancy before her mother realized it. She was getting sick on the stomach. Her mother said, "Your brother Charley was right. You are going to have a baby." Rose replied, "Mi, I thought that babies came from the tree trunk in the woods. That is what you told me." Her mother answered and said, "Well, that was not the truth. I was joking with you. We get pregnant from men and have a baby. It happened when your boyfriend stuck his thing inside you. The baby is in your stomach. That is the reason you gained some weight, and your skin became lighter. Sometimes, it will make you vomit. I did not tell the truth about the tree trunks. I didn't tell the truth about the lady eating too much beans and rice. I apologize to you." She asked her mother, "How will I get this baby?" Her mother replied, "The same hole he stuck his thing in. It is between your legs where the pee comes from." Nig became nervous about that. She could not visualize how a baby could come out of such a small hole.

One day when she was home alone, she went behind the house. She went outside to pee. Rose pulled her dress up and squatted to pee. When she had finished, she leaned over and looked between her legs. Then she prayed to *God*. She said, "God, how can a baby come out of this small hole? It is too small for a baby to come out of it. That will kill me." But she went into labor and had me. A midwife delivered me whose name was Miss Dell Williams. Rose had visited a doctor in Pompano. That was her first and last time to see a physician before my birth. Rose alleged that she was in labor about twelve hours. "It was so painful. I thought I would die."

After the childbirth, my mother swore that she would not have another child. She told the truth. I am the only one she had. I don't have any brothers or sisters. One day, Rose held me between her hands and arms. She was standing on the front porch. She spoke to the *Lord*. She said, "God, I do not ever plan to have another man. If a man asks me to be his girlfriend, I will tell him to kiss my ass and cuss him out. I do not want any more men." That didn't hold to be true because of more relationships.

She stated that she had to breastfeed me. I refused to suck milk from a bottle. I would hit and kick the bottle as if in a fight. She said that I was a real greedy baby. Rose was unable to wean me from her breast. She asked her aunt to keep me for a while. It was her mother's sister who lived in Arlington. She did that to wean me away from her breast. My aunt must have made me suck a milk bottle unless I was old enough to eat. Rose returned to Pompano to work on the farm. Money was sent by mail to Aunt Fannie for caring for me. I understand that she kept me for two years. After that, my grandmother, Mi, took care of me.

Rose told me that she attended Mt. Zion Missionary Baptist Church in Leary. All of her friends joined the church. She did not become a member right away. Her friends and classmates were not able to encourage her to join. She said, "I will join it when the *Lord* tell me to join it. She eventually became a member of the church. She asserted that *God* came to her in a dream. "God told me that it was time to join the church." She became a member and was baptized in one of the creeks or lakes. She attended it on a regular basis and was a faithful member.

In Pompano, she refused to have another relationship with my father. She told him that she was a virgin when she met him. "He is your son and looks like you." You will get a chance to see him when you come to Pompano. If you do not give any money to help take care of him, I will do it alone." She separated him and said, "I will be a fool if I let you fill a house with children. I want you to get another woman." When they saw each other, they would have a friendly conversation. She refused to go back to Par-Gross.

Rose and Annie Mae were roommates again. She worked on different farms. There was not a man in her life nearly five years. She made some new friends while working. They are listed below.

(1)　Robert Thurston, husband
(2)　Saddie Lee Benefield-Thurston, wife
(3)　Sister Benefield
(4)　Elizabeth Louise Clark, nicknamed Lou lzer
(5)　Ida Mae Mathis, wife
(6)　Lucius Mathis, husband
(7)　Gussie Mims

(8)   Samantha Flowers

(9)   Danny Gates, husband

(10) Dubbie Lee Gates (Sister), wife

In Pompano, the laborers were hauled to the farms on the rear of long large flatbed trucks. The trucks had large side railings. The workers had to stand in rows next to each other until the trucks were filled with them. They were juxtaposed.

She migrated to Clewiston, Florida, to work on the muck. Farming is a big business in that area. Most of the land is muck soil. She went to that area with the Benefields and Thurstons. It was around 1944 during the farm season. After a few months, she got a job in the Mess-Hall. She had to work in the kitchen area of the cafeteria. Most of the time, she would peel onions and ice potatoes. Rose said that she peeled so many onions until she lost its smell.

Rose met a man from Atlanta, Georgia. He drove trucks for a local farmer. His name was Nathaniel Andrews. She said that he was a well dresser in clothes. He became her boyfriend. Rose said that Nathaniel was real jealous and did not want her to talk with other men. She said that he could fight well. He was a good boxer and wrestler. A new farmworker migrated to Clewiston. He was a muscular young man. He and Nathaniel became friends. One day, they decided to wrestle. He managed to throw Nathaniel. That was the first time he was thrown in Clewiston.

Rose returned to Pompano when the season was over. She said a man walked with a cane seemed to be looking at her all the time. Nathaniel came to visit her on the weekends. The last time he came, he took her out in the business area on the weekend. Afterward, Nathaniel and Rose went to a rooming house to spend some time alone. Another name for them was a transient house. That is where blacks had to go. They were not allowed to go to hotels or motels in the white community.

Nathaniel left Rose in the room while he went to purchase some whiskey from the bar. She locked the door while he was gone. Rose said the man who walked with a cane came to the room. He knocked on the door. Rose told him to leave and tried to close the door. He forced the door open and came in the room. The man threw her on the bed and tried to rape her. Fortunately, Nathaniel returned with the alcohol. Rose told him what had happened. She said Nathaniel put a beating on the man. He was on the floor and bleeding from his mouth, ears, and nose. Nathaniel, her boyfriend, said that, "I am going to kill him with my knife." Rose begged and pleaded for Nathaniel to let him live. Nathaniel picked the man and his cane up and threw him out the door. Rose said that the man disappeared on the earth. He was not sent anymore. Rose believed that he went some place and died. Nathaniel soon relocated to his home in Atlanta. They lost contact with each other. Rose did not return to Clewiston but remained in Pompano.

Subsequently, she met a man who was much older. His name was Johnny Wright. He worked on the farms and was a part-time electrician. He was not licensed. Johnny Wright could really dance. Tap dancing was his favorite. Rose did not dance but loved to stand and watch the dancers. It was her way of having fun. She would just laugh while people danced in the bars. That is how she met Johnny Wright. He would give Rose money to spend. They got married, and she moved to his apartment. After she moved with her husband, he expected her to pay all of the bills. She left after six months and moved in the apartment with her mother and brother, Charley. They had returned to Pompano. She told her mother that Johnny Wright was playing her for a fool. She never did go back to live with him. In those days, most people separated and remarried without a divorce. Johnny Wright had been married and had not divorced. That created an illegal marriage with Rose. He was her first husband.

Around 1946, she met another man who became her boyfriend. She knew his mother. Her name was Ms. Elizabeth Louise Clark. Her nickname was Lou-lzer. They lived in Deerfield about six miles north of Pompano. He was introduced to Rose by his mother. His name was Willie Lee Dunlap. Rose was eleven years older than him. I believe that Johnny Wright was the only man to be older than her. In 1947, they were married. Their relationship was unstable. It was a "rocky" relationship. He had spent time in the U.S. Army prior to the marriage. She would accuse him of cheating with women. They would quit and get back together. He was an alcoholic but held a job as a construction laborer. The last time, quitting was from a sexually transmitted disease. She caught the claps known as gonorrhea. That ended their marriage. He died in 1980.

She continued to be friends with her husband's mother, Lou-lzer. Sometimes, her brother, Charley, would take Rose to Deerfield in his T-Model truck to see her. She loved to drink Gordon's gin. Charley would have a few shots with Ms. Lou-lzer. Rose did not drink that much alcohol. If she had a cold, she would use a little of gin as a remedy. On a Sunday, when she and her husband had quit, they went to her mother-in-law's house. Rose had a bad cold. Rose told me that Lou-lzer continued to offer her a drink. She said, "Rose, I know you don't drink, but it is good for a cold." Rose agreed and told her to pour a drink for her. She said that when she tasted the gin, it was real bitter. She threw it away and went home. She said, "Ms. Lou-lzer tried to poison me. She put some lye or quinine in the gin.

They got into an altercation several years after she and her husband had quit for good. Ms. Lou-lzer drove from Deerfield to our house in New-Town. She accused Rose of having an affair with her boyfriend. She left the house before Rose could get her gun. When Lou-lzer was driving away, a few shots were fired at her car. Rose stood in the middle of the road and fired a few more rounds. Then she put the shotgun back into the house. Rose was falsely accused, and she didn't like it. Another lady who lived nearby was going with the man. Her name was Daisy Brown. That ended the relationship with her mother-in-law.

A man whose name was Steve Smith really liked Rose. The folks in Pompano nicknamed him The Walking Radio because he was very nosey. He was a tall huge man and wore a pair of overalls. He was like a news reporter. Steve was nosey and very newsworthy. If something had transpired, he would know it. I mean, he could walk very fast. This was during the 1950s when I was in elementary school. You could see Steve walking real fast. Both of his arms would be moving backward and forth. He brought the news to our house. Steve was crazy about Rose, but she did not like him. The boys would tease me and say, "Steve is your stepfather." They knew I would get pissed off and didn't like that.

When I was in the sixth or seventh grade, she had a boyfriend named Mr. Roberts. He was from the Carolinas. He worked at a nursery on North Dixie Highway in Pompano. We lived in New-Town with her brother, Charley. It was on a Sunday night and Charley was asleep in his bed. Rose went to the house across the street to be with her boyfriend. After several hours, I heard a woman hollering for help. I realized it was my mother. I awakened my uncle and informed him about the screams. My uncle and I went to the house with our shotguns. Charley knocked on the front door and said, "Roberts, what is going on with you and Rose?" Rose said that Mr. Roberts ran out of the backdoor into the wooded area. She said that they had gotten into an argument and a fight. "He tried to shoot and pistol-whip me. But I grabbed the gun and fought him off. When you knocked on the door I managed to knock the gun out of his hand." A police complaint was made against him. He fled the area and was not seen again. They confiscated the gun. The officer told my mother that the weapon was made in Germany. It was a semi-automatic .44 caliber German-Luger. An FBI special agent came to our house and interviewed us. He told my mother, "You are a very lucky woman. He is on our most wanted list. We have been looking for that man for years. He killed his wife and children in South Carolina. Then he said, "Your son and brother saved your life. That man is a psychotic nut. If you ever see him, please contact our office." From all indications, Mr. Roberts was a nice man. He was a loner and did not talk too much. He was an excellent cook and cooked the best of hamburgers. They were real delicious.

I will share some additional information about my mother. My mother is very free hearted and a kind person. She loves to laugh and is very friendly. She will give a person her back. She loves children and has babysit many for nothing. She did not charge their parents any money. She has fed the homeless people and have let some live in our spare bedroom for nothing. They would get a job and move. Her last boyfriend was Inada Brodie. They were together for about twenty years. He died in the late 1990s. They had a great relationship. He was twelve years younger than her. She is small but hotheaded and will shoot or fight like a heartbeat. I have seen her shoot at five or six people in New-Town. She will talk you to death. She is a penny pincher with a dollar. She whole-heartedly believes in *God*. At night, before saying her prayers, she will get on her knees. It will be next to her bed. Two hands will be on her bed with the knees on the floor. That is traditional in our community. Rose is spiritual. She told me that two different spirits live on the earth. The good one is from *God*; whereas, the bad one is from the devil. I was informed that *God* has spiritual healers to combat the evil spirits. Those are the ones by the devil. She said that, "A lot of people do not think about it. It is true. Just wait until a critic get possessed and burned with it. Then they will believe it is true." She alleged that *God* talks with her frequently. She claims that she has seen a few ghosts. Most of them were family members who died. She ran them away by using the techniques of her father.

Soul food is her favorite dish. She loves fish and vegetables. She eats a lot of fruits and nuts. During her younger days, she ate fish often. She was a good fisherman. Her fishing poles were the wooden cane stick poles. A variety of cats and dogs were her pets.

Inada, her boyfriend, had served in the military during his younger days. He was in the navy. He knew how to swim. Just like Rose, he was from the country. They had a lot in common. They went fishing together. Sometimes, they would use a boat. She can't swim, but she knew her man could swim. That gave her enough courage to ride and fish from the boat. Sometimes, Fannie, her sister, would go with them. It was on a Sunday, and it was the fourth day of July. All three of them decided to go fishing. Plans were made to rent a boat. They were going to fish in the large lake near Clewiston. Rose's next-door neighbor had planned to go with his family. His name is Jimmy Dale Wright. They followed Jimmy Dale to Lake Okeechobee where two boats were rented. Their favorite spot is in freshwater. The lake is freshwater. Jimmy Dale rented a larger and more powerful boat. They had a smaller boat, which had a smaller engine. Rose told me that they got into their boat first and left Jimmy Dale and his family. She said that Jimmy Dale caught up with them. He went around their boat at a high speed. The wake from the boat nearly overturned them. Their boat skidded toward a bunch of lilies and stopped. Another fisherman used a rope to tow them out of them. Rose said to her boyfriend, "Would you have saved me and my sister had the boat turned over?" He answered and said, "I do not know because I might have not been able to save myself." That was she and her sister's last time to ride in a boat.

In the early 1950s, Rose worked for the McDougald's as a domestic worker. She cleaned their house and ironed their clothes. The house was on North Dixie Highway in Pompano. The house was a wooden plantation styled home. On the weekends, I would assist Mr. McDougald with his garden. Sometimes, I would have to rake leaves or cut the grass. The city of Pompano made the house into a museum. It was towed to the Centennial Park. They were good country folks and could cook soul food. They would allow us to eat at the table with them. He taught me a lot about farming and growing plants. While attending school, it was a nice weekend job. Today, the house is a historical site. It is called The Sample McDougald House.

The City of Pompano Beach, gave my mother an official Proclamation in 2014, on her 100th birthday. President Obama, and his wife, the First Lady, Michele, signed and mailed a birthday card. When she became 101 years old, Mark Bogen, Broward Commissioner, signed and sent a birthday card.

On June 9, 2015, Broward County government is sponsoring an event referred as the Centennial Citizens Event A photo of her can be down-loaded on the inernet as follows:

http://www.broward.org/Broward100/History/Centennial Citizens.aspx

LEARY

Leary is located in the southwestern portion of Georgia. It is a few miles west of Dothan, Alabama. In the 1800s, the Creek and Cherokee Indians lived in Leary. Leary was known for its very rich soil. The last Cherokees moved out of North Georgia in 1832 on the Trail of Tears. Some Indians remained there who were married to Black Americans. It was only a few of them. My grandfather had a few friends who were Indians. Georgia was left with only European settlers. When my folks lived there, it was known for its sharecroppers and farmers. The city of Leary was created in 1854. Calhoun is the name of the county. It was named after John C. Calhoun, the seventh vice president of the United States. Morgan, Georgia is the county seat. A few ministers, professional baseball players, and celebrities were born in Leary. My grandmother, Fennie, was a friend to a baseball player's kin-folks. A third baseman with the Seattle Mariners was born there. His name was Chone Figgins. My grandmother's friend was Jane or Carrie Figgins.

Today, the courthouse in Morgan is a historic site. Several annual festivals are held in Leary and nearby towns. They are listed below.

(1) The Still Pond Vineyard and Winery, a family-owned business host three festivals in Baker County.
    (a) Grape Stop, The Bud Break Bash, on the first Saturday in April.

(b) The Grape Stomp, on the first Saturday in August.

(c) The Holiday Festival, on the first Saturday in December.

(2) The city of Edison hosts The Billie Lane Cotton Charity Horse Show on the second Saturday of May.

(3) Arlington hosts the oldest festival in the state of Georgia. It is The May Day Festival in the first Saturday in May.

(4) Morgan hosts The Harvest Festival on the first Saturday in November.

(5) Along Highway 37, on the second Saturday, in November is The Southwest High Cotton 65 Mile Yard Sale.

(6) Leary hosts The Leary Christmas Parade on the second Saturday in December.

Today, Leary looks like a ghost town. There is only one business in the town. It is a family-owned small grocery store. All of the former businesses are gone. Some of the buildings are standing. They are dilapidated and uninhabitable. The railroad station is gone. The railroad tracks are still there. The sign is above the peanut mill. The sign have the owner's name as Jordan's Peanut Mill. That is where my mother got her first job and social security card. The artesian well is gone. You can see the sign on the fire station.

Mount Zion Missionary Baptist Church is still in the country. It is made with those red or dark brown bricks. It is nice and well kept. My grandparents and uncle were buried at the church's cemetery next to it.

According to the 2000 United Census, it indicated that 666 people lives in Leary. There were 256 households and 176 families in the city. It continues to have large farms. There are large quail and hunting plantations. A lot of creeks, lakes, and springs are in Leary. The children attend schools in Arlington and Morgan, Georgia.

When my folks lived in Leary during the late 1900s until 1940, Leary was thriving with farms and sharecroppers. Most of them lived in the plantations and did not have to pay rent. They had to work on the farms. There was a passenger train station in the town. There was a shopping district with stores. In the town, an artesian well was the center of attraction. Most of the folks did not know it was made by man. They thought that it was created by God from springwater.

Today, it is gone. A couple of times when they lived in Leary, the economy declined. That was during the Great Depression. The next time was from a famine. All of the crops died from the drought.

PATERNAL RELATIVES

My father, Alonzo Williams, was born in Wellborn, Florida. His birthday is on March 16, 1924. He was the first man to have sex with my mother. She was a virgin when she met him. His nickname was Par Gross. An educator at my high school was born in Wellborn, whose name is Dr. Eunice Harvey. She was a friend of my kin-folks. Her niece is my classmate whose name was Perida Cason. Grossman Williams was his father. He was my grandfather. For some reason, I did not get a chance to meet or know my paternal grandparents. My paternal grandmother is Jennie Caruth. I lived in New-Town with two of her kin-folks. They are my cousins and were unaware of it. They are Martha and Tina Caruth. I was attending elementary school when they were in high school. Martha, whose nickname is Mott, was an outstanding cheer leader. She was an all-American in Florida, among the segregated black schools.

I have a photograph of Grossman and Jennie in my home. They are deeply mixed with Indian blood. Jennie was from the Cheyenne-Sioux Indian tribe out of the Carolinas. Grossman is mixed with the Seminole Indian tribe. All of the folks called my grandfather Grossman. The 1920 US census put Grosvenor in parenthesis, whereas, in 1900, Grossman was in parenthesis.

According to the U.S. City Directories in 1926, he was a laborer in Brooksville, Hernando, Florida. He was about forty-three years old. The 1900 U.S. Census showed him living in Wellborn, Suwannee, Florida. He was documented to be twenty-four years old in 1900. He was born in Florida on January 1876. He was married to Virginia. She was born in Georgia and was twenty years old. They were married in 1896. Their children are listed below.

(1) Grant Williams was two years old in 1900 and born on 1898.
(2) Adelle Williams was one year old, and born on 1899.
(3) Florence Mobley was documented at the home. She was forty-five years old and born on 1865. She could have been Virginia's mother. I grew up with the Mobley family in Pompano.

The 1910 U.S. Census Bureau showed that he was living in Leona, Suwannee, Florida. It showed that he was born around 1873. He had another wife whose name was Jennie Caruth. She was twenty-seven years old and born on 1883. Their children are listed below.

(1) Adell Williams was ten. Virginia was her mother.
(2) Roosevelt Williams was six years old, born on 1904.
(3) Calvin Williams was still a baby, almost one year old.
(4) Grossman Williams Jr. was about six months old.

I have met both of Roosevelt's children who were my first cousins. One of them was Ovida W. Denson who resides in Boynton Beach, Florida. She was a retired educator. Her son's name is Marvin Denson, a second cousin. I met Roosevelt's son whose name was Lorenzo Williams. He was a mail carrier and lived in Miami, Florida. I visited him a few times before his death. He consumed an awful lot of alcohol. His wife was an educator with the school board. She was from Tallahassee, Florida, and her name was Carol Mae Williams. Both of them are dead.

I had just graduated from law school when I met Lorenzo and his wife. He always told me. "Charles, I am your uncle because of my age." I would correct him and say, "No, you are my first cousin." He would take another shot of alcohol and smile. He was fun, and I enjoyed being with him. He and his wife welcomed me to their home. We talked on the phone frequently and became very good friends. I was not aware of his death and did not go to his funeral. It was after the fact when I was notified by my aunt, Bossie. Lorenzo's wife told me something that really surprised me. She said, "My cousin and her husband just graduated from law school too. They are from Orlando, Florida. I was really surprised because I had a husband and wife team who were from Orlando, Florida. I said, "I believe that I know them." I told her their names. I said that they were Joe and Joyce Sager." Both of us were literally surprised and shocked. We knew that was a coincidence.

Ovida's mother who was married to a Holloway was from Pompano. I went to school with three brothers who were Holloways. One was called Moose Holloway. The others were named Cecil and Benny Holloway. All of them were superb athletes. Moose was one of the best running backs in the nation. Cecil was an excellent boxer and football player. Benny was a good quarterback. Another coincident is that my classmate and best friend's sister was married to Cecil Holloway. My classmate is Sammie Lee Wells. We have been friends since the first grade. Therefore, all of their children are my second cousins. A few years ago, we learned that we were related to each other. There is another one to share. It will be listed in the next paragraph. One of Cecil's boys played football for Morris Brown College.

He was the quarterback for the team whose name is Terry Holloway. My brother-in-law, whose name was Roderick Moton, had graduated from high school. He was a wide receiver and an all-American letterman. He had several football scholarships to large prominent universities. He wanted to attend college at a predominantly black college. I sent video tapes of him to my best friend in Atlanta, Georgia. He delivered them to the head football coach at Morris Brown College. They were reviewed, and Rod was given a full-time scholarship. Rod and my cousin were teammates and friends. He was the quarterback, and Rod was one of the wide receivers. Rod became an instant star as a wide receiver. He made six touchdowns as a college freshman. The coaches at the University of Georgia tried to encourage a transfer to their school. Rod refused and remained at Morris Brown College. His friends, classmates, and teammates gave him a nickname. It was Motown, the Florida boy. He was a star and very popular at the college. After graduating from college, he had signed a contract to play professional football. Subsequently, he was killed in a car accident while asleep as a passenger in a rental car. It happened near or in Palm Beach County, Florida. A college mate and friend went to sleep while driving. The car struck a disabled tractor trailer, which was parked on the shoulder of the road. The passenger side of the rental car went under the trailer and caved in on Rod. He never knew what struck him. He was fast asleep. The driver and Rod were from Ft. Lauderdale, Florida. His college mate, the driver, and father was an electrical contractor in Ft. Lauderdale. I think his last name was Hill. The driver of the rental car was not killed. A leg was broken along with a few other injuries. Rod was very popular on campus and on the football team as a savant. His college mate's minor injuries recovered, and he returned to college. He was harassed by the students.

They said, "You killed Motown." Some of them were pernicious toward the student. Others were melancholically upset with him. The behavior made the student anxious. He left the college and went home. Rod's mother filed a lawsuit against Hertz Rental car and received a big sum of money. She and her husband died a few years later.

The 1920 U.S. Census Bureau documented that Grossman and Jennie were living in Wellborn, Florida. The names of their children that were living with them in 1920 are listed below.

(1) Roosevelt Williams was sixteen years old and born on 1904.
(2) Alvin Williams was thirteen and born on 1907.
(3) Bossy Williams was eight years old and born on 1913.
(4) Annie Belle Williams was two years old and born on 1918.
(5) Bessie Williams was eight and a half months old in 1920.
(6) Jimmie Caruth was fourteen years old and born on 1906.
(7) Alberta Caruth was twelve years old and born on 1908.

The 1930 U.S. Census revealed that three children were living with my paternal grandparents. They were living in Pompano Beach, Florida. Their names are listed.

(1) Bossie Williams was sixteen years old.
(2) Annie Bell Williams was twelve years old, born on 1918.
(3) Nanndress Williams was eleven years old, born on 1919.

My aunt Bossie died in 2010 and was ninety-six years old. She outlived her parents and siblings. She was the only one I developed a relationship. I was about fourteen years old when I got to know her.

She made many efforts to get to know me. The majority of times, I would not be home. I would be playing ball at the park or at another place. She wanted my mother to let her raise me. Rose refused to let me live with her. However, I did spend two summers with her when I was in the sixth and seventh grade. She bought clothes for me to wear to school.

She and her boyfriend were living together when I was in the sixth grade. His name was Frampton Brant, whose nickname was Buddy. He had his lawn service business. They raised his niece whose name was Ruenett Carolyn Brant. She was given to them when she was eight days old. We called her Carolyn. She was not legally adopted. Although Bossie and Buddy were not married, they lived as husband and wife. My father lived in the house with them. He had the same type of business. We chatted a few times. I did not see him that much. The majority of the time, he would be with his girlfriend. Bossie did not have any children although she really loved kids.

In Pompano, Bossie married the infamous W.C. Baker's brother. They had their band. Sometimes, they rode in their cars playing music and singing. They drove on the dirt roads in the black community. Most of their songs were spiritual. They performed in black nightclubs too. She separated her husband and moved to Miami, Florida. I had a classmate in elementary and high school. Her name is Catherine Baker. Ironically, my aunt was married to Catherine's uncle. I did not know it. In elementary school, she was my girlfriend. Catherine had a friend whose name was Carolyn Rolle. My buddy would be with Carolyn while I would be with Catherine. His name is Sammie Lee Wells whose nickname was Wine. I was in my late sixties when I became aware of the marriage. Then I got on the telephone and spoke with Catherine Baker. I told her that we were cousin-in-laws. She was more surprised than me.

Bossie lived in North Miami Beach, Florida, for many years. All of her friends said, "Bossie was very gentle and kindhearted. She would give good advice when necessary." That is the way I knew her. I did not ever hear her use a bad word. She was a good Christian and attended church regularly. Bossie was a member of the African

Methodist Episcopal Church located in her community. Her name is engraved on a wall in front of the church. She was one of the board of directors. In the community where she lived, she fed many people. It would be on the weekends. She loved to cook. Bossie sold her home and bought a condo. In 2010, when she was ninety-six years old, she died. She was cremated in Miami, Florida.

My father was named Alonzo Williams. He was born on March 16, 1924 in Wellborn, Florida. My father was very handsome. His hair was black and curly. Sometimes, he would style it by having two long pony tails. He was a player with the women. The women really loved him. He died in 1960 when he was thirty-six years old. He was buried at the Lincoln Memorial in Miami, Florida.

I loved my father and would be happy to see him. He had very little impact in my life. The money given to me would not amount to five dollars. He was not forced to pay child support. When he visited us, he would be drunk as a skunk. My mother told me that he did not drink alcohol when they were together. He loved to eat fish sandwiches. One day on the weekend, he walked to our house. I was four or five years old. We walked to the business section in our community. We chatted with his best friend who was a shoeshiner. All of the folks called him Jew-Baby. He bought two fish sandwiches. We took the sandwiches where I lived. I remember when I attempted to eat my sandwich, the fish had scales on it. The cook forgot to remove them. I threw the sandwich away. I would play in his hair when he would be on our sofa. Then I would reach in his pocket and take a dollar bill. He would tell my mother, "Rose, this boy is bad. I want my dollar bill." I would get up and run with it.

My mother bought me a nice bicycle for Christmas when I was in elementary school. My barber lived in New-Town. His name was James Greene. He would cut hair on his front porch. I rode my bike to get my haircut. Mr. James said," Charlee, that is a nice bicycle she bought for you." I lied and said, "My daddy bought it for me. He brought it from Miami." Mr. James replied, "Par-Gross bought you a nice Christmas present." A few weeks later, a hit-and-run driver knocked me off it. I fell on to the dirt road in the business across from a grocery store. Ms. Harden was the owner. I received minor injuries and carried my bike home. My mother ascertained that I did not tell the barber the truth. She told Mr. James that it was purchased from her hard-earned work on the farm. Then she said, "Why would you tell a lie about this bicycle. You know that your dad don't give you anything." Then she told me, "That is the reason you were nearly killed on it. Learn to tell the truth."

Rose said that he ran the Pool-Hall in Pompano. He was the houseman. That was in the early 1940s. The pool players had to pay him fifty cents to rack the balls. Rose said that he was the best in town. He had to give odds to get a game, and he would win their money. He worked on the weekends at the pool hall. During the week days, he would pick beans for money. He would pick the most hampers of beans on the farm. He knew how to stack the beans. When the stackers pushed the beans, they would rise higher in the hamper. He didn't have to add beans to the hampers. Rose said, "Your daddy was a hustler. He worked half days on the farm."

When he died in 1960, I was not notified about it. I learned about it a few months later. I was seventeen years old. Rose said that after they separated, he became an alcoholic. She said, "*God* took him off this earth because he was irresponsible and didn't do anything for you. That is why he was young when he died. He could have done better. He kept a pocket full of money."

Rose said that he was one of the best dressed men. He loved to wear a starch and ironed shirt with his pants. He had many friends in Pompano because he was popular. Another friend and running buddy was O.C. Phillips, Senior. He was a barber and boxer in town. I have a picture of my dad in my home.

The historical side of the Williams family began when Elizabeth McGuire walked from Virginia to Florida. She brought her young son, Jimmy, with her. She met and married Thomas Williams. They had nine children. Emma Dunbar migrated from Georgia to Live Oak, Florida. She brought Charles and a sister with her. In Live Oak, Charles received his education and became a local school master. He was a farmer and owned a local general store. A member of the Dunbar family was married to a Williams. Every two years, there was a Dunbar-Williams family reunion. Grossman had a sister whose name was Iris Redman. They were from Wellborn, Lake City, and Live Oak areas. Another relative is healthy and was 107 years old in 2014. Her name is Grace Dunbar-Lincoln. He is her uncle. She lives in New Jersey with her children. They are my cousins.

Jenny Caruth had a sister who resided in California. Her name was Alberto Caruth. We have relatives all over the United States, including Puerto Rico. Claritha Allen is from the Lake City area. She was related to Carl and Douglas Allen. We lived in the same community and went to the same school. Mr. Theodore Allen was related to my father. Mr. Brown owned a grocery store in Pompano. He was related to my father. That was how I became related to a classmate and friend whose name is Renard Brown.

POMPANO BEACH, FLORIDA

When my mother migrated to Pompano Beach, Florida, it was booming with farmers and sharecroppers. It was similar to Leary, Georgia. It was substantially larger than Leary. There was far more businesses. A business district was in the black segregated community. It was on Hammondville Road. The road was named after a white successful farmer who migrated from Philadelphia, Pennsylvania. He became wealthy and moved somewhere else. He didn't do anything for the black community. Black leaders were able to name the road after Martin Luther King. They were unable to remove Hammon's name from it. His name is in small writing under MLK.

A delicate fish is named after Pompano. It is called the pompano fish. One of the largest farmer's market is in Pompano. In the 1980s, the business district in the black community became a ghost town. Today, it is being revitalized by the city of Pompano. The majority of the businesses are gone. All of the bars, nightclubs, and pool halls are gone. The same applies to the Love Land Theatre and the Dairy Cream Parlor. The Bowling Alley is gone and many more businesses.

A few known celebrities are from Pompano. One of them was Esther Rolle who played on television in *Good Times*. They called her Florida on the show. A road was named after her. The high school has been nationally rated in sports. The name of the school is Blanche Ely High school. It was built in the segregation era. The school was named after an educator whose name was Blanche Ely. Her husband was the principal at Attucks High School in Dania, Florida. Both of them were principals. She brought education in the black community. In the early 2000s, the school had produced more professional ball players in the nation than any other school. They were number one in the nation. Today, they are ranked in the top ten. Eddie Jones is one of them. He was a professional basketball player. There were many more players. Some of them were playing overseas. There was an excellent academic program at the school along with sports.

It was rare for Attucks to beat Ely High in sports. When we beat them, Ms. Ely was unable to spend that night home with her husband. She had to spend the night with one of her teachers. All of the local folks called her husband Professor Ely. It would have been a fight between them had she gone home.

In the Collier City subdivision was where freebasing cocaine started. It is located in the black community. It was the first city in Florida to freebase cocaine. In the old days, many hustlers and gamblers migrated to Pompano. I have seen and met many of them. We have had murderers and bank robbers to migrate here. In the early 1960s, two gamblers came to town. They had robbed a bank for about half a million dollars. The tall man was called Slim. The short one was called Shorty. They spent a lot of money with prostitutes. They gambled on a daily basis and had plenty of hundred dollar bills. They shot dice and pool and played cards for money. They were in Pompano about two years. I don't know whether they lost all of the money. They messed up a lot of it. I won some of it by shooting dice and pool. I was a pretty good hustler.

During the segregation era, certain subdivisions were given names. I grew up in New-Town. New-Town produced the majority of athletes for the high school. I averaged thirty-four points per game on the junior varsity basketball team. I was in the seventh grade. Me and my buddy, Sammie Lee Wells, were the only two players promoted to the varsity team. We were in the eighth grade. Our coach was Coach Clayton. I played for Coaches McIntosh and Bullard. I was assistant captain under Coach Bullard. I got pissed off with Bullard and quit the team when I was in the eleventh grade. He gave me a basketball scholarship to a school in Texas, which was named

Paul Quinn. I refused to go there. I am going to name some of the outstanding athletes from New-Town.

(1)   Booee Bivens, football quarter-back.
(2)   Robert Judson, football and academics, PhD.
(3)   The McBride brothers, football, murdered in Deerfield.
(4)   Cleveland Bethel, Sonny-Boy, played drums in the band, scholarship FAMU, was considered as the best drummer in America, made a musical record.
(5)   His brother was the Boy Scout Master, Eagle Scout, became a teacher.
(6)   Tony Simpson, football at University of Miami
(7)   Renard Brown, basketball
(8)   Martha Caruth, basketball
(9)   Chubby Bell, football
(10) Lois Bell, basketball
(11) Lela Griffin, basketball
(12) Wallace, Ira, Buggy and Purcell Blue, football and basketball
(13) Morris and Turman Grooms, football
(14) Westley, nicknamed Boose, basketball, FAMU, killed in car accident, was seven feet tall.
(15) Lucille, Jimmy, and George Greene, basketball
(16) Shirley Johnson, basketball
(17) Willis Lacey, all around in athletics
(18) Eddie Gates played for Northwestern in Miami, all around in athletics
(19) Mack Martin, football
(20) Reuven Carter, professional football with Denver Broncos
(21) Lonnie Clyde Black, football and basketball
(22) Theotis, Perry, and Henry Thurston, football and basketball

A subdivision across from Westside Park was called Ghost Town. It is near Ely High School. It is an apartment complex. We referred to them as the Ghost-Town people. Across the Seaboard railroad tracks was a labor camp. All of the folks called it The Projects-Across-The-Tracks. There were the fifteenth and sixteenth avenue section. We called them the 15th Avenue folks. They lived across the tracks too. Then we had the Collier City folks. There was a few more sections across town. Another project was on Northwest 6th Avenue. They were the Across Town Project folks. We had a subdivision named Liberty Park. They were called the Liberty Park folks. Around the comer from it was Sanders Park. They were called the Sanders Park folks. If a family lived near Northwest 3rd Avenue, they were called the Third Avenue folks. Then we had the Ogden Brothers Quarters. They were called the Ogden Brothers Quarters folks. The same applied to Peg-Leg Jones Quarters. They were referred as the folks from Jones Quarters. We had Buck- Lyons Quarters. They were the folks who lived in Lyons Quarters. All of the quarters were owned by white farmers who became wealthy in Pompano. Across Dixie Highway and the Florida East Coast Railways were the white community. Several farmers owned some property in that area. They built some houses for their farmworkers. Those folks were the Across-Dixie Highway folks. When school was closed for the summer the kids would play sports. The teams would be named from the sections that were mentioned. We played football, basketball, baseball, and softball against each other.

When it was time to harvest the crops, the school would only have half-day school sections. The students would be able to work on the white farmers' farm. They became wealthy and did not do anything for the black community. In those days, the winter season was very cold. Farmers had to pump plenty of water on their farms to prevent the crops from freezing. The folks would have fifty-five gallon drums in their yard. The drums would be filled with wood to make a fire in them. People would wear heavy wool overcoats and stand around them to get warm. I remember when the drums would turn very red from the heat. Some of the folks would drink and tell jokes. Another form of heat was to burn a worn out tire in the yard. Gasoline was poured on the tire before it was lit. Those tires made a lot of smoke while burning. When the smoke was gone, the people would stand around the tire. A lot of wire would be left on the ground from the tire. The same thing was done in the winter around the football and outdoor basketball courts. Those drums and tires were used the same way on the farms to keep the plants warm. In those days, we had four seasons in Pompano. Today, we are lucky to get one cold day per year.

It was in the winter, and I was in the fifth grade. About ten people were at our house. It was very cold. The folks stood around the drum and tire in our backyard. They were lit. The drum was red and hot. Steve Smith was one of the folks. He thought that he could throw me. I said to Steve, "You are not strong enough to throw me." We began to wrestle. He had on a pair of overalls. I grabbed him and nearly threw him into the lit fifty gallon drum. All of the folks really laughed at that. Some of them said to Steve, "Big Red is strong. It takes a man to handle him."

I was in elementary school when we got our first black policeman. His name was Criswell. The folks called him Sugar Criss. He had a master's degree in mathematics and was certified to teach school.

Today, whites are buying property in the black community. Some of the poorer ones are moving to the community. Arabs have small businesses in our community. Churches are everywhere. I think that there are too many churches in the community. Farming has dissipated, but the farmer's market continues to exist. It is controlled by the State of Florida.

CHARLEE

My name is Charlie Lee Anderson. I was born on September 26, 1941. I was born in the country. It was in Leary, Calhoun, Georgia. The midwife was Ms. Dell Williams. My mother is Rosa Lee Anderson; whereas my father is Alonzo Williams. The midwife and my father are not related. They did not know each other. The midwife told my grandmother and mother that I had to have their last name. She said, "There are two ways he can use the name of Williams. The first one is to be married to his father. I have to rule that out because Rosa said that they are not married. The last reason is an engagement to be married." My mother was too naive and honest to tell a lie that they were engaged to get married. As a youngster, that troubled me for not having my father's last name. When I was in sixth grade, I sent a letter to Vital Records in Atlanta, Georgia. I asked them to change my last name to Williams. They did not respond to my letter. I was too young to know that it was a legal issue. I did not know there were lawyers. I hadn't ever heard about them.

I was named by my aunt Fannie (Anna) Anderson. I never did like my name nor did I care for the nickname of Charlee. I graduated from high school, and Charlie Lee Anderson was on the diploma.

During the mid-1960s, I got a chance to change my name. I purchased a birth certificate from Vital Statistics in Atlanta, Georgia. When I got the birth certificate, my first name was omitted. It had on it No-Name Boy Anderson. The midwife must have forgotten or did not document my first name. That really pissed me off. The certificate omits my father's name.

Legally, I changed Charlie to Charles. Today, I am Charles Lee Anderson. I still do not like Charlee.

I only allow my classmates and folks who I grew up with to call me Charlee. I have thought about changing my name to Charles Anderson-Williams. I asked myself the question, "Why should I change it? My father did not denounce me. But financially, he was irresponsible. Nor did he have any impact in my life. I was raised by my mother and grandmother. Whenever I saw my father, he was fucked up on alcohol."

He visited me a few times. That was about the size of it. He would tell my mother, "Rose, you know you can take me to court. They will make me pay child support." Rose told him, "You were the first man I ever had sex with, and I was a virgin. Neither one of us knew what we were doing. It probably was your first time too. We did what our friends were doing. You need to be responsible enough to help take care of your child. I refuse to miss work and go to court on your sorry ass. I will take care of him along with my mother." Rose said that my father would beg her to be her boyfriend. She told him, "I am not a fool for a man. I refuse to let you give me a house full of children and don't take care of them. She told him that he could visit me and only for that reason." They never did have another relationship.

Rose said that I was a bad baby. I was born fighting. She said I was crying and hitting and kicking like a fighter. She said that I was strong and hard to handle. All of the folks in the country in Leary said, "Nig went to Florida and had sex with a white man. She brought a white baby home." My grandmother would be pissed off. She tried to explain that I was not white. She would say, "My grandson has Indian blood in him. His father is not white." The folks would laugh as if not telling the truth. They would say, "Oh really, really, Miss Fennie."

My mother said that I was a greedy baby. She had to breastfeed me because I refused to use a bottle. She said I would hit and kick the bottle of milk. Rose told me that I would fight the bottle as if fighting a man." I refused to suck milk from it. She developed a cyst on a breast and attempted to wean me from it. She was not successful and chose to leave me with an aunt in Arlington, Georgia. The town is a few miles away from Leary. My aunt's name was Fannie Davis-Crawford. Her husband was Primos Crawford. I spent two years with them. My mother and grandmother returned to Pompano. In Pompano, my mother worked on the farms. She had to pick vegetables for money. She had to crawl on her knees to pick beans. She would send money by mail to Arlington. The money was used to take care of me.

When I was a few years old, my curly hair was styled with two long pony tails. Sometimes, the Indians would come in the country to sell goods. One day when they saw me, they came to my home. I was standing in the yard. My grandmother said that the Indians picked me up. They said, "This is a pretty, very pretty boy. He has our blood, Indian blood. Where did you folks get him?" My grandmother explained to the Indians that my father lived in Florida, and he had Indian blood. They smiled and agreed about the blood issue.

My uncle, Spudge, told his mother that I was a boy, and he was going to cut my hair. He told my grandmother, "When I cut his hair, the texture of it is going to change. He is a boy and does not need that long hair. He is not a girl. When he got the opportunity, he cut it from my head. My grandmother and mother were pissed off with him. But it was too late. My uncle told them, "I don't care because you are mad. You can't do anything about it. Now, he looks like a boy."

After a few years, I was weaned from the breast and was eating food. My grandmother went to Arlington and got me. I was living with her sister. My grandmother returned to the house in Leary, in the country. It was owned by George Colley, who was a mulatto. All of the folks thought he was a rich white man. However, my research on the Internet documents him as a nonwhite man. The U.S. Census listed him as a mulatto. Throughout my maternal relatives lives, they believed that he was a white man. George was my grandfather's best friend, and he never told him that he was not white. He was able to get my grandfather out of trouble many times. George looked and acted as if he was white.

In the winter when I was young and able to walk, my mother decided to visit me in Georgia. I was three or four years old. My grandmother and I were at her son's home. His name is Edmond Anderson with the nickname Spudge. He was a married man and had two children at that time. It was cold, and the fireplace was used to keep the house warm. Wood was used in it. They had what the folks called a firepot in the house. It was made from clay dirt. They would put charcoals in it to make heat. Most people would place it in the center of the house. It would not be far away from the fireplace. It helped to keep the house warm in the winter.

I was sort of mischievous and had done something wrong. My uncle did not like it. He said, "Boy, I want you to come here. I am going to spank you." I ran backward and accidentally sat in the firepot. I was seriously burned, especially on my rectum. The imprint of the pot was on it. I was not taken to a doctor for treatment. My grandmother and uncle treated the burns. They used wild herbs and ointments to heal the injuries. I had to sleep on my stomach. The imprint from the pot remained on me for many years. It started to disappear when I was about fifty years old. I am sure that the burns were painful and traumatic. I could not recoil in my memory.

Prior to elementary school, I had not received any education. I told my mother that she was too dumb to teach me anything. She would try, but I would not listen at her. I would go outside and play with ants and insects. The ants would crawl and sting me. I would cry and say that they were my pets. Sometimes, I would play with the bird and chicken feathers. I loved to walk into the woods.

When I was six years old and able to go to school, my grandmother brought me to Pompano. I was enrolled into Pompano Beach Colored School. Subsequently, it became Coleman Elementary School. I can't remember the year when the name was changed.

After my first day of attending school, I told my grandmother I did not like the school. She said, "Son, you need to get an education and go there and make some friends." I told her that I would go to school and make some friends. My second day, I grabbed my lunch bucket and left the house. Instead of going to school, I made a detour and walked to an undeveloped wooded area of New-Town. All of the folks called it the Oak Field. I played in the Oak Field. I would play with the insects and talk to the birds. Sometimes, I would chase after a rabbit. When I thought it was time for lunch, I would eat from my lunch bucket. My grandmother would put lemonade or juice in the thermal bottle. I could see the road that the schoolkids walked on. The name of it was Hammondville Road. I would join them and walk home as if I had been to school. I played hooky during the whole school term. I was not promoted to the second grade.

My grandmother said, "Charlee, I am taking you to my sister's house in Arlington, Georgia. You lived with your aunt Fannie a few years ago. You have a cousin who lives with her. He is about the same age as you. You can go to school with him. They call him Billy Joe. The school is a small school at one of the nearby churches. It is not too far to walk. I think you will like this one." I agreed to go to Arlington with her.

I went there in the summer a few months before the school opened. Billy Joe was about the same age as me. I got to know him real good. We played in the woods and in the corn field.

I remember the enrollment day of school. My cousin and I were in the first grade. On Monday, it was going to be our first day in class. I remember leaving the house with our lunch buckets. We joined a few students who walked in a path toward the school. For some strange reason, I encouraged my cousin to play hooky from the school. My cousin and I refused to go to the school. We kind of lagged behind the other students and threw some stones in a lake.

Then we went in the woods and played. We ended up playing in the cornfields. When we could see the kids walking from the school, we would join them. We went home with our empty lunch buckets as if we had gone to school. We played hooky from school during the school term. We did not attend a day in the first grade. Neither one of us were promoted to the second. That was two years I had played hooky in the first grade. My grandmother returned to Georgia. She was very upset with me and gave me a hard time. I was taken back to Pompano with her. My grandmother said, "Son, you need an education. If you don't go and learn something, you are going to be very dumb. I said, "Grandma, I love you. Please don't be mad at me. I am ready to go to school. I will go the next time in Pompano. I promise that I will go to school." I was ready to go to school. I had a friend who lived across from us. His name was Johnny Gates. He was in the second grade. His sister was in the first grade with me. Her name was Gladys Gates. There were more sisters and brothers who were in a few grades higher. After enrollment, all of us walked to school together. I attended school this time without playing hooky. I was anxious and ready to go to school. I kept my promise with my grandmother.

It was a very large first grade class of students. The school had to hire more teachers for the first grade. The name of my teacher was Miss Washington. Miss Bradley was another teacher along with Miss Thomas. Miss Thomas limped when she walked. Those teachers were mean and put a lot of fear in our hearts. In the rear of the classrooms was an enclosed area called the cloak room. All of the teachers had a wooden paddle with a handle carved on it. They were thick and about three inches thick. Many students were taken in the cloak room. The living shit was beaten out of them. I am surprised that I did not play hooky again. I was lucky because I was not taken into the cloak room.

Those teaches had their students and taught in the same classroom. Sometimes, they would teach all of the students in one class. They used those paddles daily. If a student could not answer a problem correctly, they were taken in the room and beaten. Sometimes, we had to whisper the answer in their ear. I remember when Miss Bradley came to me, and I had to whisper the answer in her ear. I was so scared and nervous. I could not whisper the answer but said it correctly out loud. Miss Bradley said, "Anderson, you do not have to be afraid. You solved the problem and got it right."

Our first grade class was huge. Many of them did not return after that year. I sat directly behind Paulette Robinson. I played with her two ponytails. She did not tell me to desist from doing it. Across from me was Sammie Lee Wells. He became my best friend. A sign was hanging from a string next to the door. On one side of it was In and on the opposite side was Out. If a student had to go to the bathroom, the sign was flipped where you could read Out. It had to be turned to In when they returned to the room. If a student failed to do that, they would be beaten in the cloak room. That room was supposedly used to hang clothes.

My buddy was in a row on my right side. I remember two brothers who were in our class. Their last name was Newkirk. One of them stuttered in his speech. They brought sardines and a fish sandwich to eat. It was in their lunch buckets. My buddy and I made friends with them. Sometimes, we would walk to the store owned by the Blue Family next to the school. Other times, we would walk to Mr. Par-Jake's grocery store. I was promoted to the second grade. I had an A average and was the number one student in our class. After our first year of school, the teachers placed us in sections according to our grades. My second grade teacher was Miss Winfield. She limped when she walked. One of her legs was shorter than the other one. She was an excellent teacher. I really liked her. My grades continued to be outstanding. The teacher asked the principal of the school to give me a double promotion. Miss Ely refused to give it. I was promoted to the third grade. I was the number one student with an A average.

The school used an O which as equivalent to an A. The O meant outstanding. I think my third grade teacher was Miss Spiva. She taught me in elementary school, but I am not sure about the grade. She was another excellent teacher. Again, the principal refused to grant a double promotion. In the fourth grade, my teacher was Miss Grisham. Her husband owned a dry cleaning business in the community. He was a prominent successful entrepreneur. He was Harry Grisham. She had a pretty good reputation with her paddle. She used it quite often. She did not ask for a double promotion.

In elementary school, I became very athletic. I was the tallest and largest student in my class. Villis Sworn was an outstanding student. She was the largest girl in our class. I was one of the best wrestlers in Pompano. I had a reputation in New-Town. I encouraged my mother to buy me a basketball for Christmas. There was a vacant lot next to our house. I got a five gallon paint can and cut the bottom from it. I got a wooden pole and nailed the can on it. I dug a hole in the ground and placed the pole in it. It was almost as tall as the basketball goals at the school. I played basketball on that vacant lot until darkness with my neighbors. I became the best shooter in my neighborhood. I was the best wrestler in elementary school and in New-Town. I have never given respect to anyone who was smaller than me.

I had a friend who was a year ahead of me. He taught me how to swim in the Pompano canal. His name is Purcell Blue. His older brother had a reputation whose name was Wallace Blue. Purcell wanted to be like Wallace. He was much smaller than me. We were lucky because the canal was infested with alligators. The canal ran from the Atlantic Ocean into our community. We would swim in it butt naked. If any girls or women came in the area, some of the boys would stand on their hands in the water. Before head standing, they would say, "Do you want to see the sun or the moon?" To see a swimmer's butt was the moon, whereas to see his penis was the sun. Purcell was the main one to do it. One day, we were the only ones to swim in the canal. We got naked and placed our clothes on the embankment of the canal. I would swim across to the opposite side of the canal. Purcell grabbed my clothes and hid them. He said, "If you do not swim on the other side with me, you are walking home butt naked." That was my first time ever swimming across the canal. I went across it with him. He got our clothes, and we walked home.

Another day, he decided to challenge me while walking through the Oak Field from Miss Harding's grocery store. It was a small family store in the community. He wanted to wrestle with me. I would pick him up and throw him like throwing a marble. I said to Purcell, "You had better leave me alone before you get hurt. He was a game little fellow. As soon as I would get off him, he would bother me again. We ended up in the rear of his cousin's house whose name was Brother Graham. Brother Graham saw me throw Purcell on the ground. When I got on top of him, his cousin rushed in the Oak Field and pulled me off Purcell. He told Purcell, "You know that you cannot beat Charlee. Leave him alone." Then he said to me, "If you beat my cousin, I will help him out." Purcell went home. I remained with Brother Graham and watched him practice how to repair transmissions on cars.

In the fifth grade, my teacher was Miss Williams. She was another excellent teacher. I continued to be a straight A student and remained the number one student. The school board decided to use students on campus as crossing guards. The principal and my fifth grade teacher made me the chief. Some of the other students who were picked were given different ranks. There were a few captains, lieutenants, sergeants, and officers. Again, Miss Ely refused to grant a double promotion.

When I was in the fifth grade, I was walking from school with my friend, Purcell, and Ronald Westley. We were in New-Town on 10th Avenue near Freeman's Funeral Home. Both of them decided to double team me. I hit Ronald and knocked him on the ground. He got up and ran home. I told Purcell, "Your cousin ain't around today. That didn't scare him because he was game and wanted to have a bad image.

I slammed him on the ground all the way to Perry Jean McBride's house. We drew a crowd of children. One of Perry Jean's brothers pulled me off him. We ended up at the house where Morris and Turman Grooms lived. They were sitting on their back porch and watching us fight. They did not intervene. My classmate was their sister whose name is Clementine Grooms. I picked up Purcell and slammed him to the ground. Ronald Westley lived next door to the Grooms family. He was too scared to come out of his house. I had really gotten mad with Purcell. I was on top of him and choking the shit out of him. We grew a big crowd of children. Someone went and told Wallace and Ira Blue that I was beating up their brother. They ran where we were and saw me choking their brother. They pulled me off him. When Wallace was holding me, Purcell jumped up and bit me in the eye. Carolyn Bell whose nickname is Bunky went to the house and told my mother that they double teamed me. When I arrived at the house, Rose grabbed her pistol. She put it in her purse and went to their house. I did not want to go there with her. But she made me go with her. She confronted their mother whose name was Essie Mae Blue. Rose told her that if one of them should beat me fair and squarely, it would be all right. She said, "I am not standing for my boy to be double teamed, and if it happens again, someone is going to get shot." They soon moved out of New-Town. I never could catch up with Purcell to pay him back. In high school, we became friends again. Today, the only thing he remembers was biting me in the eye. All he needed to do was to ask his brother, Ira, or Turman Grooms what really went down. Morris mentioned it to me before he died. I don't remember losing any fights when I was in elementary school. In New-Town, all of the older folks said I was bad. But I did not start any fights. Wallace became my friend when I was in high school because we played a lot of basketball together. He apologized to me for enabling his brother to bite me. He said, "You were too big for Purcell. I had to pull you off him." I did not have any brothers and sisters. I got into a lot of fights. I did not have any one to help me. I was on my own and beat a lot of kids. I was as strong as an ox. I remember when a bully from Jones Quarters came into New-Town. His name was Cyrus Mclemore, whose nickname was Big Buddy. We were playing basketball. He got mad when I shot the ball and scored over him. We got into a fight. I threw him down and whipped his butt. Willis Lacey pulled me off him. He got up and ran toward Jones Quarters. I told him that he had better not come to New-Town anymore. That was his last time coming to New-Town.

Our school was closed for the summer. I had gotten promoted to the sixth grade. Willis Lacey and Robby Gates, his brother, came to our house. They came to play basketball. Robby was a classmate and good friend. His cousins saw us and came to the house. They were Johnny and Par Gates. The four of us played basketball. I got into a fight with Robby who never could beat me. His brother, Lacey, did not help him. He watched us fight. However, his cousins chose to help him. I knocked Par Gates out, and he fell on the ground. Then Johnny was thrown to the ground. Par and Johnny got up and ran home. Lacey stopped the fight. Lacey told Robby, "The three of you are sorry. Charlee beat all of you by himself." Robby said, "Charlee is too strong for one of us."

The last fight I got into with Robby, a movie could have been made. He was mad because I had won his marbles. He threw an iron golf club. It hit me on the leg. He ran toward his aunt's house. I picked up the golf club and was standing in the center of the dirt road. He jumped on the wood porch. He was in stride and opened the door to enter the house. As the door was closing, I threw the golf club. The iron portion of the golf club struck him on the side of his head. It knocked him down. He was bleeding profusely. It happened when he was running in a stride; and while the door was closing, Ernestine Gates, his aunt, brought him to our house. She told Rose, "Charlee is bad, and I am calling the police." Rose bargained with her and told Ernestine that she would pay the medical bill. I was pretty accurate when I had to throw something. I threw rocks at birds and would kill them. I could really shoot sling shots. Sometimes, I went hunting with a BB gun, rifle, or a shotgun. I became an excellent shooter. With my BB gun, I have shot small pieces of wood from my neighbor's mouth and hands. Nobody was shot.

Sometimes, we would get into a fight and throw rocks at each other. We would stand on the dirt roads and get a hand full of rocks. I was smart when I got my rocks. I would not throw them. I would duck and duck and dodge their rocks. They would not have any more rocks. Then they would bend over to pick up more rocks. When they bent over, I would throw my rocks. The majority of times, they would be struck on the head with a good-size rock. Rose would have to pay another medical bill to keep the police away.

Once, I got into a fight with Alvin and Gertrude Taylor, his sister. I whipped Alvin. He threw a broken broom handle at me. When he was running, I picked it up and threw it at him. Gertrude got in front of it and was struck on the head. Unfortunately, the splintered edge of it entered into the front of her head. She was taken to the doctor with the stick stuck in her head. Gertrude stopped talking with me for many years. Finally, she started to talk with me when she was a senior in high school. I gave her an apology.

I was promoted to sixth grade and was in Mr. Bentley's class. He was an excellent mathematics teacher. I learned a lot from him. I was the only student with a straight A average. I have a copy of the transcript to corroborate it. I was the number one student. Our teacher would have us to give an answer to the quizzes in the math book. The first student to answer it correctly would get an A. I would get the majority of them right. He told the principal that I was the best math student he had ever taught. Miss Ely was no longer the principal. She was the principal at the new high school. It was the first high school in the black community. He made contact with Miss Ely and the dean of boys when I was promoted to the seventh grade. The dean was Joe Smith. Barbara King who was an excellent and outstanding student was my classmate. Her mother whose name was Miss Bennett became the principal of Coleman Elementary School. They told the dean and principal that I was the number one student with an A average. There were a bunch of excellent and outstanding students in our class. I will name a few of them.

(1) Paulette Robinson
(2) Villis Sworn
(3) Leonard Swain
(4) George Sanders
(5) Eve Martin
(6) Henderson Hunter
(7) Gladys Gates
(8) Clementine Grooms

(9)   Maxie Pete

(10) Barbara King

In elementary school, Mr. Braynon was the physical education teacher. All of the black elementary schools had basketball teams. The program started when I was in the fifth and sixth grades. My buddy and I made the team in both grades. He was on the first team. I was on the second team and the number sixth man. Robert McGirt was the star on the team. I always thought that I was better than him and should have been on the first team. However, the coach did not think so. In the sixth grade, we were undefeated.

A school in Hallandale was undefeated. They were the top seed in the tournament and considered as the best in the county. The name of the school was Lanier Elementary. We were beaten by Lanier in the semifinals. They played against Roosevelt Elementary from West Palm Beach, Florida, for the championship game. A star basketball player was on the Palm Beach team whose nickname was Red. This was the championship game. In the last quarter, Lanier had an eight point lead with about a minute to go in the last quarter. A time out was called and during that time, Red told the coach and players to let him shoot the ball. He was fouled and had to shoot free throws. Red played a one-man game. Roosevelt Elementary won the championship game. They refused to give him the MVP trophy. It was given to a Lanier player. The officials refused to give it to Red. They said, "Red had played a one-man game. They won by one point. Lanier was a powerhouse in basketball. Red became a star in high school and college. He went to Arkansas State College. He played in the Olympics and the professional league. Roosevelt High was a super power in high school basketball. I went to Coach Boynton's funeral when I was in my mid 60s at Antioch Baptist Church. At the end of the funeral, Coach Braynon approached me and my best friend. During the conversation, I told him, "Coach, I should have been on the first team in elementary school. I was better than some of those players. You know me and my friend were the only players to make the basketball team in high school. If I had been on your first team, I believe we would have beaten Lanier Elementary School."

In the sixth grade, a spelling bee contest was held at Antioch Baptist Church. The boys were told to wear a white long sleeved shirt and a black or blue pair of pants. The girls had to wear the same colors. My mother was at the farm. I did not have anything to wear. I rushed home from school and ironed a shirt to wear. I had a dark blue pair of silk pants. I washed them. When they were dry, I ironed the pants. They were made with silk and were supposed to be dry-cleaned. They looked real bad on me. They had drawn shorter because I had washed them. I wore them to the spelling bee. Only three students were left in it. I was one of them. The other students were Paulette Robinson and Eve Martin. They were outstandingly excellent students. They could not spell the next word which was "faucet." They were eliminated. I had to spell it to prevent a three-way tie. I spelled it and won the spelling bee contest. The winner was supposed to be given a cake as an award. I never did receive the cake, and I continue to remember it. That is the reason why role models or adults should fulfill their promises with children. Children will not forget it. I was put in the trick by those teachers.

In the fifth and sixth grades, I did a lot of wrestling. I was the best wrestler. A friend whose name was Woodrow Shivers would challenge me daily. My best friend was afraid of us. He would watch us wrestle. Woodrow never did manage to throw me. The toughest challenger was Joe Reddick prior to contracting polio. He was strong and I caught hell throwing him. Henderson Hunter was a decent wrestler. Our basketball court was directly behind the cafeteria. When I was in the sixth grade, during our lunch break, several of us went to the basketball court. We played basketball during the break. All of the students left except Sammie Lee, Lancaster Rolle, and me. Lancaster and I began to wrestle. I thought that he was weak because I threw him down three times. My friend left while we were wrestling. Mr. Bentley was my homeroom teacher. I started walking toward the school. Then Lancaster got up and ran behind me. He jumped on my back and managed to throw me. I did not see him when he ran behind me. He threw me that time, but it was not fair. In 1970, I was a policeman. I went to the dog race tracks. I was at the Biscayne Kennel Club in Miami. Lancaster was there, and he recognized me. He came over; we chatted and had some fun together. He was living in Miami. Lancaster was well built and a body builder. He was built like Charles Atlas and Jeannie Boy. Jeannie Boy was from Pompano and moved to Miami. Lancaster remembered when we wrestled in the sixth grade. He said, "Man, I underestimated how strong you were, and you threw the shit out of me. He said, "I got you the last time. I had to sneak behind you and get dirty." We smiled and I said, "Today, I would not want to wrestle with you. I know you have been pumping plenty of iron." He told me that a classmate named Henry Heath lived in Miami. Then he said, "Henry is a body builder too. His built is better than mine. Sometimes, we work out together. Henry works in the warehouse for Publix Super Markets."

In the fifth grade, there was a raffle. The prize was a rabbit. He was white with pink eyes. I won the rabbit. I named him Pinky. He was a wonderful pet. I would let him out of his cage. He would wonder away in the woods and return home. One day, he did not return home. I believe that somebody killed my rabbit and ate him. It really broke my heart. Pinky was a good pet. He was a smart rabbit. My dog was very smart too. The dog was named Shane. The dog was killed chasing a car.

I started working on farms when I was in the first grade. That was when the school was closed in the summer. When I was in the fourth grade, I made a shoe-shine box. I would go on the farmer's market and shine shoes for money. I would go into the white community and work. They would pay me to cut and rake their yards. That was my weekend job. There was a peg-leg man whose name was Chief. He would get a load of oranges on his pickup truck. I was one of the young boys who sold buckets of oranges for him. Chief would travel into Broward, Dade, and Palm Beach counties. Another hustle was to sell the Pompano newspaper. They had an office next to the Greyhound Bus Station on Dixie Highway.

A soda water bottling company went into business. It was named Nehi Soda Company. The drivers would drive on the dirt roads and sell them by the crate. Twenty-four bottles were in a crate. I would buy a few crates and sell the sodas in New-Town. A white man came into our neighborhood and sold boxes of candy. After he got to know me, he would leave some boxes on consignment with me. I ate plenty of it and sold most of it to my neighbors. I was mechanically inclined. I would take my bicycle apart and put it back together. I built a wagon to pull behind my bike. I would ride on it to the packing houses and fill it with vegetables. They would be sold to the local restaurants in our community. When I had time, I would go fishing in the Pompano Canal. I used the old-fashioned cane pole. I was a pretty good fisherman. Sometimes, I would catch more than one hundred fish. I would sell about half of them to my neighbors.

We had the Loveland Theatre in our community. Sometimes, I would pass out leaflets to get free passes to the theatre.

When I was in the sixth grade, Willis Lacey became my friend. I could not beat him. He was stronger than me. He taught me how to play many games. Some of them were with cards. Others were checkers, ping-pong, and basketball. We did a lot of swimming in the local rock pits and canals. A few times, we rode on the Greyhound Bus to the downtown area in Ft. Lauderdale. It was on Andrews Avenue. We were not allowed to sit next to whites on the bus. We would have to give them our seat and go to the back of the bus. The same applied to the public beaches. We were not allowed to go to their swimming areas. In Ft. Lauderdale, a public beach was developed for black folks. It was behind Port Everglades. We were transported on a ferry boat to the beach. If a person did not return on the last ferry, they had two choices: remain on the beach until the next day or swim across the waterway to the port. There were one or two lifeguards on the beach. The rules were very lax. I remember quite a few times when we would go very far into the ocean. The water was very deep. We would gather shells with conch fish inside them. It was very plentiful in those days. It is a county or state park in Dania today. A fee is charged to enter the park.

I joined the Cub Scout when I was in the fourth grade. The meetings were held in the projects at the labor camp. Louis Mingo, a friend, was in it. His mother was the Cub Scout master. Her name was Miss Mingo. I became a member of the Boy Scout in the fifth grade. I was an Explorer Scout in the sixth grade. In Ft. Lauderdale, the uniforms were sold at Burdine's store. I rode the Greyhound Bus alone to buy my uniform in the fifth grade. They did not sell the Explorer Scout uniform. It was sold at Burdine's store in Miami. The store was located in the downtown area of Miami. I rode on the bus to Miami when I was in the sixth grade. I went alone and bought my uniform. I received many awards and became an Eagle Scout. I was an Assistant Scout Master for a year. I gave my Explorer Uniform shirt to my oldest daughter. Her name is Adrianne Yvette Anderson-

Coward. She keeps it as a souvenir. I got out of it when I was in high school.

I started having sex at a young age. I was in the second grade when it happened. The Gates family lived across the street from us. The children were my friends. One day, I gave them a visit when I was in the second grade. I was talking with the oldest girl in her bedroom. Her name was Carolyn Gates. She was about six years older than me. Carolyn said, "Have you ever had any pussy, Charlee?" I did not know what she was talking about. Then she said, "I am going to teach you how to get it." She pulled down my shorts and underwear. My little penis was massaged until it got hard. Carolyn put me on top of her and stuck it in her vagina. She kept me on top of her a few minutes. She was real tall, fine, and cute. I remember seeing her butt naked in the bed. She had a lot of hair around the pussy. After that, my mother could not keep me away from them. Whenever, she was alone, I would go to their house. I made love with her all through elementary school. From the fourth through the sixth grade, I had plenty of sex with Carolyn Bell. Her nickname is Bunky. We would do it in their outdoor toilet. Her father caught us having sex. He ran me home. He came to our house and talked with my mother. He said, "We are related to your son. Tell him to leave his cousin alone." That was the last time ever getting involved with her. I was in the sixth grade when I met Carolyn Bell's cousin. She lived in Oakland Park and became my girlfriend. I had sex with her a few times. I had my first orgasm when I was in the sixth grade.

It was with a neighbor. Her name was Clementine Mclemore. Her father was a preacher. She had a sister whose name was Mamie. She lived in Lynn Walton's quarters. Mamie was invited to a party and asked her to stay with the children. Clementine told me about it and asked me to come to the house. The children went to sleep. We took our clothes off and got into the bed. We had sex. I had my first orgasm. After that, I had sex with her frequently.

I loved to play mommy and daddy and have a playhouse with the girls. One day, I almost scored with a classmate whose name is Clementine Grooms. We built a playhouse under some trees in the rear of their house. It was hid from the view of their house. Her brother Morris was sitting on the porch. Clementine was the mommy, and I was the daddy. Her sister whose nickname is Doll was the baby girl. Purcell was the baby boy. We pretended that it was night. I said, "It is time for the babies to go to bed and sleep. I grabbed Clementine and started kissing her. Then I zipped my pants down and took out my penis. When I pulled her underwear down, her brother was behind me. It was her brother, Morris. He made her pull them up and made her go into the house. Then he ran me home and told me not to come there anymore. The Mathis family lived across the street from the Grooms. Joanne Mathis was our classmate. One of her sisters was named Tiny Mathis. We played mommy and daddy frequently. I am surprised that she did not get pregnant. We had sex frequently for a long time.

In the sixth grade, a family moved into New-Town, and they were from Texas. The oldest sister was nicknamed Texas. Her sister was named Helen Shaw. They rented an apartment from Reverend Black who lived in 10th Avenue. Their father or stepfather was nicknamed Sonny. Helen became my girlfriend. I had plenty of sex with her. Sonny was our softball coach. I played left or right field. Carl Allen and I were the only two players who could throw the ball to the home plate. I am referring to left or right field. During that summer, there were two undefeated teams. Our team was undefeated and ranked number two. The Third Avenue Team was undefeated and ranked number one. We played them for the championship. Their coach was Willie Newbow. The game lasted two days. We played on the vacant lot across from the Baker's house. Maggie Baker was my classmate. Today, the owner of Poitier Funeral Home has a house across from the vacant property. I remember a few players on their team.

(1) Bobby Glenn
(2) Jimmy Glenn
(3) Ralph Adderley

Some of the players on our team are:

(1) Charlie Anderson
(2) Carl Allen
(3) Willis Lacey
(4) Henry Thurston

Those are the only players I can remember.

We started playing in the championship game on Saturday evening. I played in left field, and Carl was in right field. Darkness came, and we had to stop playing. The game continued the next day on Sunday. A lot of spectators were at the game both days. I remember catching the ball in the ninth inning. It was their third out. We won the game by one point. It was an upset. We became number one that summer.

Helen Shaw was from Texas. When I was in the sixth grade, she became my girlfriend. We had sex until my seventh grade in high school. She returned to the State of Texas. During my sophomore year in school, she returned to Pompano, Florida. She was living in the Carver Homes area in Pompano. Her brother told me that she had returned to town. We had sex for about six months before ending the relationship. I had sex with quite a few other girls when I was in elementary school.

My grandmother died when I was nine or ten years old. She was really my mother, indirectly. My mother worked too hard on the farm. It would be night when she would get home. Before going to work, she would cook breakfast for me. Then she would give enough money to buy me something to eat during the day. I became a decent cook. I cooked eggs and biscuits often.

We were poor and did not realize it. In New-Town, we were the last family to get innovative technology. We were the last family to have electricity in the home. My mother used kerosene lamps and heaters. Candles were burned too. We were the last family to get an indoor bathroom. We continued to use the ice-box a few years after the invention of the refrigerator. We never did get an air-conditioner. I remember when it was invented. In the summer, we kept our windows open. We had electric fans after getting electricity into the wood-framed house. The home was never air-conditioned with a window unit. We were the last family to get a television or telephone. I remember when we got a phone it was on the party line. Anybody on your line could listen to your conversation. We listened to the radio most of the time. I was in high school when we got our first black and white television. That is the reason why I went to the Love-Land Theatre for amusement.

A lot of evil, mean-spirited people lived in Pompano. I remember hearing Steve Smith, The Walking Radio, deliver the news. Sometimes, I would hear my neighbors talk about what had happened. A lot of people got killed from ice-pick wounds. They would get into a fight. One of them would be punctured with an ice-pick. That person would end up dying from the injury because the punctured area would close back up. Internally, they would bleed to death. The punctured area would not be visible.

Sometimes, potash would be mixed with honey or syrup. It would get thrown on somebody. It was because of madness or mere jealousy. Sometimes, it resulted from a fight. It would be thrown into the victim's face and body. The honey or syrup allowed it to stick to the skin. It would be serious and traumatic. The injured person would be running and screaming. It often ended into death and blindness. The survivor's skin would never returned to its color. The surface of the affected areas would be whitish looking. It would be similar to colored clothing with bleached spots. Their complexion would not return to normal. That would be the talk of the town. Most of the times, it would happen near the bars. There was no police involvement. The folks were reluctant to report crimes. It was rare to see an officer in the community. That was before getting a black officer.

I remember seeing people who were supposed to have had a spell put on them. I have seen some people scream and cry. Some would speak in an abnormal manner. They would destroy property and attack people for no reason. Prior to this, their mannerisms had been normal. Sometimes, people would hold them to prevent them from harming themselves or others. I heard some of the older folks say, "An evil person has cast a spell on them. They went to the root lady on the Ring Line Canal and got something to put on that person. We need to take him or her to see the spiritual doctor in Ft. Lauderdale. He will be able to heal him or her." The name of the spiritual doctor was Dr. Sweeting. A road is named after him today. The victim would be transported to his office. When they returned home, the victim would be acting in a normal manner. The folks would say, "Dr. Sweeting removed or cast the spell off the person."

My mother earned a small amount of money from the farms. She was a frugal spender and was able to save some money. She kept the money in a trunk that was in her bedroom. She converted it to fifty and hundred dollar bills. When I was in the fourth grade, I would help her count it. She had about $3,000 saved. I learned to distract her while counting it. Then I would put a hundred dollar bill into my pocket.

She wouldn't see it. I kept plenty of money while I was in elementary school. I did that three to four times per year. My cousin Renard Brown thought that we were rich. If I did something wrong, he was going to tell my mother. I called him a snitch. He told Rose, "Charlee have a lot of money in school. He spends it on other children. I am his cousin, and he refuse to spend some with me. You must be rich, Miss Rose."

At that time, Leonard Swain and Maxie Pete were in my homeroom. We became friends and would spend money on each other.

During the school semester, after a certain number of weeks, we would get our report cards. All of the neighbors had ascertained that I was an excellent student. As I walked from the school to my house, I would be confronted by them. They would call me into their house and ask to see my report card. They would say, "Charlee, you are so smart. All I see is As." I mean I had to stop at every neighbor's house for them to see my card. When you took the report card home, a parent or guardian was supposed to review and sign it. I don't think my mother ever reviewed or signed any of my cards. I had to sign her name on them. She did not know she had a very intelligent son. She had to work too hard and would be tired. She did not know any of my teachers. She didn't visit them at the school and never had a conference with any of them. The only time she had something to offer was negative. She never did say anything positive to me.

She is one of the most negative persons I have ever known. I love my mother and understand the ramifications behind her negative personality. She is a sweetheart and very kind person.

When I was in elementary, my mother would do things that embarrassed me. To me it appeared as if she was bragging. We had our sixth grade graduation in a large building at the labor camp. It was a long large building used for assembly. She brought a large sum of money in a grocery bag. The money was given to the principal, and my mother said, "I am saving it for his college education." It was nine hundred and seventeen dollars. She was the only parent to do that. It embarrassed me. Everything was funny to my mother.

She would laugh and giggle. Her voice had a strange unique sound, and it would make me mad. She bought a large record player. Some of my friends would visit me. My friends would dance and sing. She would not laugh. When I did it, she would laugh and giggle at me. It sounded so crazy to me. It would make me stop doing it. I was embarrassed. That is the reason I grew up not knowing how to sing or dance. My mother had a friend whose name was Samantha Flowers. She had a few children and was able to get a welfare check. She told my mother that she could get one too. Rose applied for one when I was in the fifth grade. She was given about $25 per month for a year. I remember listening to the principal, Mrs. Ely, and a teacher talk about it. The teacher said, "He gets a welfare check." It made me feel bad. I went home, and when I got a chance, I told my mother about the conversation. I tried to encourage her to get the check cut off. She refused to do that. However, when I was in the sixth grade, the welfare check was cut off by the counselor. She told my mother that I was large enough to pick beans and earn money. I was so happy. I did not like the stigma of receiving a welfare check.

I remember when I walked to the high school campus. Two people met me when I entered the campus. The first person was the principal, who was Mrs. Ely. She knew I was a straight A student and number one in our class. I have a copy of my transcript to verify it. After she finished talking with me, she introduced me to Dean Smith. He had a degree in mathematics. I remember some magical words he said to me. I don't know whether or not he was joking. However, he said, "You are the number one student." Mr. Bentley told me, "You are a genius in mathematics. When you graduate from this school, you will not be number one in your class." That was my first day on campus. I thought those were terrible words to say to a young kid. I do not know whether or not they were bad intentions by the dean. I have never forgotten those words. One thing for sure, they were not positive, motivating words. I am grateful to *God* for enabling me to be a positive thinker. We did not have middle schools. There was an elementary school with grades one through six. After that, you went to high school from the seventh grade through the twelfth grade. At both schools, the students were divided into groups according to their grades.

In the seventh grade, my homeroom teacher was Mr. Nathaniel Valentine. He was an excellent math teacher. He was a short man, and it was rumored that he was gay. On our first day, he gave us an aptitude math test. I was the only student to make a perfect score. The teacher told the students that he expected me to make a perfect score. "That didn't surprise me because Mr. Bentley had told him I was a genius in mathematics." Mr. Valentine said, "Anderson, you are the only student who remembered how to compute problems with decimals. My best friend was not in any of my classroom groups. We remained friends and would be with each other daily.

We were the only basketball players from the elementary team to make the junior varsity team. Both of us played on the first team. We played for Coach Boynton. I averaged thirty-four points per game. My buddy got the most rebounds in the basketball games. We were number one in the district and lost only one game. We split the winning games with Roosevelt Junior High from West Palm Beach, Florida. The basketball tournament was held in Dania, Florida, at Attucks High School. We had to play Roosevelt Junior High School for the championship game. It was played on a Saturday. I did not awaken in time to catch the bus. I walked to the school. The bus had left for the game. They lost the game because I was not there to play. Some of the players who were on the team are listed.

(1) Charles Anderson, co-captain
(2) Sammie Wells, captain
(3) Maurice Poitier, center
(4) Elijah Larkins, point guard
(5) Phillip Davis
(6) Red Daniels
(7) Hazel Givens
(8) Alvin Phillips

My mother did not know how to tell time. We did not have a clock. I told her to wake me up at seven o'clock in the morning. We had a lot of chickens fenced into our yard. The chickens would crow at certain times of the day. That is the way my mother would compute the time of day. Evidently, the chicken did not crow at the correct time for me. When I arrived at the school, it was ten o'clock in the morning. I turned around and walked home. I was real mad and upset. I bought an alarm clock and taught her how to tell the time of day. On the night prior to the game, I went to the teenage center at Miss Bessie Irvin's Place. It was on a Friday night. I was with my best friend, Sammie Wells. I bought my favorite snack. It was a honey bun and a sixteen ounce soda. I bought the same thing for my friend. A few minutes later, I repeated the order for myself. My friend asked me to give him half of it. I said, "I am not giving you shit because I already have bought you something to eat and drink." I had eaten half of my honey bun. He snatched it out of my hand and ran to eat it. I did not like that so I made some plans. I drank what was left of my grape soda. I went into the store and bought another one. I drank half of it. I went outside around the corner from the teenage center. I urinated into the bottle on top of the grape soda. One half of it was my piss, the other half the grape soda. I shook the bottle to mix it up. I walked near my friend and said, "Here is a bottle of grape soda. You need it to wash the honey bun down your throat."

I took off and headed home to prevent a fight. I knew it would have been a nasty tough fight. But he couldn't beat me. All of the boys told me that when he had drunk half of it, my friend said, "It taste like piss and threw the bottle down." I had hid the shotgun on our front porch under the sofa. About an hour later, my friend whom I call Wine came to our house. He was mad and furious. He knocked on the door at the front porch. I asked him to come on the porch, but he refused. He wanted me to come outside, and I refused. It went on for a few minutes. Afterward, he removed a black rusty butcher knife from his pants' pocket. He shook it at me and said, "I am going to get you!" I grabbed the shotgun and said, "I have something that is better than that knife." Even today, he asserts that was the reason I missed the game. That was bullshit because he could not beat me, and I was not afraid of him. I went to school the whole week and did not see him. He knew I went to the theatre on the weekends. He saw me go into the Loveland Theatre on the following weekend. It was on a Saturday night. He paid his fare to enter the theatre. He sat in a row directly behind me. I was unaware of it. Then he tapped me on a shoulder. I turned around and looked directly into his face. I was reaching for my pocket knife. He smiled and said, "Charlee, why did you play such a nasty trick on me?" I smiled and said, "You created the problem and deserved it. We shook hands and have been friends since the first grade. I am too mature to do something like that today. I have given him an apology. I care for him as if he was my brother.

We often played basketball with the older boys at the park and on the outdoor basketball courts. A new gymnasium had been built for the school. The principal planned to open it at the beginning of my eighth grade term. On a Sunday, before the school term, some older boys broke the padlocks open and entered the gym. They were playing basketball in the gym, and one of them was Wallace Blue. My friend and I were walking from his sister's house. She lived in the project near Sander's Park. We had eaten food with Louise, whom we call Mama Lou. We were headed to play ball at Westside Park. When we walked by the gym, we could see the boys playing basketball. We joined them and had a good time. When the school term resumed the next day, Mrs. Ely became aware of the burglary. Somehow, she ascertained that the two of us had been in the gym. She made a police report with the only black officer, Criswell. We were interviewed, and we told them what happened. The principal took my National Honor Society pendant for punishment. Wallace Blue was interviewed after our dismissal from the office. I do not know what happened to him.

I was the seventh grade class president and continued to maintain an A average. We had a bunch of excellent students in our class. I maintained the number one ranking. Mr. James Jones was my homeroom teacher in the eighth grade. I continued to be the class president. I was a member of the National Honor Society and Student Council. Several of my classmates were in it. They were Leonard Swain and George Sanders. The physical education teacher for the girls was the chairman. Her name was Miss Yopp and was related to Miss Ely, our principal. Our science teacher was an excellent teacher and he was called Doc Davis. He had a reputation in the science community. He took George and Leonard under his wings and became their mentor. After a few years, Mr. Davis got a huge government job and resigned as a teacher. His job was in the science field. I did not have to take any midterm or final exams in mathematics. The reason was because of making a perfect score on them. The teacher told the students, "If you let Anderson take the exam, he was not going to put their grades in the curve. All of the students would say, "No." I automatically had an A in math. I was promoted to the ninth grade and continued to have an A average and the number one student.

When I was in the eighth grade, my best friend and I were the only players to advance to the high school varsity basketball team. Coach Clayton was the coach. We played on the team with Thomas Mclemore, Joe Nathan Armbrister, Jerry Bullard, Willis Lacey, and Lumboe Smith. Our first game was against Attucks High School. I played on the first team with Thomas Mclemore. A tall player by the name of Charlie Brown played for Attucks. I remember him because of a record with his name on it. It turned out to be a popular song. We really beat them in their gym. I scored thirty-four points. Thomas Mclemore was the star. He made thirty-three points. Both of us got a number of rebounds in the game. I went to my agriculture class the next day. The teacher lived in New-Town. When I got to his classroom, he gave me a compliment in front of the students. Mr. Sworn said, "We have a new star on the basketball team."

My math teacher was Mr. Ola Williams in the ninth grade. He was my homeroom teacher. My fifth grade homeroom teacher was his wife. He already knew my intellectual capabilities from his wife and the other teachers. Mr. Williams was an excellent math teacher whom I really admired. After making a few perfect math scores, I did not have to take a midterm or final exam. In high school, we had to take tests every six weeks. We called it the sixth week examination. I did not have to take a midterm or final exam in any of my high school math classes. I automatically had an A. The same thing happened in my physics class. I would put my mother's signature on the report card. She never looked at it and did not visit any of my teachers.

When I was in the ninth grade, the varsity basketball team was coached by Mr. McIntosh. My friend and I were on the team. In some of the games, I played on the first team. I averaged about thirty points in some of the games. My mother got a live-in domestic job in Glenn Cove, Long Island, New York. She worked for a rich Jewish family. I lived with her brother Charley in New-Town. He was a construction worker. The Jewish family wanted me to move to Long Island. They had planned to pay for my college education. Unfortunately, my uncle became ill and died in 1958. My mother did not return to her job. She decided to remain in Pompano.

I met a girl at every high school when I played basketball. Each year, they would meet me when I played at their school or at our school. We talked on the phone and wrote letters. I had sex with some of them. I had become a real player when I reached the seventh grade. Our friend Phillip Davis drove his father's car. It was a 1956 Power-Pack Chevrolet. The car was beautiful. The color of it was bronze.

Phillip was our riding buddy. In the seventh grade, our height was similar to our height as adults. In our era, we had to be twenty-one years old to be an adult. I remember when I became twenty-one years old. I bought a cigar. I lit it and walked up my street and said, "I am a man." I became as sick as a skunk and never smoked again. We had to be twenty-one years old to enter bars and nightclubs. The same thing applied to the pool halls. I made a fake identification card, which showed that I was twenty-one years old.

I helped my best friend make an identification card. He did not learn how to shoot pool and did not enter them. We went to the bars and nightclubs all over Broward County. Sometimes, we would go out of the county to them. We would hitch a ride with the older boys to and from those places. We used our fake identification cards. We hung out at the Melody Bar in Pompano and other establishments. In Deerfield, we went to the Blue Chip and Diamond Clubs. We went to the Corner Store Bar on State Road Seven Highway and Hillsborough Road in Deerfield. Sometimes, we went to the Paradise Club in Delray. In Ft. Lauderdale, we went to Little Joes, The Piccolo Tavern, The Down-Beat, Embassy, the Jazz Lounge, and the Elks Club with our fake identification cards. We went to the Paradise club in Dania. My favorite club was the Palms in Hallandale. I had an older female girlfriend at all of those spots. When I was in the fifth and sixth grade, we hung out at the local teenage centers. When it got late at night, my mother would make me come home. I would argue at her and be pissed off. When I entered the seventh grade, I put a stop to it. We would hitch a ride with the older boys, and she could not find me. On the weekends, I would spend a night with one of my women. I had plenty of sex with them. One of them was related to Rob Jones. Her name was Annie Ruth. She loved to wear tight shorts. She called me the pretty little boy because of her age. She was hot and fine as hell. Willis Lacey was one of my running partners. He taught me how to shoot pool. We hung out in the pool halls all over the county. We had to use fake identification cards. All of the clubs had a band and piccolo machines. People would drink, smoke, and dance in them. We got plenty of second-hand smoke. We came out of them smelling like smoke. Our clothes would smell like it. I have seen a large number of entertainers perform. I have seen Sam and Dave, Joe Tex, Jackie Wilson, Otis Redding, James Brown, Ray Charles, and many of them perform.

My personality was suppressed. On campus, I was quite, shy, and bashful. It changed when I reached the tenth grade. It was like that throughout elementary school too. I began drinking alcohol in elementary school. I would drink gin, moonshine, homebrew, buck, and wine. My mother gave me some to drink a few times. My friends and I started drinking in the seventh grade. We bought beer and wine. We had a drink which we called the schoolboy drink. We mixed White Port or Thunderbird wine with grape or strawberry soda.

Since the seventh grade, l worked to earn money. I worked on farms and the farmer's market. The majority of times, I was with Willis Lacey. Sometimes, my buddies and I would work at Port Everglades. We have helped unload cement, fertilizers, and bananas from the ships. I was playing bolita, which was called the Cuba number when I entered seventh grade. It was a form of gambling and was illegal.

The only grade I have ever made was an A in elementary or high school. I got a copy of my transcript from the school board. I was surprised to see some Bs and Cs on it when I was in high school. There must have been a mistake in the documentation. My elementary grades are correct. The problem happened in high school. Mrs. Ely, our principal, did not like me. She knew that I did not like her. If a student made anything lower than B, I thought they were dump. My standards were that high. After becoming an adult, I learned that I was wrong. Most people in the world are average, which is a C grade.

When I was in the eighth grade, a pair of tailor-made pants became popular. They were bell-bottomed pants and were called Ts. They were very popular in South Florida. A tailor called King-The-Tailor made them in Miami. He was located on Second Avenue in Overtown. It was a popular business district for blacks during segregation. I caught the Greyhound bus to Miami and had two pair made for me. The bell bottom would be between eighteen to twenty-two inches. When we went to school, we were dressed to kill both the boys and girls. It is nothing like today. We were not allowed to wear shorts to school unless it is physical education. I met a boy who was a few years older than me. He lived in Miami and was visiting his brother in Pompano. His name was Roosevelt George. He became my friend, and I hung out with him in Miami. He was real sporty and popular with the girls. I wanted to be like him. I met quite a few women when I would be with him. I hung out with him in the popular bars and nightclubs in Miami.

When I was in the ninth grade, I read an advertisement in a magazine. It was related to a tailoring company. They made tailor-made suits and pants for men. I subscribed to be one of their representatives. They sent me all of their samples in a small attaché case. I had my own small business. I had to measure and order two suits to get a free suit. When I measured and ordered four pair of pants, I would get a free pair of pants. I would take the case of samples in its case to school with me. The student would be taken to the boy's bathroom. They would select their sample. I would measure them and place their order. They had to make a deposit on their order. I was selling Ts when I was in high school. There were numerous selections, and the quality of the material was excellent. Some of the samples were silk. It turned out to be a good hustle. I was rewarded with quite a few free pants and suits.

I played on the varsity basketball team from the eighth grade until the eleventh grade. In the eleventh grade, I got mad with Coach Bullard and quit the team. I was co-captain of the team. I was young and did not know better. Moses Wilkes was the captain. The coach made me the point guard, and I did not like that position. The coach came to my house many times and begged me to return to the team. I was foolish and did not come back. I could really shoot the ball from any spot on the court. I have made fifty points in scrimmage. Sammie Lee and I paid Bullard a visit in Ft. Lauderdale, a year before his death. He said to me, "Charlie, you really let me down because of your potential on the court. I believe that we would have won the state championship your junior and senior years had you returned to the team." I told him that it was a mistake when I was young. I gave him an apology.

I remember the happiest day of my buddy's life. It happened in the ninth grade during the summer. We decided to wrestle in front of a group of boys. He managed to throw me his very first time. I got up and told him that I slipped down. I wanted to wrestle again. He refused and ran away. I was pissed off and knew the next time would be different. The next time we wrestled, I threw the shit out of him. It was not a slip. He played on the football team, and I didn't play. I was good enough to play because I was an excellent sandlot player. I went out for the team. Coach Boynton and Houston wanted me to be a quarterback. I did not like that position. I wanted to play as an offensive end, which is a wide receiver today. That is the reason I did not play on the team.

In high school from the seventh grade through my senior year, the school had a Student Government Day. It was for a week. The best academic students were selected to teach a class. I was always selected to teach mathematics. The only score I've ever made was a perfect one in mathematics. I was exempted and did not have to take the midterm or final exams in math. My transcript had a few Bs in math, which I know is not true. In physics, I made an A in both semesters. The transcript shows a C and a B, which is not true. Today, I have questions about the authenticity of my grades. In our era, the black principals had a lot of power. They did what they wanted to do, and sometimes, it was wrong. I usually made the highest grade in the class. That is why I have questions about the accuracy of my grades. The educators were not smart enough to use numerical scores with the grades. Instead, they utilized your grade with an alphabet. By using a student's numerical scores is the best way to rank students. It has been learned that it is the best way to compute averages.

During my senior year in high school, Mrs. Yopp approached me. She said, "You are the number one student in your class. If you make an A in each class, you will be the number one student. I made an A in all of my classes; however, the transcript is different. When I graduated, I was ranked as the number six student. That was a low blow, and I did not give a damn. I knew something was wrong. I took bookkeeping from Mr. Norbert Williams, my senior year. I was the only student who was exempted from the final examinations. I earned an A in both semesters. He had given us a weekend project. He said that whoever completed it correctly would not have to take the final exam. I was the only student to get it right in both semesters. It took the whole weekend to complete the project. He was at one of our class reunions. Frankie Flakes and her brother Sumpter were in the class. I was talking with Mr. Williams about it, and he concurred with me. Sammie Lee and Frankie Flakes were standing with us. For some strange unknown reason, Frankie became mad with me. It really does not matter, and I could care less. No love was lost over it.

Prior to our graduation, two of my classmates approached me in the hallway. They were Villis Sworn and Paulette Robinson, and they said, "Charlee, the principal and her secretary are changing some of your grades." I told them that I could not stop them, and I did not plan to attend college. I had earned two academic scholarships to college. They were at Howard University and Morehouse College. I showed the scholarship letters to some of my classmates. I think Villis was one of them. I earned the scholarships by taking an aptitude test at Northwestern High School in Miami, Florida. Only the best academic students took the test. It was given state-wide in certain locations. Among all of the black schools in Florida, I made the highest score on the test. I made a perfect score on the mathematics section. Miss Ely and Miss Martin, her secretary, brought me into the office and told me about the test results. They told the teachers about it too.

My homeroom teacher in my senior year was Miss Deliford. She was an excellent English teacher. Prior to the graduation, she had a private conversation with me in her classroom. Miss Deliford said, "Anderson, you know that you have been absent from school a whole lot of days. Miss Ely had planned not to give you a diploma." However, Miss Deliford and a few more of my teachers encouraged her to give it to me. Many years after graduating, Mrs. Deliford came to my restaurant in Ft. Lauderdale. We had a nice conversation, and I thanked her for the favor. She told me she was married and had twins. She had earned a PhD in education and worked for the school board.

I rode with Woodrow Showers on the night of graduation. He was pissed off because he did not get a diploma. He received a blank folder. Woodrow had to take additional classes to get his diploma.

The Bahamian girl who lived near my girlfriend came to my graduation. Her name was Eva and had a crush over me. She came from Ft. Lauderdale to see me. My girlfriend, Cynthia, was at her home in Ft. Lauderdale. I got into Eva's car. She gave me the keys. We had a few drinks and went to the Paradise Inn Transient House. We spent the night there and had plenty of sex. She called me a month later and told me she was pregnant. I lost contact with her.

I refused to take a beating from the dean of boys. Joe Smith was his name. I was kicked out of school for twenty-five days. I could not return to school until I received the punishment. We were given an examination every six weeks equaling to thirty days. I slipped on to the campus to take the exams. One of the students told the dean. He made me stop taking a test. I went into his office and told him I was sorry. I said, "I am not taking a beating. I asked him to let me wash and clean all of the windows." We bargained, and he allowed me to do that. After cleaning a few windows, he allowed me to take the rest of my exams. I was absent from school for five-sixths of that term. I made the highest score on all of the exams. That was talked about for a long time. No one could understand how I managed to do it. When I was out of school, I continued to study. Some of my friends would share their notes with me. Some of the underclass students continue to talk about it today. I spent most of my time with a girlfriend named Carolyn Swain. She had two children. I had a ton of sex with her and could care less about school.

I did not see eye to eye with the principal or the dean. We did not get along with each other. I avoided them as much as possible. I took most of my courses with the advanced students. I took trigonometry with them my senior year. Coach Bullard was the teacher. I did not have to take any of the tests after the first semester because of making a perfect score. In fact, I did not have to participate in the class. His wife and children would be in Delray. He would give me his car keys and let me transport them to Pompano. It happened in most of the second semester. In the second semester, I did not have to take the exam. Instead of an A, I have a B on the transcript. On the transcript, each teacher was supposed to write their names next to the course. My transcript is not consistent with the signatures. In the segregation era, all of the black principals were given a tremendous amount of power by the school board. Most of them were religious and made their rules. Students were abused by the beatings with those thick paddles. A lot of fear was in the hearts of a large number of students. They made some of the rules and could do whatever they thought was right. I knew that it was a no-win situation between the administrators and me. Hell, I knew the power of the old mighty ink pen and paper. The principal personally told me she was going to change my grades. I was told that I did not deserve the valedictorian award because I would be a bad representation for the school. I told her, "I could care less because I did not plan to go to college. I was going to become a professional gambler. I threw both of my academic scholarships in the garbage can." I earned an academic scholarship to Morehouse College and Howard University. The best students at all of the segregated schools in Florida were allowed to take the test. Our area was represented by Northwestern High School in Miami, Florida. I made the highest score in Florida with a perfect score on the mathematics section. I already knew that Mrs. Ely was going to change some of my grades. She told me that she could do it based upon my unexcused absenteeism. It was nothing I could do because I was a powerless student. In Coral Springs, since I have been an adult, that rule was challenged by a white student. I think she prevailed in a lawsuit. In my era, I did not know anything about filing a lawsuit. That was unheard of in our community.

The school held a spelling bee contest in the agriculture class-room. It was when I was a junior or senior. A classmate won it who was the valedictorian in our class. His name was George Sanders and was an outstanding student. I have an utmost respect for him. He had a scholarship to Morehouse College and became an excellent physician. He made a perfect score on the SAT. During my senior year, I came to school late when the SAT examination was given to seniors. I was unaware of the test. Nobody told me about it. When I arrived at school, the test was being given to the seniors in the library. My homeroom teacher, Miss Deliford, took me to the library. One fourth of the test had been taken by the students.

I was not allowed to take that portion of the test. The principal and librarian told me I had to start on the second section along with my classmates. I only took three-fourths of the senior exam and made an excellent score. It is possible that I could have made a perfect score on it. I believe that the librarian and principal were glad I was late.

The chairperson who administered the spelling bee contest was the librarian named Miss Smith. When she spoke, her accent was very polished and proper. She was a very good friend of the principal. She went to the office frequently. Miss Deliford encouraged me to get in the contest and felt that I would be the winner. It turned out to be false because I was eliminated in about the third round of it. I have never forgotten about it. The librarian tricked me. I really believe that it was intentional even today. I was eliminated with a very simple, easy word to spell. The word was either shirt or skirt. I spelled the word correctly, and she alleged that I did not spell it right. In fact, I spelled both words because you have a second chance to spell a word. I spelled both of them correctly. From that day on, I hated that lady because she eliminated me improperly. George was the principal's favorite student, and the librarian knew it. I really believe it was a setup. Miss Deliford had questions about my elimination. She said to me, "I do not understand the elimination because you spelled both of the words." I told my homeroom teacher that the woman was a thief. I really believe I would have won that contest. I was Miss Deliford's favorite student. I believe I could have scored with her. But I gave her utmost respect and cared a lot about her.

In the ninth grade, I got into an altercation with my friend in front of the agriculture classroom. It was about some hubcaps that were stolen over the weekend. At this time, Woodrow Shivers was another friend. He was allowed to drive his brother's car. We would steal hubcaps from cars parked at the bars and nightclubs. We did it during the night. Woodrow and my buddy stole them while I remained seated in the car. We went back to Pompano. When we got home, I told them how we were going to divide the hubcaps. I said, "Half of them belong to me. You will have to split the other half between you." It was raining, and we were parked in from of an apartment. Sammie Lee's sister lived there. He was in the backseat of the car with the stolen goods. He did not like my formula. He grabbed all of the hubcaps and ran into the apartment. I chased him and cursed him out. On Monday, the next day, I went to the front of the school where bicycles were parked. I stole one of them and rode it to his sister's apartment. Mama Lou was not home. It was in the projects next to Sanders Park. I got a piece of wire and picked the lock on the door. I took all of the hubcaps to my house. Another friend whose name is Lorenzo Nelson saw me on the bike. He mentioned it to my best friend. He went home and didn't see the hubcaps. He knew I had gotten them. When I arrived to school the agriculture students were on their break. A group of us were standing in front of the classroom. My buddy approached me and said, "I want you to return the hubcaps," and I said that, "I am not going to give you shit." Sammie Lee became upset and went and got a large hoe from the classroom. When he drew it back, I ran away from him. He threw it down, and I stopped running. We stood on the grass and were getting ready to fight. I told him that I was going to beat his ass. "You are going to need that hoe now." Coach Boynton and Collier ran on to the grass and stopped the fight. They took us to the office to the dean and principal. We were interviewed by them. My buddy told them that I had broken into his sister's apartment. He said, "Then he stole something out of it. We don't know how he got into it. The doors and windows were locked when we got home." Mr. Smith, the dean, was so happy. A while back when I was absent from school, we had an encounter. He came to the house to talk to my mother. I told him that I was the man of the house. I told my mother, "You sit down while I go into my bedroom." She said to the dean, "He is going to get the shotgun, and you had better leave the house." He ran out of the house and got into his car. I ran into the street and fired a shot at his car. He was driving so fast, and I don't think he heard the shot. When he arrived at the school, he told the principal and some teachers about it. He said that I was bad and needed some help. After learning about the burglary, they said, "If you broke into his house, you will do the same to our house." Oh boy, he was happy. He said, "I have your bad ass now. We are going to call the police." They left us in the room alone. I became a politician on that day. I leaned over and whispered in my buddy's ear. I said, "If I go to jail, I will no longer be your friend." I said, "When I get out, I will beat your ass." Then I said our friendship is important. "You keep your mouth closed. I will give the hubcaps plus a ten dollar bill." He liked that offer and agreed with me. When the black policeman arrived, they returned to the room with us. They had made a crucial mistake by leaving us alone in the room. Officer Criswell asked me had I broken into the apartment. I said, "No," and there is no proof that I did it." Afterward, he attempted to question my buddy.

He told the officer that he was not sure I had broken into it. The officer told the dean and principal that there was no evidence against me. He made a report and left from the school.

I was absent from school most of time from the tenth grade through my senior year. I missed school every Friday and Monday. I was shooting pool for money at the Pool-Rooms. I had become an excellent shooter and won plenty of money. I went to school on Tuesdays, Wednesdays, and Thursdays. I had to be a gifted student, but that was unheard of in those days. My homeroom teacher and the principal confronted me in the office. They asked me, "Who is your role model and who would you like to pattern after?" I said, "I want to be like Poe-Counter, the houseman at the pool hall." Then I said, "I want to be a hustler and gambler just like two-spot Tom and Wallace Blue." The dean heard the conversation and said, "You are going to waste a very talented mind." Miss Deliford said, "You have two scholarships. Why don't you take advantage of them?" I said to them, "No." I will get rich as a hustler before my classmates finish college." I was wrong about that issue. One day when I came to school on a Tuesday, my classmates had posted some signs on campus. The signs stated, "Impeach the senior class president. He is always absent to attend meetings." I made an announcement and told them, "That is the reason I have a vice president." However, they were unsuccessful with the impeachment. My vice president took over the meetings.

When I was in the tenth grade, some of my classmates had met some girls from Ft. Lauderdale. They lived in the Golden Heights area. Renard Brown, Lonnie Clyde Black, Lemuel Allen, and Woodrow Showers were the classmates. They bragged about the Golden Height girls. It was a newly developed area, and the homes were made with cement. They were nice homes with a lot of teachers living in them. A birthday party was given on a Saturday night. The girl was from the Bahama Islands, and Eva was her name. Woodrow was unavailable to transport the others to the party. One of them saw me driving my stepfather's car and asked me to take them to the party. A lot of teenagers were at the party. I must have gotten a dozen phone numbers, and two of them were from sisters. I didn't know I had hit on two sisters until looking at the phone numbers. Eva was crazy about me. She did all she could to get me, but I didn't care too much about her. Renard and Lonnie alleged I had taken their girlfriend from them. A young lady who was four year younger than me became my girlfriend. Her name was Cynthia Marie Moton. Many years later, she became my wife. When I met her, she was a virgin. She became pregnant when I took her to my senior prom. We had a daughter who is Adrianne Yvette Anderson born on 1962. We were not allowed to go to hotels. A room was rented by the hour or by the night for the black folks. They were called transient rooms. When the prom had ended, I went to one of the rooms. Its name was the Paradise Rooms. It was located on Powerline Road just north of Hammondville Road in Pompano. I had a few drinks with my friends before going there. I left Cynthia in my car and paid for the night. When I returned to my hot rod car, she told me she was not going in there. She locked the doors. I encouraged her to unlock the doors. Then I grabbed her and picked her up and carried her on my shoulders into the room. I locked the door to our room. I took both of our clothes off. We made love with each other and went to sleep. Since it was on my prom date, I thought she was supposed to give it up. Today, it would be rape. I took her home the next day. She was about seven months pregnant when her parents learned about it. They were upset at both of us. Cynthia had to drop out of school to have our daughter. In those days, if a girl had a baby, she could not return to her school. The principal would not allow them to return to the school. She was attending Dillard when she became pregnant. I had to pay seven dollars per week for child support. She enrolled in Dania at Attucks High School. Her parents bought her a car to go to school. She spent several years there and graduated. After that, she went to Bethune Cookman College in Daytona. She had a wonderful mother who had a few years of college education. She said that I was very bright and should go to college. Cynthia was my main girlfriend, and I loved her dearly. Those were some of the best days of my life. I was real sporty and popular with the girls. I thought you had to have more than one to be a sport. I had plenty of them. I dated a few of her classmates and upper and under classman. One of them was Harriett Grant. She told me that she was pregnant by me. She dropped out of school and moved to Philadelphia. I lost contact with her. A girl by the name of Francis Sutton was another girlfriend. I had a lot of sex with both of them. There were many more relationships.

I attended summer school recreation in my junior and senior years. In both summers, I won the first place trophy by playing table tennis, which is ping-pong. It was won in Deerfield and in Ft. Lauderdale. The reason I won because the best players did not attend the summer recreation program those years. The best players were Eugene Gillis, Elijah Larkins, and Thomas Mclemore. I was not as good as them. When I was in the eleventh grade, Mr. Swom had a two-man basketball team tournament during the summer. Sammie Lee and I were teammates. The teams had to win by two points or more than the losing team. The game would be won with twenty points. The winning team had to have two points or more than the losing team to win. In the third round, we beat and eliminated Thomas Mclemore and Joe Nathan Armblister. We played the championship game against Rufus (Tree) Hughes and Peter-The-Gun. The games were played on the outdoor basketball court at West-Side Park. Both of the teams were tied with eighteen points. We had the ball, and I passed it to my buddy. He drove the ball to the basket, and Rufus blocked his shot. They got the rebound, and Pete made a left hook under the basket and beat us. We won the runner's up trophy. I told my buddy that I should have taken the last shot. I believed that we would have won the game.

In Pompano, I was dating Carolyn Swain and Mary Ann Harris. I had a ton of sex with both of them. Mary Anne was one of the most special women I've dated. She was my girlfriend when Cynthia was attending college. I was in love with both of them. I was drafted by the U.S. Army during the Vietnam War.

I went to the office where I was registered. I told the white lady, "I am the only son in the family. I thought that would prevent me from being drafted." She told me, "All of us have problems." As I was leaving, she called me into the office. She told me, "There is a law to keep you out of the military. You would have to be twenty-five years old and have a child under five years old." I met the criteria. I called Cynthia in Daytona at her college. I told her, "If you want to keep me, we have to get married. Then I said, "I am like Muhammad Ali. I have not done anything to those folks in Vietnam. After that, I went to Mary Ann's house and told her the reason I had to get married. She was badly hurt. We cried and had sex in the passenger seat of my 1965 Stingray Corvette. It had the 427 engine in it. Cynthia would soon be on her summer break from college. We went and did our blood work for marriage. We were married in Light House Point, Florida. It was a secret marriage. Our parents were not aware of it. The reason was I did not earn enough money to support my wife. I took a copy of my daughter's birth certificate and marriage license to the Selective Board of Registration. It kept me out of the Army. When Cynthia was attending college, I had women all over South Florida. Some of them wanted me to be their pimp. I was a good gambler and hustler and did not need their money. I refused to be their pimp. A lady named Barbara Major was another girlfriend. She was from Dania, Florida. She loved me dearly and would give me her heart. Along with shooting pool and dice, I sold some pot. I would go to Liberty City, Opa Locka, and Over-Town in Miami. I would buy about three small matchboxes with the weed in them. We had some undeveloped property next to our house in New-Town. It was grown up with weeds and trees. I would get leaves from certain plants and let them get dry. Then I would buy some tea that were in bags. When the leaves were dry, I would mix the leaves, tea, and the pot together. Then I would roll about two hundred joints and sell them. I charged one dollar for each joint. I sold the pot at the bars, nightclubs, and gambling facilities. At the bars, I would go into the restrooms. When some of the males came in there, I would light up a joint. After getting a puff from one of them they would say, " Charlee went to the city in his vette and bought some good shit from Miami." After that, I would sell all of my grass to the smokers. Along with that, I was a numbers banker for a year. My friends accused me of growing pot on the vacant lot. I kept my friends blasted with it. Sometimes, we would mix cigarette ashes in our booze to get high. I made all of my women get high except Cynthia and Mary Ann. I went to Orlando to visit some of my relatives. My first cousin whose name is Fannie Bell took me out. I met a fine chick who was her friend. We went on a double date to several clubs and bars on Church Street. A drug was used, which was not used in South Florida. It was ammonia-nitrate. It was in the pharmacy department and could be bought without a prescription. The vials were wrapped under a mesh like cloth. Then we would put it to our nose and squeeze it. The fumes were inhaled after the vial was broken. That shit gave us a "boss ass high." Since the vials were crushed after squeezing them, I referred to them as pops. When I returned to Pompano, I introduced it into our neighborhood. They were packed by the dozen into a tin container. The cost was three dollars per container. I turned out to be a regular customer. I would purchase ten of the containers for thirty dollars. Then I would sell each vial for a dollar. I made a ninety dollars profit on the purchase. I think that the drug was intended to be used for respiratory diseases. After introducing it to our community, I would sell out on the weekends. When I went to one of the transient houses to have sex, a lot of those drugs would be in my possession. I would sniff that shit and get messed up. Most of my women used it too. I went to every transient house from West Palm Beach to Miami. In Pompano, I went to the Fat-Man Rooming House, The Red Cherry, Booker-T's Inn, and The Paradise. Sometimes, on the weekend I spent the night with one of my women.

A lot of women became pregnant by me. It was illegal to have an abortion. One of our teachers was married to a laboratory technician. We called him Doc-Robinson. He learned how to perform illegal abortions. He charged about eighty dollars for it. Three of my women had five abortions over a period of time. Each one had five abortions. That was a total of fifteen. I am not revealing their names for their privacy. One of them is dead, and her name was Barbara. That is the only reason to mention her name. When abortions became legal, three women had abortions. Two of them were married and separated from their husbands. They had not gotten a divorce were the reason for it. One of my girlfriends would have had twins. I was married when she was my girlfriend. I was about twenty years her senior. I was forty years old while she was twenty. She had a religious mother who wanted her to have the twins and was unable to discourage the abortion. I always wanted a lot of children. I am not happy for what happened during my past. I wish those kids had been born. I would have had nineteen children. I am not happy for having been a womanizer. I have had over five hundred one-night stands. I had some of them all over the U.S. and in foreign countries. If I had to do it all over again, it would be different. I was living too fast. There was plenty of gambling, selling drugs, and sex. I have prayed to *God* and asked for repentance and forgiveness for all of those sins. I pray daily during the day.

Sometimes, two of my buddies and me would drive to Miami on the weekends. We would buy some sex from the black prostitutes in Liberty City. It was done quite often with them. I met a former physical education teacher who was a pimp in Miami. He was supposed to have been an expert in judo. When he was at Ely High School, he introduced a spring board into stunts and tumbling exercises. He knew that I was popular to women. He gave me his number and wanted to introduce me into pimping. I did not like him, and he never knew it. When I went out on dates, I would take Sammie Lee, my friend, with me. We went to the Diamond Club in Deerfield. When we returned to my car, the battery had been stolen. I told my girlfriend that I was going to teach her how to steal a battery. Cynthia and Mary Ann were not treated like that. I told my woman I was too clean to carry the battery. All of us located a car. I popped the hood open and gave her the tools. She used the tools and removed the battery. Then I made her carry it and put it in my 1954 Ford. She was a nice classy woman. On another occasion, Sammie Lee went out with my girlfriend and me. It was a different one that lived in Delray. We had a flat tire on the way to her house. I gave her the jack and spare tire and made her do the work. I have always used bad words. I told her that was her job and said, "Bitch, I am too clean to change that tire." She did it without an argument or fight. If she hadn't, she would have gotten a good old ass beating. She was fine and pretty. I dated her for many years. Delray, Deerfield, and Pearl City were my stomping grounds. I had a lot of women in those areas. Most of them lived in Palm Beach County. One of my "basketball girls" lived in Delray and went to Carver High School. Her name was Betty Williams. We played basketball against her school. I was with her and got left by the bus. She and a family member drove me home. She was very attractive.

A year later, Lorenzo Nelson met her in Pompano. He never knew I was spending time with her. He said she was his girlfriend. She did not give him the time of day. In the seventh grade, I had a big crush over Shirley Holmes. My buddy and I would go to her house. I was too shy and bashful to get her. The relationship did not materialize. She is a special person to me, and I continue to care for her today. I think that she is so fine, sexy, and good looking.

When I played basketball in the tenth grade, Thomas Mclemore was a senior. We played on the same team and became friends. The home economics teacher was his girlfriend. We have been in her classroom when school had turned out. I have seen her give him money, hug, and kiss. Both of them are dead. I think she was married. I would make sure no one was coming to the classroom. She and the French teacher were friends. We had a gay, male teacher whose name was Mr. Goggins. He went on a sabbatical leave to Paris, France. The position was filled by a female French teacher. She had a huge crush over me. When I was in the eleventh grade, she became my lover. When school was turned out, Thomas and I would go to the economics teacher room. They would spend some time together. Then we would walk to the French teacher's room. She would be waiting for me. Sometimes, she would give me a twenty dollar bill. I think she was separated from her husband. I refuse to reveal their names for privacy reasons. I took French II from her when I was a senior. Thomas had graduated and was attending college. I think some of the classmates knew about the crush over me. One day, when school was dismissed, I was in her classroom. We forgot to lock the door for privacy. All of a sudden, we started kissing each other. She massaged my dick with her hands. She told me how much she loved me. I put my hands between her legs and felt that fat pussy. All of a sudden, my cousin came into the classroom. We were shocked and surprised. I don't think he saw our feelings for each other. His name is Renard Brown. He chose to blackmail the teacher. He said, "If you give Charlie Lee an A, you had better give me one too. He said, "He is always absent from school." She promised that he would get an A too. He caught us when we were hugging and kissing. The teacher asked me to drive her car during the homecoming parade for the football team. When I was driving the car, she would feel my penis and put one of my hands in her vagina. I made love with her a few times. We went to the Harris Guest House in Hollywood. She was a sweetheart, and I would love to see her today if she's still alive. I am not revealing her name. My cousin remembered the incident when he caught us in the act. After graduating, I lost contact with her. I would love to see her today.

We had a boys and girls varsity basketball team. A player whose name was Etta Flu-Ellen became my girlfriend. All of us called her

"ET". She was two grades ahead of me. She lived across the tracks in the labor camp. I would walk her home after the games. Sometimes, I would go to her house on the weekends. I had plenty of sex with her. Charles Ellington's wife whose name is Emma remembered the relationship. I lost contact with her after my graduation. She was a nice young lady.

When I was in the tenth and eleventh grades, I had quite a few underclass girlfriends. My favorite girlfriend was Nardine Blue. I became very friendly with her mother, Mrs. Inez Blue. Nardine's brother, James and I were very good friends. He spent a couple of weekends with me at my aunt's house in Miami. We met quite a few young ladies in Miami. They thought we were brothers. The only thing I did with Nardine was to hug and kiss her. I was crazy about her. I gave my class ring to her. Her mother told me I could take her to the junior prom. She changed her mind and refused to let Nardine go with me. I took a girl from Ft. Lauderdale whose name was Joyce Shields to the prom. I didn't have any sex with Nardine. She was young, and I was saving her for a later date. I was having sex with different girlfriends. I would leave Nardine's house. Then I would go to Carolyn Swain's house. She had two children and was giving it up. Sometimes, we would sit on the porch. Nardine became very upset with me and separated me. She would not give a reason for it. Nardine really broke my heart. A little after my 70th birthday, we became friends and only friends. I asked her to tell me the reason why she separated me. Nardine told me, "Your friend Rufus Hughes told me about Carolyn Swain." He said that we would be sitting on the porch. Nardine walked near the house and saw Carolyn and me. We were hugging and kissing each other. She told me that she was really hurt. She said that was the reason why she separated me. I gave her an apology. Rufus was dating Carolyn's sister whose name was Clairetha Swain. We were supposed to be friends. We played a lot of basketball together. His nickname is Tree. We were running buddies. He loaned me his 1956 Power-Pack Chevy for the prom.

Another girlfriend was Ruthie Mae Jones. We dated for several years. She refused to have sex with me, and that is the reason why we separated. It was mentioned to her father, and he discouraged her from giving it up. When I was in my mid-sixties, I became friendly with her. She kind of scared me away from her. She told me that she was very hot natured and like plenty of sex. I was not sure if I could satisfy her. I think she liked it too often for me. I chose not to get involved with her. I took her out several times and treated her with class. Another underclass girlfriend was Lillian Samuels. She was real tall. One of her nephews is a professional football player. On Saturday and Sunday nights, we would walk to West-Side Park. We had plenty of sex on the benches. Several times, we had it on the embankment next to the swimming pool. We would be on the blind side of the pool. We broke up because of having too many girlfriends. A classmate whose name is Lloyd King became her next boyfriend. She had a few children by him. Another one was Annie Ruth Wimberley. The only thing we did was hug and kiss. That did not last too long. The same thing applied with Mary Philpart who lived in Deerfield. I never had a chance to score with them. The last one was Ruby Lymons. She was from Deerfield. I dated her for several years. She had real big beautiful eyes.

I took her to the movie theatre several times. Her mother would go with us. The only thing I did was to hug and kiss her. I got tired of that shit and let go of her. Ruby and Frankie Rose Taylor were best friends.

She ended up marrying my cousin whose name is Douglas Allen. At that time, a classmate whose name is Vernon Robinson was her boyfriend. Sometimes, all of us would be together. A friend whose name is Raymond Shivers became her boyfriend. I think she had a couple of children by him. I supposed that her mother had stopped riding shotgun with her daughter.

When I was in the eleventh grade, I had another friend whose name was Carroll Jackson. He worked as a dishwasher at Howard Johnson's restaurant. He owned a nice Ford car. Sometimes, I would borrow it to go to my girlfriend's house in Ft. Lauderdale. During that school term, he got me a job as a dishwasher at the restaurant. The school was dismissed at 3:30 in the evening. We had to be on the job at four o'clock. Sometimes, we worked as late as 2:00 in the morning. The starting pay was about twenty-five cents per hour. It took a year to save ninety-nine dollars. I saw a 1954 Ford which was for sale by a private white owner. I got my money and had my stepfather transport me to the car. When we arrived at the house, the owner's selling price was one hundred and thirty-two dollars.

My stepfather told the man, "It took him a year to save ninety-nine dollars." Then I said, "I'm in high school and work as dishwasher at Howard Johnson's restaurant. He said that was his favorite eating place, and I could get the car for ninety-nine dollars. That was my very first automobile. When I graduated from high school, I quit the job. I hung out at the pool room and won a lot of money. I was able to pay my child support, which was twenty-eight dollars per month.

I was on the high school basketball team from the eighth grade through the eleventh grade. In the eleventh grade, I quit the team in the middle of the season. I was on first team and was the co-captain.

Our coach was named Coach Bullard. In the ninth and tenth grade, I played on the first teams. Our Coach was Coach Mcintosh. When I was in the eighth grade, I was on the first team. Our coach was Coach Clayton. I was in the seventh grade when I played junior varsity basketball. I averaged thirty-four points per game. My friend, Wine, was the best rebounder I was the best shooter on the team. We lost only one regular season game. Our coach was Coach Boynton

When I was in the eleventh grade, a tall beautiful lady moved in an apartment in my neighborhood. She was a redbone, and her name was Minnie Hargrett. She was married to Clarence Hargrett. She became my girlfriend. I went with her until I had graduated from high school. She was from North or South Carolina. She was a relative or friend of Nettie Griffin who was her neighbor. I had sex with Minnie three or four days a week. She would meet me when I walked in the area. Her husband would be at his job. Nettie was a previous girlfriend too.

During the 1960s, Sammie Lee and I became interested in law enforcement work. We submitted applications with Deerfield, Pompano, and Ft. Lauderdale police departments. We failed the test with all of those agencies. Whoever graded our test papers were dishonest with the scores. Deerfield Police gave us a score in the mid-twenties, and I knew that was a lie. I answered more than twenty math problems on the test. We couldn't do anything about it. People were not suing for discrimination. The City of Ft. Lauderdale really stuck it to me, and it was really a low blow. A minimum of seventy points had to be scored on the police test. When I received my results, it was sixty-nine and a half percent. That was another lie. In those days, the police departments had already handpicked a black for the job. I submitted an application with the City of Coral Gables for the police officer position. It was identical to the test given by the City of Ft. Lauderdale. The City of Ft. Lauderdale sent me a score that was 69.5.

It left a bad taste about the City of Ft. Lauderdale. You had to make a minimum of 70% to pass. In Coral Gables, I made the highest score on the test. It was 98%. My mother talked against the job. She said it was too dangerous, and she was afraid I might get killed. I didn't take the job offer.

When Woodrow returned to school for the makeup courses, he finally got a diploma. Purcell Blue had to do the same thing. He was a year ahead of us. Woodrow planned to go into the air force and asked me to give some tutoring lessons. He was very illiterate and never passed the entrance test for the military. One day, we rode our bicycles on the beach and looked for a job. We rode on them from Deerfield to Ft. Lauderdale and stopped at every business. The only thing we got was promises. I always read the classified section in the newspaper. In 1961, a truck driver position was advertised in the classified section of the newspaper. It was with O'Brien Associates. It was a wholesale supplier for air-condition and refrigeration businesses. The business was open at eight in the morning. In this line of business they were the largest in Florida. I drove my car to Ft. Lauderdale and arrived at the office at five o'clock in the morning. I was the first and only black to apply for the job. A few minutes later, a white man arrived for the job. When the manager arrived and opened the business, about fifty people stood in a line. The manager asked the white man who stood next to me, "Who was the first person to arrive for the job?" He pointed at me. The manager took me into his office and interviewed me. His name was Mr. Shanahan. After the interview, he introduced me to his assistant manager. He was a young Frenchman or Canadian and a few years my senior. They were impressed with my level of intelligence and having a high school diploma. They took me into the warehouse and gave me an application to complete. The manager told me that I had the job and to stick around until the others were interviewed. They were finished within a matter hours. I was paid thirty-five dollars per week and had to work five and a half days. It was forty-four hours for thirty-five dollars.

That was less than a dollar per hour. The managers took orders over the phone along with counter-sales work. I made deliveries primarily in Broward County. After working hard after my first week, I was given a pay raise. My salary was increased to forty dollars per week for the forty-four hours. I was making almost a dollar per hour. It was about ninety-three and a half cents per hour. Both of the managers told me that I would be promoted when a position became available as a counter-salesman. They didn't know that I read the classified section in the newspaper every week. After working there for four years, I was earning sixty-five dollars a week. On a Sunday, I read the job section in the newspaper and saw their advertisement. It was a counter-sales position that offered a salary plus commission and additional pay for merits. When I arrived to work on Monday, they interviewed a number of white applicants for the job. They hired a white male who was about my age. I had learned everything about the business. I did not remind them about what they had told me about that job. After hiring the new employee, they told me, "We want you to teach him everything about the business." I did not like that and did not intend to teach him everything. The company did not hold back any pay in arrears. We were dead even when I received my pay. I got my check when I finished working on Saturday and did not return there for work. I had applied at Chris-Craft Corporation in Pompano to work as a fiberglass laminator trainee. My starting pay was seventy-five dollars per week for forty hours. It was less hours with more pay. We made the first forty-seven feet long yacht for Jerry Lewis, the entertainer. After becoming a skilled laminator, I was able to get several part-time jobs along with the work at Chris-Craft. The boat business was booming in 1964. I continued to read the job section in the newspaper.

I was working for O'Brien Associates. The Pompano Canal was across the street from my house. One day, when I was on route to my house in the pickup truck, I saw about ten cars parked, and people were standing on the embankment next to the canal. I stopped to see what was wrong. I saw a car in the center of the canal. A woman and three or four small children were in the car. It was Nettie Griffin's sister and her children. I believe they were her children. All of the folks were standing and looking at them. Nobody attempted to help them. I got out of the truck and took off everything except my underwear.

I jumped into the canal and swam to the car. It was still floating on the surface of the water. I told Lela Griffin that I was getting the children first and to be calm. I was able to get Lela Griffin and all of the children out of the canal. The car got filled with water and sunk to the bottom of the canal. The water was very deep and infested with alligators and possibly some crocodiles. They got into the truck, and I took them home. She was my neighbor and lived a few houses up the street from my house.

My friend Woodrow would challenge me by wrestling. He was never strong enough to throw me. After tutoring him, we would wrestle about ten times next to the Love-Land Theatre. I would place one hand behind my back and throw him every time. He was real weak or I was strong as hell.

I have had some relationships with women much older than me. Most of my women would buy me nice gifts and plenty of money. Some of them were younger than me. A few years after high school, I had a girlfriend who was older than me. She had a daughter about my age. They lived in Liberty Park. I don't remember her name. She had a daughter by a man who became gay. He is dead and his name was Jack Swain. I believe I could have scored with the daughter because of the way she looked at me. We dated for several years. The sex was good. I have always had a rule with women. If I did not get it within ten days, it was over. I did not have that rule with my first wife and Nardine Blue.

I had become a very good hustler by shooting dice and pool when I was in my early twenties. When I was twenty-four years old, I won nearly $80,000 over the weekend gambling. I won most of it in a dice game against the manager of the Hess Gas at Hammondville and Powerline Road. I paid cash for a brand-new 1965 Stingray Corvette. It had the big 427 engine with a four-speed standard shift transmission. The car was red with a white convertible top. I stopped shooting pool for money because of having to give odds to get a game. I could run the table without a miss. I was in my prime and had become a pool shark. I made more money shooting dice and didn't have to give odds. Along with that, I would hustle a little pot for money. I regret giving up billiards because I really enjoyed playing the game. I was in my prime. When I had that vette, I had women all over Florida. The legendary famous singer performed in

Ft. Lauderdale on Thanksgiving. He was Otis Redding and put on a great show. We were in a building that was once a bowling alley, which was turned into a nightclub. Prior to the show, I went to a friend's house. They were Woodrow and Joan Showers. A real beautiful chick was at their residence. They introduced me to her, and we really hit it off. I took her to the show in my car. After the show, I took her to Harris Guest House in Ft. Lauderdale. It was a transient house. I paid for the whole weekend. Oh boy, did we have some great romance and sex. I don't remember her name, and I never saw her again. Many years later, I asked Joan if she remember the young lady. She answered negatively. I was too busy to keep in contact with the young lady. It just turned out to be another one-night stand. I forgot to get her address and phone number.

A few years prior to getting the Corvette, I owned a 1936 Ford Hot Rod with a 283 Corvette engine. The engine had three two-barreled carburetors. The rumored seat was removed when the car was customized. The paint was a beautiful dark blue and in small alphabets was painted TNT along the edge of the two doors. All of the folks called the car TNT. One day, I was getting ready to drag race against R C Baker. We faced West on Northwest 15th Street just west of Northwest 6th Avenue. A City of Pompano police officer hid and observed us. As soon as we took off in the race, he chased us with his lights and siren on. I decided to make a U-turn and went the opposite direction. I drove east on Northwest 15th Street very fast. I was smoking the police car. I got into an accident with another car when I was getting ready to go across Northwest 3rd Avenue. It was a three-way intersection with stop signs. A car traveled in a different direction entered the intersection, and my car collided with it. As a result of the accident, I was apprehended. My car slid on to the vacant lot on the north side of 15th Street which intersected with Northwest 3rd Avenue. Today, there's a kindergarten for children and homes in that area.

About five or six white policeman snatched me out of my car. They handcuffed and arrested me. Their adrenaline was pumping, and they used derogatory words at me. They said, "You are a bad ass nigger, and we are putting you in jail." That was around 1962 or 1963. They threw me into a squad car and took me to jail. I was charged with the accident along with fleeing, careless, and reckless driving. I was placed under a $1,500 bond. In front of a jail cell, they took the cuffs off. While we were in the hallway, the officers intimidated me and tried to provoke a fight. I was called a dump stupid ass nigger. They were getting ready to beat and rough me up. The only black officer came into the room. He was officer Criswell, and he told them that he knew me. *God* must have sent him to the station. I am sure they would have beaten me up and charged me with a felony. The felony would have been resisting an arrest with violence. Fortunately, I had a bank account and bailed out of jail shortly. Ironically, I got to know one of the policeman and the owner of the car involved in the accident. I got to know them many years later.

During the summer after graduating from high school, I met Joan George. She was from Sebring, Florida, and lived with her father in Sanders Park. He was employed by the Sheriff's Department. I took her out in my hot rod 1936 Ford. We went out the whole weekend. She had to return to Sebring to attend school. I didn't try to score with her. The only thing we did was to hug and kiss each other. She promised me that she would contact me whenever she returned to Pompano. I forgot to give information, and she was unable to contact me. The next time I saw her was at the homecoming football game at Ely High School. She was with my friend who was Woodrow Shivers. Mamie Lee Flakes had fixed him up with her. My girlfriend was with me, and she was from Dania, Florida. Her name was Barbara Major. Woodrow and I took a walk and left the women behind. I said, "Woodrow, you have my woman." He said, "Charlee, you have a foxy, fine, and pretty woman with you. Please let me have her and don't bother her." I kept the promise. They invited me to their wedding. Joan was dedicated and loyal to their marriage. She loved her husband dearly and remained with him until his death. I taught him everything he knew, and he always wanted to be like me. We were friends and have been with many women on double dates over the years. One date really stands out in my mind. It was in Sanders Park and on the weekend. We have a classmate whose name is Jimmy Lane. His sister is Elizabeth Eaton. She was a teenager and much younger than us. She had a party at the house. Her boyfriend was from Ft. Lauderdale and was at the party. The party lasted two days on the weekend. There was plenty of alcohol and pot. I had a deck of cards. It was rather late and only eight people remained at the party. I came up with the ingenious idea to play a game with the cards. The game was called strip-me-naked. Liz, had two female friends at the party They came by themselves. It was perfect for me and Woodrow. Woodrow and I came along. The other two girls were Elizabeth's friends. They came to the party together. Prior to playing the game, I made a statement. I said, "When we are nearly naked, we would go to a bedroom. I took a young lady to a bedroom whose name was Gladys. She was much younger than me. I think she was a virgin. That was my first time meeting her. I had sex with her for two days at the party. I didn't know where she lived and never saw her anymore. Many years later, Elizabeth told me that she became pregnant at the party. She said that it was my child. When I was almost sixty years old, I stumbled across Gladys in Collier City. It turned out that our mothers were friends. She refused to talk with me and alleged that I raped her at the party. I tried to reunite with her with negative results. She refused all of my inquiries about the pregnancy. I really wanted to score again with her. Her oldest son did resemble me. She moved, and I lost contact with her.

I attended college at Florida Atlantic University in Boca Raton in 1971 and 1972. I was pursuing a Bachelor's Degree in Criminal Justice. One of the arresting officers from Pompano attended a course with me. He was really shocked to see me and know that I was a policeman. We joked about the arrest and became friends. His name was Terry Sullivan. He retired as a captain. During my last year in law school, I came across the person involved in the accident with me. His name is Benny Johnson and his nickname was Dap. We talked about the accident, and he said, "You never did pay me for the damages to my car." I think he said that it was about $2,000 in damages. We were in Pompano, and it was about ten years later in 1972. He told me that he had submitted a few applications for law school. I encouraged him to apply to my school in Texas. I submitted a recommendation letter to admissions for him at Thurgood Marshal School of Law at Texas Southern University in Houston. He was accepted, and we were roommates for one year. We became very good friends. After graduating, he returned to Florida. I did not pay him because of the statute of limitations. Benny is a great guy, and I really like him.

In early 1965, I got a job as the assistant warehouse manager for a film and chemical company. The name of the business was Chemco Chemicals. They sold supplies to photo engravers and newspaper companies. The warehouse manager was a old white multimillionaire. His name was Andrew Logan and did not need the job. He lived in Pompano near the ocean in the security gated sea ranch community. He taught me everything about the business, which included inventory control. We used bills of laden for shipments. Sometimes, I would make small deliveries to local businesses.

While working at Chemco, I took the police officer test in Hollywood, Florida. I made a score of 96 percent on the test. That was in 1968. I passed the physical agility, oral interviews, psychological, and background checks and tests. They hired and sponsored me through the Broward County Police Academy in 1969. At that time, law enforcement was not considered as a profession. It was considered as a skilled position. The federal government decided to make it a profession. The U.S. Department of Justice created a Law Enforcement Educational Program known as LEEP. Grants were awarded to educate policeman with a college education. Colleges and universities offered courses and degrees in law enforcement and criminal justice. A few officers took advantage of the grants. In 1969, there were only a few black officers in Florida. I was the third one with the Hollywood Police Department. I was the first black officer to work in the white community in Hollywood. Both of the other black officers worked only in the black community. I broke the ice for all of the other black officers in Hollywood. I took advantage of the LEEP grants and enrolled into Broward Community College in 1969. I entered into the criminal justice program at the college. I was the only black officer in the criminal justice program at the college. The police department placed me on a permanent shift to attend college. My ambition was to become a special agent with the FBI. My wife was getting ready to graduate from college as an elementary school teacher. I worked full-time as a police officer while attending college full-time. I encouraged a classmate to apply for a job in Hollywood, near the end of 1970. His name was March Lee, and his nickname was Red. He failed the written test. The personnel officer was Lieutenant Sandalier. He came to me and asked for advice. He said, "If March Lee fails the next test by a few points, should I hire him?" I said, "Yes, he is a nice respectful young man. He failed it by four points and was hired based upon my recommendation. He was hired by Lieutenant Sandalier and sponsored in the academy. He did not know that I was the reason he was hired. He graduated from the academy. We had a conversation and he told me, "I am going to do whatever it takes to excel on this job." It didn't take me long to get the message.

We had a white supervisor whose name was Sergeant Kraft. I think he was from Georgia. He had been into an accident, and it left a scar on the side of his face. He led me to believe that he was prejudiced. One day, when I had to turn my reports in to him, he asked me, "Why do you write your tickets to white people? And I notice that you don't give black folks any tickets." I said, "Sgt. Kraft, I do not work in the black community, and I have a limited amount of contact with black people. That is the reason I don't write them up." Then I told him that if he harass me, I would go to the state attorney's office and file a complaint.

"If you want me to give some black folks a ticket, let me work in their community." Shortly afterward, he and Officer Lee became the best of friends. I thought that March Lee was a friend. He kissed a number of the white officers ass, brown-nosed, and stabbed me in the back. I stopped fucking with him after learning what he had done against me. A few of the white officers thought that I was radical. I told them that I was not radical. It turned out that Red was not a friend. He was a pretender. He damaged my character and reputation, and I did not like it. I think he tried to make me look like a racist. It left a bad taste in my mouth. He would not have gotten the job had it not been for me.

I attended college with Officer Claude Covino and Assistant Chief of Police LeRoy Hessler. We formulated a car-pool to ride to Florida International University in Miami. The round-trip was one hundred-ten miles. We became excellent friends, and I really like those guys.

In Hollywood, I was an accident investigator for a year. Prior to that, I rode on the three-wheeled motorcycle and worked in the downtown business section for about six months. They wanted me to join the traffic division. I refused the offer and remained in the patrol division. I didn't like motorcycles. In the Road Patrol Division,

I worked on the busiest shift, which was from 3:00 to 11:00 PM. I had that shift in order to attend college. During my first year as a rookie officer, I made an arrest, which was a felony. I think it was on a Sunday when I was on patrol. I drove through the alley in the business and residential area of Hollywood Hills. The alley was on the south side of Hollywood Boulevard and between 44 and 52nd Avenue. I saw a black male beating and hitting a black lady next to a car. The woman had on a white nurse uniform. She was bleeding, and the uniform was bloody. I got out of my car and placed the man under arrest. Sergeant Kraft backed me up. I knew the lady because she was from Pompano. Her name was Clementine Mclemore. She was not the Clementine who I had my first orgasm with when I was young. They were cousins. The man was her husband. His wrists were too large to get handcuffed. He was charged with aggravated battery. If it were not for me, he would have killed her. The paramedics transported her to the hospital. Many years later after resigning from the police field, she became my girlfriend. She was tall, fine, and cute. The other one was fat. We dated for about eleven years. She became my girlfriend some years after divorcing my first wife.

I remember patrolling in West Hollowood near The Corral Bar. It was a troublesome Redneck Bar. A nearby 7 Eleven convenience store had been robbed. A description of the suspect was given, and they thought he went into the bar. I went into the bar and found the suspect in the bathroom. I had him under arrest before any backup help arrived. He was in handcuffs when they arrived. I did a pad search on the suspect. He was armed with a semiautomatic .45 caliber. It was ascertained that the offender had robbed stores from Washington, D.C. to Florida. The detective division took over the case. One day, when I was on patrol on Northwest 56 Avenue, I observed a white male acting in a strange abnormal way. I approached and questioned him after getting his identification. It turned out that he was stoned on LSD. He was placed under arrest. During the search, he possessed some more of the same drugs. On another occasion, I arrested a white female for driving while intoxicated. She was on Northwest 56 Avenue at the intersection with Johnson Street. The traffic light caught her, and she fell asleep. She and her husband owned a bar. They were separated, and she had planned to get a divorce. She took all of their money out of the bank. It was quite a few thousand dollars. She had it in the trunk of the car. Sgt. Kraft backed me up when I put her under arrest. The car was towed, and all of the money and additional property were secured with an inventory receipt.

I was on patrol on a Saturday or Sunday, and we were very busy. I had an Auxiliary scout riding with me. He was a high school student. I was near Young Circle when a call was made and that an officer was in trouble and needed help. All of the officers were busy on calls. I took the call. It was in the projects in the black community near Attucks High School. It was quite a distance from my location. When I arrived at the scene, a large mob of angry black folks were in the area. It was a huge crowd of people. I could see a police vehicle that was from the Davie Police Department. They chased a stolen 1955 Chevy from their jurisdiction into Hollywood. The suspects jumped out of the car and ran away. The folks alleged that the officers shot into their apartment, which created a disturbance. The officers were surrounded by the angry mob of people. It was two white police officers, and they were scared. When I got out of my car, the mob overturned the Davie Police car. I was communicating with the dispatcher. Somehow, I was able to prevent any harm to the officers. They got into my car, and we cleared the scene. The car was set on fire and burned to the ground. It was nothing we could do. There were at least a hundred or more mad people around the officers. Both of the white Davie officers were transported to our headquarters. Subsequent to that, a riot was in that area. It was cooled down within a few days. Lieutenant Mowers wrote and placed a letter in my file based upon my bravery. Those are a few things I did that were considered as outstanding work.

At Florida International University in the criminal justice curriculum, if you earned honors credit (HC) grades, it was computed with five points on a four-point grading system. The student was given an extra point. My police friends and I took a political science course from Dr. Greenberg. The course dealt with the aggressive behavior of animals and people. We took the midterm examination. It was a huge class and was taught in the auditorium. At least a hundred students took the class. I was the only black student in it. When the class resumed after the midterm exam, I had a court case and was absent. The professor wanted to know Charles Anderson. My friends told him that I was a cop and worked together. The reason he inquired about me was because I had made the highest score in the class. I made an A which was 100 percent on the test. The class was very large, and we were only a number. During my last semester at FIU, I needed twenty-five more credits to graduate, and I wanted to go to law school. I resigned from the police department in 1973 or 1974. I took twenty-five credits in that semester. Twenty of them were taken at FIU with ten of them in independent studies. I had course work with the other ten credits. Along with that, I took a five-hour class at Barry College. It was taken as a transient student. It was an advanced course on a graduate level in statistics. I made the highest score in the class at Barry, which was an A. At FIU, I made As with the additional twenty hours. In one semester, that was a total of twenty-five credits. I was accepted to Thurgood Marshal School of Law at Texas Southern University, Houston, in 1974. The law school required three letters of recommendation from professionals. One of my letters was from one of my professors at FIU. He was a lawyer and college professor whose name was Dr. Snow. Another one was written by Alcee Hastings. He is a former federal judge. Today, he is a congressman. I did not have any ambitions or intentions to practice law. What I wanted to do was to excel in law enforcement.

I earned an associate science degree and a one year police science certificate from Broward Community College in 1971. I enrolled in the criminal justice program at Florida Atlantic. The course work related to too many social sciences for me. I did not like the curriculum. A new school opened in Miami, and I transferred to it. The name of it was Florida International University. It had an excellent criminal justice curriculum. I worked as a full-time police officer and attended college full time. I did that at both institutions. On a four-point scale, I graduated from FIU with a 3.75 grade point average. That was with outstanding honors. It was magna cum laude. I earned both of the degrees and certificate within a three-year span. In order to do it, I had to attend school the whole year, which included going to school in the summer. I helped make history at FIU by graduating in their first class in 1973. I did not see any other black students in the criminal justice program. I got an ingenious notion to do some research on that issue. I wanted to know if I were the first African-American to earn those degrees. I made contact with the appropriate administrators at both institutions. It took a year to do the research at both institutions. On November 17, 2008, I received a notarized letter from Broward Community College. It was authenticated by the associate vice president of student affairs in the registrar's office. His name is Willie J. Alexander, Junior. The letter stated specifically that based upon their research, I am the first African-American to earn a criminal justice degree and police science certificate from Broward Community College. A notarized letter was received from FIU on December 1, 2008. It was authenticated and signed by Dr. Rosa L. Jones, vice president of student affairs and undergraduate education, administrator. It stated specifically that I'm the first African-American to earn a bachelor's degree from FIU. Some of my professors believed that I might be the first black to earn such degrees in Florida, United States of America or worldwide. I didn't complete that research project because it was extensive. It would entail many years and hours of research.

Prior to entering law school, I worked for six months as a parole and probation officer for the State of Florida. I resigned and drove to Houston, Texas, and enrolled in law school in 1974. It was at Thurgood Marshal School of Law. My youngest daughter was about fifteen months old. I felt guilty by leaving my wife and two daughters in Ft. Lauderdale. When I got to Orlando, Florida, I thought about making a U-turn and return home. I didn't do it and continued driving to Texas. I had submitted an application with the FBI in Miami, Florida, to become a special agent.

After completing my first year of law studies, I came home. A special agent contacted me from the office in Miami. I was interviewed by him and was given a job offer. He was a Latin special agent with the FBI. At that time, the maximum age requirement was forty-four years old. I told him that I had just completed my first year of law school. Then I said, "I am 32 years old. I will reapply when I finish law school." He literally begged me to drop out of law school. Then he said, "The law degree was not going to help you that much." I turned the job offer down and returned to law school. I knew that I would be in my mid-thirties when I graduated from law school. I took legal research and writing from Professor Honore. I made the highest score in that class. It enabled me to become a member of the TSU Law Review. I was thirty-four years old when I graduated from law school. Within three months, I would have been thirty-five years old. The FBI had made some changes in their hiring requirements. They had reduced the maximum age limit from forty-four to thirty-five years old. The reduction created a mandatory retirement at age fifty-five in quite a few federal agencies including the military. I made the mistake and applied with the FBI in Houston, Texas. I returned home in Florida. I had just graduated, and I needed to earn money. I did not get a response from my application.

Perhaps, my age was too close to maximum age limit, or they were upset because I didn't take the first job offer. I passed an examination to enter the US Coast Guard to work as a military lawyer. I would have been a commissioned captain. The starting salary was $18,500 in 1977. I would have handled military cases in the JAQS. At the last moment, I chose not to take the job offer. I felt that it was too transient and did not want to leave my family again.

I got a job during my second year of law school. It was with one of the wealthiest Jewish families in Houston. I was employed by Jerry and Ana Battelstein. They had children whose names were Adam and Ana. Adam was in the seventh grade, and his sister was in the sixth grade. They attended a private school, and its name was Kin-Kaid. In 1975, it was ranked as the number one private school in America. Their home was on Memorial Drive in the suburbs. The house was huge and situated on quite a few acres of land. The outdoor swimming pool was half as large as the house. They were separated and needed someone to be with the children. The husband had moved into another house. They were very bright kids and did not need any tutoring. I was hired and moved with them. I lived in a separate facility, which was about a hundred feet from their home. The building was once used as a servant's house. It had a bedroom, dining room, kitchen, and a bathroom. It had a central air-conditioned unit.

The property had a lot of large tall trees on it. My job was to spend some time with the children when they were out of school. I, more or less, had to entertain them. We played a lot of table tennis. I was better than all of them. When the wife went out of town, I would sleep in the huge house with the kids. I was paid $50 per week.

The maid washed and ironed my clothes, and I ate there too. It was a great job for a college student. The wife owned a brand-new Mercedes Benz, and it was the sports car. Sometimes, she would let me drive it to law school. I came home for the Christmas Break in

1975. I received a phone call that someone had robbed and shot Mrs. Battelstein. The perpetrator wore a mask and took her near the pool. She was shot in the head. She was lucky because the bullet had grazed her on the head. The injury was superficial. Her diamond wedding ring was taken. It was worth more than $200,000. They bargained with me to return to Texas. My salary was increased to $100 per week. They moved me into their family home with them. I lived in the house with Mrs. Battelstein and her children. She was a year older than me and was very attractive. Mr. Battelstein was an entrepreneur and owned a few successful businesses. He was in the banking industry, steel industry, and real estate. They owned department stores in Texas similar to Saks Fifth Avenue. They were named Battelsteins Department Stores. His wife was a model and had performed in their stores. She had been on the front page of *Vogue* magazine. Mr. Battelstein became a very good friend and gave me a grant, which paid for my tuition. That was the reason I refused to date his wife. I had the opportunity but refused it. I have seen her wear thin lingerie outfits with nothing under it. I have hugged and kissed her when she was upset. She wanted me to make love to her, but I refused it. Today, I regret refusing making love to her. I didn't want it to conflict with my law studies. I had a wife and family in Florida and a dozen or more women in Texas.

One of them was a model at Foley's Department Stores. Another one was a Cajun from Louisiana. She is the first black woman I had ever seen with natural green eyes. I told them that I was from Atlanta, Georgia.

I had two women with the same first name that was Sherry. One of them was about my height. She was a model and in the air force while attending college at TSU. She was bisexual. The other one was named Sherry Brannon and attended college. She was from East Texas. Her husband was a mail carrier and unable to have sex. She was my main girlfriend. She had beautiful hair with a lot of body to it. It hung down her back almost to her hips. I refused to elaborate about the other women. I destroyed their phone numbers and returned to Florida. I did not date any of my classmates. I dated two women who were administrators on the campus. A few years after my graduation, I ascertained that a classmate had a crush over me. Her name was Arnetta Moye and was from Panama City, Florida.

I wish I had known that because I liked her too. She attended college with my first wife at Bethune Cookman College. Gosh, what a small world.

During my last two years of law school, Mr. Battelstein helped me get a job in the Harris County District Attorney Office. I did legal work while I was in law school. Mr. Battelstein's nephew was a district attorney, and his last name was Sussman. When I graduated, he got a job with the federal government.

I was offered a nice large salary by Mr. Battelstein after graduation. He wanted me to work for him and handle his divorce. Instead, I returned to Florida. Around 1979, I met two white lawyers from Houston who knew them. They told me that they had gotten a divorce and stated, "Mr. Battelstein had so much money, and all of it could not be traced. A settlement was granted. He kept the children and the house.

Ana was awarded $5,000,000, along with the Mercedes Benz. She wanted to become an actress and probably relocated to California. On her leisure time, she was an artist and jewelry maker at her studio.

When I was in law school, sometimes I would shoot pool in the recreation center. I entered a tournament and won it. I was the best pool shooter on the campus. Houston is one of the largest cities in America. I attended quite a few concerts. Some of them were in the astrodome; while others were outdoors. I got a chance to see a number of professional entertainers. The heavyweight champion Ali was one of them.

When I returned home during the summer or any break, I would work. I got a job with the City of Lauderdale Lakes as a part-time police officer. The chief of police was Albert Kline. When I graduated from law school, the city was consolidated with Broward Sheriff's Office. I was involved with a large number of women when I was a policeman in Lauderdale Lakes. I had sex with so many of them. In 1974, I was hired under a CETA grant by the Broward County Human Relations Department. Several white lawyers were hired with me. We had to conduct a legal research study for a year. It entailed writing a civil service hand booklet for Broward County employees. The Board of County Commissioners had something to do with the project. At the end of the CETA Grant, I was hired by the Broward Sheriff's office as a deputy sheriff. A circuit court judge resigned to be appointed to the vacant position. He became Sheriff Butterworth. Many years later, he became the attorney general in Florida.

While employed as a deputy sheriff, I became an entrepreneur. I formulated a marine corporation. I sold and installed boat equipment to the boaters. Then I opened a restaurant in Ft. Lauderdale. Both of the businesses were fairly successful. I became a licensed property and casualty insurance agent. I made a perfect score on the exam. I opened my own insurance business. I planned to become a financial planner and took additional state exams. I became a licensed mortgage broker and real estate broker. I had an office in Ft. Lauderdale.

As a law enforcement officer, I dated many women. One of them was when I was with the City of Hollywood. She was a registered nurse and her name was Lilly Mae Greene. It lasted a few years. She lived in Dania, Florida. She was from Monticello, Florida. Her best friend was a teacher at Attucks High School in Dania. Her name is Almetta Wynche. I believe she became pregnant by me and had a baby. I had a large number of one-night affairs while employed as a cop in Hollywood.

When I worked for the sheriff's department, I was reassigned at the airport. I worked as a law enforcement officer and had a business. I sold my marine corporation and went into the restaurant business. I owned the property and had the restaurant on it. The name of it was Frenchy's Pit Bar-B-Q.

Both of my businesses were very successful. I earned enough money to pay cash for a large piece of undeveloped property contiguous to the restaurant. I had planned to build a small shopping center on it. Both of them were incorporated in Florida. A large number of my customers inquired about beer and wine. I got a beer and wine license. At the restaurant, I became ill and called in sick. A supervisor came to the restaurant and told me I had to come to work. His name was Sergeant Herb Potsdam. He told me that I had to be home when I get sick. I said, "That is a lie, and I had no control where I became sick." We got into an argument, and I ran him off my property. My oldest daughter, Adrianne, was at the restaurant helping me work. She smiled when I ran him away. Sergeant Potsdam and another supervisor hung out at the airport. His name was Sergeant Slichter. He appeared to be a redneck" and had recently transferred to the airport. He was at the airport for about a week and never had any contact with me. He gave me an evaluation report, and I refused to sign it. It was a bad evaluation. The score was sixty. He had not supervised me. How could he give me an evaluation? One of the areas was for report writing, and I am an excellent report writer. I challenged the evaluation with a letter to appropriate authorities. They made him do another evaluation. Within a few days, I received another evaluation, and the score was eighty. The bad evaluation was supposed to have been removed from my records. Instead of that, it remained in my file. In reality, it reduces the 80 percent score to a 70 percent when the two scores are averaged. I don't think it was a mistake. I believe it was an intentional act. Both of those sergeants had something to do with it. A copy of my rebuttal letter should be in my personnel file. I have always said that *God* does not like ugly. Sergeant Potsdam contracted cancer and suffered. He eventually died. Both of those sergeants were a piece of shit. I wonder how many other minority officers were treated unfairly by them.

I had a lot of female friends who were employed as representatives for rental car businesses. The majority of them were white. One of them I had taken out a few times. My supervisors did not like me because I had won on the evaluation. They retaliated against me by alleging that I was sexually harassing women at the airport. They were trying to get me fired and made up that lie. One complaint came from an old ugly white female. She worked at Delta Air-Lines where food was sold. I never had any contact with the lady and didn't know her. I fought the complaint and never heard any more about it. I had recently made Sergeant Potsdam leave from my restaurant. Instead of coming to me like a man, he chose to make a complaint with a state agency. He had seen the beer and wine in my restaurant. Florida had an antiquated law on the books. It prohibits law enforcement officers from having any business that sells alcohol. It is a third degree felony. An investigator made contact with me. He told me that the sergeant had filed the complaint with them. The investigator thought it was a nasty idea to do that. He said, "He should have told you that you were violating the law. Your business is incorporated, and you could have been a silent partner." The investigator gave me two choices. One was to resign from the sheriff's department. The other was to keep my job and give the beer and wine license up. I resigned from the sheriff's department to end the harassment. They did not like it because I am outspoken. I believe they were jealous because of my business and nice home. The state refused to file charges against me.

At the Hollywood-Ft. Lauderdale International Airport, I was stationed at National Airlines until they went out of business. A young beautiful young lady was the manager of Hertz Rental car. She had graduated from Mercer University or College in Georgia, a few months prior to the job. She became my girlfriend, and her name is Virginia Roland. She was very bright and intelligent. She resided in Dania, which was near the airport. We have had countless hours of sex. We dated for several years. She fell deeply in love with me and did not want me to have another woman. I was married and had a home in Coral Springs. She was hurting because I was married and hated it when I would leave her residence. I spent a few nights with her. One day, Virginia approached me and said, "Baby, I love you too much. Please let me break away from you." I agreed to give her the freedom and ended the relationship. Then she said, "I would like to make a promise with you." The promise is for us to have sex twice a year as long as we know each other. I would like for it to be on my birthday and on New Year's Eve." I concurred with the agreement. That lasted for a few years until we lost contact with one another. She resigned from Hertz and became a mail carrier for the U.S. Post Office. During the relationship with Miss Roland, we went to my friend's house in Georgia. We drove one of Hertz Rental cars, which was a brand-new Lincoln. Managers could drive any car and did not have to pay for it. My buddy Wine really liked her. She was a very fine attractive redbone and about twenty-five years old. I was around forty years old. I think we were in Georgia about a week.

Sometimes, I would drive to Georgia alone and stay for a week or two. One time, I had sex with seven of my buddy's girl friends. Both of us were married. Once, I arrived at 2:00 o'clock in the morning. We had a few drinks in his bar room, which was in the basement. I said to him, "Make a few phone calls because I want some pussy." He said, "I wish you had told me that before your arrival." He made a few phone calls, and one of his women came to the basement. The only thing I remember is her first name, which was Shirley. She was an accountant and had her own business in Atlanta. After socializing and having a few drinks, I told her something. I leaned over to her and said, "Baby, I like you with your fine sexy-ass self." I said, "I want to make love to you." Shirley said, "I can't do that because I am Wells' woman." Then I thought of a fast, quick scenario. I said, "Honey, let me tell you something. We are like brothers. When my friend comes to Florida, I let him screw all of my women, except my wife." Shirley said, "If it is like that, all of us can get started." I took her into the bedroom, which was in the basement. It was a waterbed. We had a threesome. It was on a Sunday, and my friend had to work the next day. He left us in the basement. We were still having sex when it was time for him to go to work. Shirley took Monday off from work. She liked it so good and told me to pretend I was going home. Then she invited me to her house. I told my buddy I was ready to go home. Instead of returning home, I went to her house. I stayed there for a week. She said during that threesome, it was the best sex of her life. About ten years later, I told Wine that I had spent a week with Shirley. He didn't like that, but we are still friends. I have had more women in Texas and Georgia than one could count. Florida probably should be included. I had a girlfriend who lived in Decatur, Georgia. She was married and a very intelligent principal at a school. She fell in love and was planning to divorce her husband. I had planned to relocate to Georgia. At this time, I was single. I had gotten my first divorce. She was the most lubricated woman I've ever had sex with. I thought she was using a lubricant. The sex was very good. Over the years, I have learned that regarding sex, all of it is different. When I make love with a woman, she must give me a special thrill. If she can't do that, I will not return. I have failed to return with a few of them. I do not like it when a woman is pretending to feel good. I like the real deal. I hate women who are phony. Another thing I don't like is an oversized woman. The type I can put my fist in it. A classmate by the name of Lonnie Clyde Black had one like that. She lived in Ft. Lauderdale, and her name was Mary Sue Riley. She was real tall and gave it up easily. Hell, I had more sex with her than my classmate. I remember when I got it my very last time. I took her to West-Side Park on a Sunday night. I decided to give her a massage in the middle of the vagina. We had our clothes off on the rear-side of the pool. We were on the embankment. I put a few fingers up it. I decided to see how many would get in that thing. I ended up with my fist up her. We began to have sex. She started to moan, whine, and cry. It pissed me off because I knew it was a fake. I stopped and took it out of her. I cursed her out and beat her ass. I said, "You big sloppy, pussy whore, you know I am not hurting you. I made her walk or catch a ride back to Ft. Lauderdale, Florida.

After the relationship had ended, Virginia got in touch with me. It was on her birthday. We spent most of that day together and had plenty of sex. We left her house in her rental car. She decided to visit her best friend who was a correction officer in Pompano. Her name was Becky. I was literally shocked and surprised when I entered the apartment. A friend and classmate was her boyfriend. He was Woodrow Shivers. Neither one of us knew about their friendship. All four of us had a great time. She became pregnant and had a child with Woodrow. Their relationship ended because he wouldn't pay any child support. He was a correction officer, and they worked at the same facility.

When National Airlines went out of business, I was transferred to work at Eastern Air Lines. While working at the Airport, I had a large number of one-night relationships. I dated several white flight attendants who were married. Most of the one-night stands were with passengers who became stranded. At the airport, I worked from 6:00 PM to 2:00 in the morning. It was about 7:00 PM, and I observed a black female walking. She appeared to be bewildered, and I approached her. She said that she was from Freeport, Bahamas and came to purchase a windshield for her car. She told me that a cab driver drove her around and beat her out of money. When they arrived at the business, it was too late. They had closed for the day. She was debating about returning without the windshield. I made a proposition to her. I told her that I worked until 2:00 in the morning and that she could sit near my desk. I said I am married, but I am willing to take her to a motel. "I will spend the night with you, and you will be able to buy the windshield the next day." She was gorgeous, and we made love most of the night. She purchased it and returned home. Her job was with the Bahamian government. She made contact with me frequently. Another one-night affair was at National Airlines. There were many more, but this will be the last one. An Oriental lady was stranded. I approached her and asked her, "What was wrong?" She said that she was from Washington, District of Columbia. "My boy-friend was supposed to pick me up." I told her about my hours at the airport. Then I said, "You will not be able to get a flight until tomorrow. If your boyfriend is not here when I finish work, I can take you to a motel. He did not show up, and we spent the night in a motel. She was gorgeous and was from Cambodia. Her father was a brain surgeon. We had sex most of the night. I took her to the airport the next day. We eventually lost contact with each other.

In my day, I have dated many professional and nonprofessional women. I have had a large number of low-class thugs. When I was in my late teens and mid-twenties, I was a sport. I dressed well and was rather cool. I had a twenty-eight inch waist and weighed about 220 pounds. During that period, I hung out at the bars and nightclubs. On the weekends, I would go out alone. When I entered those places, if a man was with a woman, he would get worried. I had a reputation of ending up with another man's woman. I've seen some men look at his woman, and then look at me. Every weekend, I would end up with another man's woman in a transient house. In the bars and clubs, I would dance slow with women. We called it slow-dragging. Then I would hit on her and tell her where I was parked. I would leave the club soon and wait for the woman. The majority of those women lived in Palm Beach County. A lot of them lived in Broward and Dade Counties. A lot of that transpired when I owned my hot rod and Corvette. A tall big woman from Delray was crazy about me. She was not fat but was a big tall nice-looking woman. Her name was Bernice. Rufus, whose nickname was Tree, was her boyfriend. Just like me, he was a player. When he did not come to the club, she was my woman. I had a ton of sex with her. She is dead. Another nice girlfriend was from Pompano. Her mother was an entrepreneur and owned a fish market. The name of it was Siss's Fish Market. The young lady's name was Clara-Mae. When I had sex with her, she was a virgin. That was when my wife was in college.

My mother is a super negative person. I am a mega-positive thinker and happen to be very competitive. I have always tried to be a few steps higher than a challenger or competitor. When I was attending law school, we were advised that the rate of attrition was high. I heard someone make a statement. My philosophy was that I am returning and will not be among that attrition group of students. I looked at all of the students and said to myself, "I will be back next year." I gave that advice to a student who was struggling with grades. He was much younger than me. I think his first name was Benjamin. He was from a state in the South, and I believe it was Tennessee or Mississippi. When he observed me at the graduation ceremony, he approached me. He said, "Charles, I want to thank you for the advice. I used that philosophy, and I am graduating from law school." I wished him all of the luck in the world as a lawyer.

I remember when I arrived to Houston, Texas. I had three roommates who became friends. One of them was a few years older than me and was a former cop too. He was from St. Louis, Missouri, and his wife was a lawyer. His name is Andrew Hodge and his wife is Peggy Hodge. Another roommate was Barry Ford. He was from Pontatar, Mississippi. His brother was a judge in Mississippi. The third roommate was younger than us. He was from Detroit, Michigan, and had worked for one of the largest black law firms in America. His name was Ray Hullum and became a very good friend. Andrew and Barry became judges in their hometowns. It was my very first day in Houston. I told Andrew I was going on a tour in the town. It was nearly nighttime. He went with me. I said, "I am a Florida boy. I plan to get some pussy." We stopped at a fast food restaurant, which specialized in chicken. An attractive black female took our order. I believe it was on a Saturday, which was my first day in town. She had the most beautiful dark skin I've ever seen. She told me that she was from Colorado and had two jobs. I placed an order that had some breasts and wings. After paying her, I said, "I am a breast and thigh man." Then I inquired about her time off and asked to take her home. I told her I had been accepted to law school. She got off from work at 11:00 that night. I told her that I would return and take her home. She was off from the second job. Andrew and I went to a couple of nude clubs in downtown. When we finished watching the women perform, we went to the restaurant. The young lady got into my car. I took her to an apartment, which was a duplex. It was where she lived. I hit on her and told her that it was love at first sight. She told Andrew that she had a roommate. When we arrived at the apartment, she had gone out on a date. The young lady invited us into the apartment. She prepared a drink for us. We sat in the living room while she took a shower. Then she entered the living room with a red lingerie outfit. It was beautiful, and it turned me on. I told my friend that he could watch the television in the living room. The attractive young lady and I went into her bedroom. We chatted and got acquainted along with a few drinks. I am so sorry because I don't remember her name. She said, "I will make love with you on one condition. I don't want a one-night sex game. I am from Colorado, and I am looking for a boyfriend. Promise me if I give you some, you will be my boyfriend." I agreed with her, and we had the greatest amount of romance. She was a queen and on a scale from zero to ten. She would be given a fifteen. This chick was a knockout. Her roommate did not return home. She wrote her name, address, and phone number on a piece of paper. We returned to our apartment. Andrew told our roommates that I was real cool and how I had scored. On Monday was the orientation day at the law school. The classes were very demanding and a real challenge. I had to study for many hours. Sometimes, it was all night long. I forgot about the young lady I had met. After about a month of law studies, we got a break. I had lost the information that was given to me by her. I drove to the restaurant where she worked. She had quit the job. I hadn't realized the size of Houston. I thought I could find her apartment. The whole time I was in law school, I was unable to find her or the apartment. All of the apartments looked alike to me. After that, I learned the size of Houston. It bothered me because I did not keep my promise to her. I didn't know that law school was going to be that hard. About half of my classmates graduated. A bunch of them flunked out or transferred to another school.

Houston is a huge metropolis. There are many black businesses in the black community along with a large university. There are so many places to be entertained. Concerts are held on a weekly basis by professional entertainers. One of my women took me to an outdoor concert on a large piece of undeveloped property. It appeared to be about a hundred thousand people at it. It started in the morning and lasted until night. It was an all-day long ordeal. Quite a few black and white professionally known entertainers performed at it. A lot of the spectators were smoking weed. Some of the performers smoked some too. The police could not do anything because they were outnumbered. I had a large stable of women that were serviced by me. All of them thought I was a single man. That was not true because I had a wife and children in Florida. It would have been different if they were with me. In Florida, I was stable and owned a duplex in Ft. Lauderdale. My mother lived in Pompano. For those reasons, I chose not to relocate to Houston.

A classmate and friend brought his family with him. His wife and children came with him to Houston. His wife was a teacher just like my wife. His name is Belvin Perry, and he is the chief justice of the circuit courts in Orlando, Florida. He became a celebrity from the Casey Anthony criminal trial. He was assigned to that case. It was on national television. He did an awesome job with the trial. I think that Orlando is his hometown.

About six months after graduating from law school, I bought a nice custom-built house in Coral Springs. It was loaded and had everything you could dream of in it. It had an oversized fence enclosed swimming pool. I made a down payment of $50,000 on the purchase price. After that, I encouraged my wife to go to graduate school and get a master's degree in administration and supervision. I advised her that would enable her to become a principal. She continued to work as an elementary school teacher and attended college. She earned two degrees. One was a master's degree and the other a specialist degree. She earned them from FIU and Nova Southeastern University. The only thing she wanted to do was to teach in school. I encouraged her to become a principal. Our house had four bedrooms and three bathrooms. Marble was all over it. We had a double car garage. You could BBQ in the center of the kitchen on a specialized pit. We had a formal dining room. The house was equipped with an intercom system. We could hear our kids when they were breathing during their sleep. When I was forty years old in 1981, I gave myself a big birthday party. I invited my classmates and some other friends. I spent about $10,000 for it.

I learned a lesson from a teacher in the eighth grade. He was my industrial arts teacher, and his name was Mr. McGee. He had a speech impediment but was an excellent teacher. One day, I was in the woodwork shop alone. I started horse playing around with some of the electric saws. He returned to the shop and caught me in there, and some of the saws were turned on. He turned them off and wanted to know the reason I was playing around with them. I said, "Mr. McGee, I was having fun, and I am sorry." He ran me out of the shop, and I have never forgotten some of his magical words. The teacher said, "Boy, let me tell you something. It is too late to be sorry. You could have gotten injured or killed by those saws." If someone happens to give me an apology, I use those words. I would tell them, "It is too late to be sorry." I've used those "magical words" quite a few times. If I loan a person some money, I want it back. I don't want it back if I gave it to them. If I loan a penny, I want it back.

When a woman does something that is not approved by me, I put a strike by her name. It is done mentally. When I quit a woman, I usually will not compromise with her. During my marriage with my first wife, Cynthia, I quit her after the third mental strike. Around 1984 or 1985, I filed for a divorce. I refused to compromise or get marriage counseling. I am going to list the mental strikes by her name. Firstly, she was too jealous and nosed around in my personal life too much. Secondly, she knew I talked in my sleep. One night, I had gone clubbing with the boys. I was awakened in my sleep. She was whispering in my ears. I pretended to be asleep. I heard her whisper in my ear and she said, "Charlie, where were you and who were you with?" I said to myself that this woman must be crazy. I really did not like that shit. After the last strike, I filed for a divorce. I had planned to relocate to Atlanta, Georgia. I drove to my friend's house in Decatur, Georgia. I lived with him about two months while I was applying for work. I made plans to take the Georgia Bar Exam and applied for some governmental positions. When I returned home from Georgia, my wife had failed to make two mortgage payments. I received a foreclosure letter from the bank. The mortgage payment was around $1,500 per month. A third payment was due in a week. I withdrew $4,500 from my personal account and caught up the mortgage payments. After that, I listed the house for sale and filed for a divorce. Since I had known her since we were teenagers, I thought we would have a friendly divorce. I think I was sixteen years old and she was thirteen when we met. Wow, was I wrong with the friendly divorce suggestion! I told her it would be cheaper because I was a lawyer. I told her that we would split the proceeds when the house was sold. The restaurant and property along with the undeveloped land were in my mother's name. The home in Pompano was in her name too. I had recently purchased about $100,000 worth of furniture in the home. I told my wife you can have all of the valuable furniture in the home. I will keep the restaurant and vacant land. She agreed with me. After that, I drafted the uncontested divorce petition. It had to be notarized by both of us. I took it to her school and left it with her. Several days later, she returned it with red marks on what she disapproved. I did another petition and made it a contested divorce. She did not have to sign it. I filed for the divorce in Broward County. It took several years to reach the divorce. During that period, I had about four girlfriends. One of them was from Miami, Florida. She was Dianne Johnson. She was in the process of a divorce too. When I saw her wearing those Victoria Secret panties and bra, it turned me on. Her body was so beautiful. Our relationship continued after my divorce. It was a wonderful and special one. The relationship lasted about seven years. We had some of the greatest sex. She separated me because I wouldn't marry her. We are still friends today. Another girlfriend was Yvonne Donlap who was from Deerfield, Florida. We attended the same high school, and she was a few years behind me. Cynthia found out about Yvonne and went to her house. She messed up that relationship, but it continued. A spiritual singer attended her church. He was the reason why we quit. He noticed that I did not come to the house on holidays. On a holiday when I was not at her house, he told Yvonne, "If Charles cared anything about you, he would be here." He was from Ft. Lauderdale, and his name was James Hudson. I quit Yvonne and told her she could have him. She wanted me back and came to me several times with complaints. She told me he had raped her. I believe her because she is a square. Yvonne is a Christian and is very intelligent and attractive. *God* does not like ugly because he is dead. I have never talked against another man to get a woman. If I can't get her on my merits, I do not need her.

Dianne lived in Opa Locka, which is in North Miami. Her daughter was named Janine. A number of years after we had quit, I met a young lady who lived in South Miami. A lot of miles are between North and South Miami. The young lady I met had the same name as Dianne's daughter. Her name was Janine too. She was eighteen years old and became my girlfriend. What a small world! My girlfriend's mother and Dianne were friends. I had sex with Janine a few times. She was a virgin when I had sex with her. When I met her, I was almost fifty years old. We had a great relationship, and her parents liked me. Somehow, Dianne ascertained we were dating. She called me on the phone and gave me a hard time. That was the reason I quit Janine. I was crazy about Janine, and it appeared to be mutual.

Another girlfriend during my divorce was Clementine Mclemore. She is not the one from my neighborhood, but they are cousins. This one is tall and fine and about six years older than me. We dated for eleven years and continued to date after my divorce. When I got my divorce, the court ordered me to pay $45 per week for child support. I was supposed to pay it to child support enforcement. I chose not to pay it to the agency. Instead of that, I would give the cash money to my daughter who was Brigitte. My ex-wife observed me give the money to my daughter most of the times. After it built up to nearly $8,000, she went to the court. She told them that I had not paid the money. The judge who led me to believe that he was a racist was named Harry Hickler or a similar last name. He told me, "The money that was paid in cash became a gift." He gave me thirty days to pay it or be jailed for sixty days. I didn't pay it and moved into Clementine's house. When the thirty days had expired, law enforcement officials looked for me. They came to my house to put me in jail. I decided to return to my house to check on my mother. I went into the bathroom to shave. I heard someone knock on the door. I looked through the window and saw two deputy sheriffs in front of the door. I went to the back door to run away. There were two more officers at the door. I could not escape. That was when Dianne Johnson chose to quit me. I spent the time in jail and was discharged. My ex-wife picked me up and drove me home. I came out of jail with a jailhouse virus. When I was discharged, the indebtedness was substantially larger. I was given two months to pay it or return to jail. I sold the business establishment in order to pay the money. I didn't have the money and didn't have another choice. The buyer got an excellent deal because he knew I was in distress. I was attending BCC when I was arrested. I had an A average in two math courses. I had planned to get certified in mathematics and become a teacher. My ex-wife and the judge messed that up. We had joint custody of my daughter. If that had been me, I would not have had her jailed. Some people are just money hungry.

I filed for a contested divorce. It made me realize that a friendly divorce is a fantasy. Believe me, it does not exist. Afterward, Cynthia hired George Allen Law Firm to represent her. A white lawyer who had graduated from Nova's Law School was her legal representative. His name was BJ Cummings. He was a real asshole, and I did not like him. I told him that to his face. He and the judge were friends. I hired a lawyer whose name was Steven Cole. He told me, "BJ Cummings and him were classmates at Nova. I do not like him and plan to tear him apart with this divorce." He lied and half-assed represented me. My wife even said, "You hired an incompetent lawyer to represent you." He acted as he was afraid to talk in the courtroom. I should not have paid him the legal fees. When I was married and living in Coral Springs, my wife got a signature loan from a teacher's association. It was about $20,000 or a little less. She stopped paying the debt. We owned another house in Pompano. The association's lawyers represented them. We were given thirty days to pay the debt or lose the second house. My mother lived in the house. We had to get an appraiser to get a loan. The bank had planned to give a new first-year mortgage on the property. They changed their mind after twenty days. I had only ten days to get the money. I made contact with a Jewish mortgage broker. He loaned the money under one condition. We had to use all of our property as collateral. It would be a balloon mortgage with a two-year call. I was in distress and had no other choice. I did not want my mother to lose the house. We were about to get the divorce when the two years were up. It was almost time to renew the mortgage, and it had been signed jointly. Cynthia contacted me and said, "I want you to give me the vacant land next to the restaurant. I know it is time to sign another contract on your mother's house. If you don't do that, I am not signing another contract with you. Please don't get another woman to sign my name on one. I know how you are and if you do, you are going to jail. If you don't give me the property, I will make you lose every damn thing you own. I don't care if Rose will have to move." I called her bluff and waited until the mortgage was up.

All of my property was wrapped around the loan. I did not want the Jew to get all of it. On the deadline of the balloon, I made contact with my ex-wife. The land was in my mother's name, and she signed it over to Cynthia. We took her name off the house in Pompano and got a new first-year mortgage from another bank. My mother told me that Cynthia was a real nasty woman. She became upset with my mother after the divorce. They have not had any contact for quite a few decades. Cynthia visited my mother when I was not home. It was after getting the vacant land. Rose said, "She had some papers and wanted me to give her this house. I told her that I am not a fool. Did your mother give her house to my son? If I give you this house, Charlee will kill both of us." She left and never returned to our house. She had gone ballistic and wanted everything I had worked for, and I probably would have been on death row. There is no such thing as a friendly divorce. Her poker hand was better than mine. She is the only person to beat me and get away with it. I believe in payback or revenge when I get beaten by someone. I chose not to do anything because of my children. I have a clear conscience.

In 1992, I met a twenty-five-year-old woman from the ghetto in Miami. She lived in Liberty City. I was fifty-one years old. Her name is Paulette Hayden. She became pregnant and had my son. His name is Koffi Hayden. She is a real thug that is why I quit her. We dated off and on until my son became fifteen years old.

In 1985, I was employed by the State of Florida, HRS, as a district intake counselor. I was a child abuse and juvenile delinquent counselor. I had the job a little more than six months. I had passed my probationary period. I had a job offer with the City of Dania as chief of police. I was the first African-American to be nominated as a chief of police in Broward County. I became a public figure. I was on national television and newspapers. At this time, Steven Cole was my lawyer. He represented me in my first divorce. The *Sun Sentinel* and *Miami Herald* newspapers made many mistakes. They alleged that I was fired from the sheriff's department and City of Hollywood. That was flat out a lie. I resigned from both agencies. The resignation letters are in my personnel file with both agencies. The news reporters decided to get an average score from my evaluations. The evaluation which I fought should not have been included. It was supposed to have been removed and destroyed. The reporters printed an incorrect evaluation in their papers. There were many additional errors in those newspapers. I became very controversial in the news, and the city did not want to be involved. Along with the lies in the newspapers, a bunch of rumors developed. A lot of them were from anonymous black folks. I was in the news, 24/7, on a daily basis. I became real controversial. Some black folks called the City of Dania and said that I was a drug dealer and user. Some black folks alleged that I had beaten them out of insurance premiums. I had gone out of that business more than a year. I had a property and casualty insurance agency and had the insurance broker license. I trained and hired a black female and promoted her to office manager. She ran the business after getting trained by me. I checked on her once or twice a week. I had another job while I was building my business. The State Department of Insurance filed charges against me. All of this was in the news on a national level. I made nearly $10,000 in payments as restitution. The newspapers printed The Chief of Police Have Paid Restitution. The manager whom I had trained stole a large number of insurance premiums. I was unaware of it. The City of Dania wanted to fire me. My lawyer who was Steven Cole advised me to let them fire me. Then he said that he would represent me and file a lawsuit. It was on a Friday, and I was supposed to be sworn in for the job on Monday. On Saturday or Sunday, the city chose not to give me the job. The news was like a cancer and it said, The City of Dania Chief of Police Have Been Fired. The state requires that when a lawsuit is filed against a governmental agency, they must be notified within a year. My lawyer did not notify the city. He was either incompetent or afraid to file a lawsuit. I didn't care. All I wanted was to let everything cool off. No matter what transpired, I am still the first black chief of police in Broward County. The charges by the insurance commissioner's office were tried in Miami, Florida, in the state building. I represented myself and prevailed. The agency revoked my insurance broker license. They based it upon the mismanagement of insurance funds. I was responsible because I was the broker. The manager had relocated to California and was unavailable. A large number of black folks were at the trial.

The friend who backstabbed me with the police department became their first black sergeant. I am not sure if he became a lieutenant. I learned a few things about him. He was a good ass kisser and pot-licker. If I had to do that to get ahead, I will never get there. I am too independent to do that. I met him at a Narcotics Anonymous meeting in Miami in early 2000. This was many years after he had gotten fired for using drugs. He had gotten a divorce from his wife. She was from Louisiana and had a boy and girl by him. She was a teacher in Broward County. He would get off from work and beat her up. The last time she left, she refused to return. She gave him the house and everything in it and got a divorce. After that, he married a nurse. When he was fired, the City of Hollywood gave him his money from the pension. His brother, Billy Lee, told me they gave him nearly $100,000. He said that Red messed up all of the money by using cocaine and heroin. After that, the nurse divorced him. When he was fired, he had been employed nearly twenty years. I met several white officers I knew who were still with the force. He could have entered himself into a drug treatment program for a year. After that, Red could have retired with twenty years on the police force. He would have been set for life. At the NA Fellowship, he wanted to be a friend again. I mentioned to him, "Did you know that I am the reason you got the job?" He replied that he was unaware about it, but he knew he had failed the test. He was sick and suffering from cancer. We exchanged telephone numbers and spoke on the phone frequently. I introduced him to one of my girlfriends. Her name is Bonnie Fussell. She is a real sweetheart. I have been dating her for a long time. He made a call to her one day. We had broken up, and she told him about it. She told me something he told her before he died. When Bonnie told Red we had quit, she told me this, "Your classmate told me that I had done her a favor. He said that slick ass Charlee would have beaten you out of every dime you have. You are too nice and classy for him." Boy, he was really a good friend. Now he was backstabbing me with my woman. Thank *God* I did not know it when he was alive. Again, *God* works mysteriously. He made him suffer and took him off this earth. I don't have to worry about him anymore. I know his backstabbing have ended.

If I could count my relationships with women, it probably will be more than a thousand. I thought that was the way to become a sport. I have made a tremendous change with my attitude. Today, I am not like that because of all the contagious diseases. I am blessed to be free from them. I cannot change what happened in the past. That is what happened and the way it was.

I have had a large number of skilled and unskilled jobs. I was the chief of security for BJ Wholesale Club. I was trained for three months in the New England states. I was trained a month in each state.

They are Massachusetts, Connecticut, and New Hampshire. The company paid all of my expenses. I had a rental car and lived in a high-class hotel. When I was in Hartford, I paid a visit to a class-mate. He was an entrepreneur and owned several shopping centers. His name is Emerson Blatche. His sister was my classmate too. I gave her a visit at the Jai-Alai where folks gamble. This was around 1987, and I had not seen them about twenty-five years. Emerson acted in a strange manner. He led me to believe that he thought I worked for the internal revenue. Hi sister was friendly when we met.

After my divorce from my first marriage, I've had a few more of them. They were from the islands and did not have papers to live in this country. One was from Panama and the other one from Grenada. They were able to get papers to live in our country. Since the year of 2000, I have had some things that happened that was phenomenal. All of this happened when I was not drinking or using drugs. My normal faculties were not impaired or incapacitated. I was sober and had a clear and sound mind. I am not a psychiatrist or a spiritual healer, but I do believe in meditation and spirituality. I try to meditate and pray daily because I am a believer of *God*. The phe-nomenal things occurred to me in my mid-sixty years. I shall share them to you. I have been arrested three times with cocaine. Each time, I was charged with two felonious charges. They were for posses-sion of cocaine and purchasing cocaine. Each charge carried a $5,000 bond. I could have been sentenced to five years in prison on each count. I think that was in 1991 when I was fifty years old. Since I'm a lawyer, I represented and defended myself in the court. I did the legal research and filed motions to suppress the evidence and a dismissal of the evidence. I said that the police had planted the evidence on me. I fled from the police in my van into the projects. They blocked it out and caught me. I got two notarized statements from two of my friends who lived in the projects. It was in Liberty City in the heart of the ghetto. They did not care that much for a cop. The witnesses said, "We saw them plant that shit on you, and we have your back, Pop." Along with the statements, a certified affidavit were filed in court. At the pretrial hearing, all of the charges were dismissed. The rationale was from the motions in court.

Something happened that was extraordinary prior to the arrest. It was on the fourth of July about 2:00 in the morning. I was fast asleep and had a vision. During that vision, I repeatedly spoke to

Jesus. I said the same thing repeatedly, "Jesus, Jesus, Jesus." He lifted me into the air from my bed and spoke to me.

While I was floating into the air, Jesus said these words, "If you do not stop using cocaine, I am going to kill you with a bolt of lightning." After that, I hated to hear it thunder and lightning. However, late in the evening, I had forgotten about the vision and went to Miami. When I got arrested, it felt like lightning had struck me. It pays to listen to *God*. I had another vision five or six years later and in it, I was arrested. I was in Miami. In the vision, two unmarked police cars followed me on Northwest 79th Street. They made me park at a gas station which was at a street that intersected with 79th Avenue. It was 22nd Avenue, which intersected with Northwest 79th Avenue. I went to Miami and got arrested. The location was identical to the vision or dream. The officers arrested me and charged me with two felonies. One count was for possession of cocaine and the other one for purchasing cocaine. I could have gotten five years in prison for each count. Again, I chose to represent myself and filed all of the legal paperwork in court. At the pretrial hearing, I was confronted by Judge Jeffrey Rosinek who ran the drug court program. He really liked my motions and my defense strategy. He said, "Mr. Anderson, what you need is an education about illicit drugs. The legal work presented by you is better than most lawyers in this courtroom. You should consider practicing law." He said, "I am dismissing one of the charges based upon one of your motions. I am not going to adjudicate on the other charge because I want you to attend my drug court program for a year. After you successfully complete it, I will drop that charge." He is known nationally. I believe that he is the first judge in America to start such a program. I commuted to the program for a year. The last charge was nolle pros, which meant not prosecuted. I got it expunged from my records. In 2007, I was arrested again in Miami, Florida. I did not have a vision this time. I gave a friend a ride to an apartment complex named The Blues off 135th Street in Miami, Florida. While I was there, I visited a friend. Within a few minutes, I left alone in my car. After driving several miles away from the complex, a traffic light caught me. Four police officers got out of an unmarked car and arrested me. They alleged that they confiscated some cocaine from my car. I said that the passenger probably left it in the car. I was arrested and charged with two felony counts. I represented myself and filed the appropriate documents in court. Prior to the pretrial hearing, I enrolled into a private drug treatment program. It was in Ft. Lauderdale and lasted three months. My health insurance paid for it. Another judge had taken over the drug court, and he was Judge Thornton. He really liked my motions at the pretrial hearing. He dismissed one of the charges. Then he advised me to hire a lawyer because I did not qualify for a public defender. Another hearing was scheduled. A lawyer represented me for $5,000. He used my legal work in court and told the judge about the private drug treatment program. The judge was impressed with my background and credentials. He was not aware of my prior arrests. They were not on my record.

He agreed with me and my lawyer that the charge would be dropped after completing the program. It was completed, and the charge were not prosecuted. After three strikes, you are out, and I am smart enough to know that. Now, I try to shy away from troublesome spots. I do not intend to get caught in the "spider-web" again. I know the police have a booby-trap waiting to arrest minorities. I refuse to fall in it again. I have seen an image of Jesus in the rear of my house. There is a large Catholic church behind my house. An enclosed fence divides the property. An evergreen Florida pine tree is next to the fence. I have seen an image of Jesus in that tree a few times. I believe that this property where I live is sacred. The rationale centers from those images and sights.

I had a lawsuit between 1997 and 2000. I was talking with my mother at our home. I stood in front of the carport while she stood in front of the front door. It was almost nighttime. While we were talking, something happened that was extraordinary. It scared me, and I ran from under the carport. While I was talking with my mother, a bird flew and landed on my right shoulder. The bird was invisible, but I could feel it on my shoulder. The bird flapped its wings several times. That really scared me. I do not remember whether the bird flew away when I was running. I have presented the scenario to two psychiatrists and a couple of ministers. Both of the psychiatrists said, "It was an angel from heaven." The ministers believed it was an angel or a relative who had died and returned to visit me. They said it had to be a relative who really loved me and came as a spiritual ghost. If that is true, it had to be my maternal grandmother.

I am concluding this book with my last extraordinary experience. It happened when I had my last lawsuit from an injury. On a clear night, I enjoyed looking up into the horizon. I liked to look at the moon and stars above. I viewed them often. It was approximately two o'clock in the morning. I was standing on the driveway and looking in the sky. It was a very clear night. It was on a Sunday, and I was the only person outside. A fence divided our yard from the neighbors. I had some potato chips to eat along with a bottle of cold spring water. One of my neighbors was Bishop Jimmy Dale Wright and his wife, Daisy Wright. I was leaning against my car eating some of the chips. A man was standing in front of their house. He was in front of the entrance door. He stood with his face in front of me. This was my first time seeing this man. I had not seen him before that night. We were approximately thirty-five feet apart from one another. His complexion was dark, and he was a short black male. He had a large medallion around his neck. The hair on him had receded in the top of his head. I refer to its shape as a horseshoe. His pants were dark, and he wore a striped vest and shirt. The anonymous man faced me and waved at me with one hand. I would wave at him too. After looking and waving for a few minutes, I made a statement. I said to him, "You are probably a private investigator that is spying on me. Where is your camera? I have not done anything to you, and you are doing nothing to me." After seeing that man for a few hours, I got into my car. I could see him standing. I started my engine and drove in front of the house. I turned my bright lights on, and the man would disappear. Afterward, I would drive to my house and park at the same spot. The man would reappear in front of my neighbor's house doing the same thing. I drove from one house to the other one about six times. The same thing happened. I remained against my car until almost daylight. After that, he disappeared. I really thought he was watching me because of a lawsuit.

I went into the house and got into my bed. I slept about six hours. I got up and took a shower. Then I had a meal. I walked to my neighbor's house and knocked on the door. My neighbor, who was Daisy, opened the door. I told her about the man and described him. She said, "Oh, Charlee, he is my father. He visits me all the time. When I buried him, he was wearing that medallion and clothes you described to me."

They had a son whose nickname was Kee-Lee. He was kind of bad and would abuse himself with drugs and alcohol. Shortly after observing the mysterious man, Kee-Lee was home alone. I saw him bring a woman to their house. They closed the front door and entered the house. I was in my front yard doing something with my back to their home. After a few minutes, I heard their front door make a noise. It sounded as if a person had slammed the door. I said to myself, "That was a quick piece of sex." I heard the noise but didn't see them leave the house. I saw them walking from the house an hour later. In the same year, Kee-Lee became ill and died. He was twenty-eight years old. I spoke with Daisy, his mother shortly after Kee-Lee's death. She told me, "My father knew that Kee-Lee was going to die. He paid him a visit before his death." She died a year or two after her son's death.

I have lived to see an African-American become the president of the United States of America. His name is Barack Obama. In my opinion, he and President Clinton were the brightest presidents among all of them. I grew up in the segregation and Jim-Crow eras in America. We were discriminated against and treated unfairly. That included employment, education, and housing. A few blacks escaped the cycle of poverty. If you are born poor according to the law of average, you are going to die poor. The white folks knew that formula. I have had a few different race classifications. They are negroes, colored, black, and African-American.

This country is always going to have racial tensions as long as people are classified by race. We need a color-blind society. If a person has their citizenship, they should be called an American. If you do not have it, they should be called a non-American. The majority of countries do not use the black or white race classifications.

FLORIDA INTERNATIONAL UNIVERSITY ALUMNI ASSOCIATION

Lifetime Member

Dr. Charles L. Anderson '73

With recognition and sincere appreciation of outstanding loyalty and dedication to the programs, activities, and ideals of Florida International University's Alumni Association and its mission to proudly support the academic excellence, best interests and traditions of Florida International University and its alumni worldwide.

ALUMNI
ASSOCIATION

June 2014

BROWARD
COMMUNITY
COLLEGE

We keep you thinking.

Office of the Associate Vice President for Student Affairs/College Registrar
Willis Holcolmbe Center ▪ 954-201-7471

WILLIS HOLCOMBE CENTER
111 East Las Olas Blvd.
Fort Lauderdale, FL 33301

RE: Dr. Charles Anderson

DATE: November 17. 2008

**INSTITUTE FOR
ECONOMIC DEVELOPMENT**
111 East Las Olas Blvd.
Fort Lauderdale, FL 33301

To Whom It May Concern:

This is to certify that the above named person applied and was
accepted as a student on January 7, 1969, to Broward College
formerly known as Broward Junior College. Dr. Anderson earned
an associate of science degree and a technical certificate in July of
1971.

**A. HUGH ADAMS
CENTRAL CAMPUS**
3501 S.W. Davie Road
Davie, FL 33314

NORTH CAMPUS
1000 Coconut Creek Blvd.
Coconut Creek, FL 33066

Please accept this letter as an official verification that, based on our
research, Dr. Charles Anderson was the first African American
student to complete and earn an Associate in Science Degree in
Criminal Justice from Broward College.

**JUDSON A. SAMUELS
SOUTH CAMPUS**
7200 Hollywood/Pines Blvd.
Pembroke Pines, FL 33024

If there are any questions regarding this letter, please feel free to
contact this office.

PINES CENTER
16957 Sheridan St.
Pembroke Pines, FL 33331

Sincerely,

WESTON CENTER
4205 Bonaventure Blvd.
Weston, FL 33332

Willie J. Alexander, Jr.
walexand@broward.edu
Associate Vice President for Student Affairs/
College Registrar
(954) 201-7471

MIRAMAR CENTER
7451 Riviera Blvd.
Miramar, FL 33023

TIGERTAIL LAKE CENTER
580 Gulfstream Way
Dania Beach, FL 33004

WJA:mm

FLORIDA INTERNATIONAL UNIVERSITY
Miami's public research university

December 1, 2008

RE: Charles Anderson

To Whom It May Concern:

This letter serves to verify that Charles Anderson was the first African American to graduate from Florida International University, in Miami, Florida with a bachelor's degree in Criminal Justice, in June 1973. This information has been verified by Florida International University's Office of Planning and Institutional Effectiveness.

Should you have any further questions, please do not hesitate to contact me.

Sincerely,

Rosa L. Jones, Vice President Student Affairs
And Undergraduate Education

c: Jeff Gonzalez, Associate Vice Provost
      Planning & Institutional Effectiveness

MANNY MENENDEZ
Commn DD0514047
Expires 5/2/2010
Bonded thru (800)432-4254
Florida Notary Assn., Inc.

January 20, 2009

Office of the Vice President
Student Affairs & Undergraduate Education
11200 S.W. 8th Street, GC 219 • Miami, FL 33199 • Tel: (305) 348-2797 • Fax: (305) 348-1957 • www.fiu.edu

Florida International University is an Equal Opportunity/Access Employer and Institution • TDD via FRS 1-800-955-8771

ABOUT THE AUTHOR

Charles Anderson earned his Juris Doctor degree in 1977 from Thurgood Marshal School of Law. He graduated from Blanche Ely High School in 1961. The school is located in Pompano Beach, Florida, and is nationally known for sports and academics. Pompano is a famous small city just twenty miles north of Miami. In the early years of 2000, its high school was number one in the nation in the production of professional athletes. The author was the first African-American to earn criminal justice degrees from Broward Community College and Florida International University. Research is in the making to ascertain if he is the first black to earn such degrees in America and worldwide. Several college professors believe that he is the first one. The author was the first black chief of police in Broward County, Florida.

A movie and mini-televised series is in progress. In 2014, the author dedicated this book to his mother, Rosa Dunlap-Anderson, who was born on 1914. She is one hundred years old in 2014, and alive, and well in 2014. She and Martin Luther King were born on the same day. The proceeds from this book will be donated to his mother for a good cause. After that, a new unknown celebrity will be on the map. May God bless all of the readers of this interesting and exciting book!

I have always struggled for not having my father's last name. In my opinion all children should have their father's name. On May 1, 2015, my name was changed from Charles Lee Anderson, to Charles Anderson-Williams. The Final Judgment was ordered in the Family Division of the Circuit Court, Broward County, Florida. I will have both of my parents last name. Finally, the doors were closed on that issue and I am very pleased with the outcome.

CPSIA information can be obtained at www.ICGtesting.com
Printed in the USA
LVOW07s1024310815

452179LV00001B/38/P